# Wild Bill

## Bill Hunter's legendary 65 years in Canadian sport

With Bob Weber

Foreword by Wayne Gretzky

Johnson Gorman Publishers

*The Publishers*
Johnson Gorman Publishers
Distributed in Canada by Raincoast Books

*Credits*
Cover design by Boldface Technologies Inc.
Text design by Full Court Press Inc.
Printed and bound in Canada by Friesens for Johnson Gorman Publishers

*Acknowledgments*
Financial support provided by the Alberta Foundation for the Arts,
a beneficiary of the Lottery Fund of the Government of Alberta.

COMMITTED TO THE DEVELOPMENT OF CULTURE AND THE ARTS

5  4  3  2  1

*Canadian Cataloguing in Publication Data*
Hunter, Bill, 1920 May 5–
Wild Bill

ISBN 0-921835-54-X

1. Hunter, Bill, 1920 May 5– 2. Edmonton Oilers (Hockey team)—Biography. 3.
Sports team owners—Canada—Biography. 1. Weber, Bob, 1960– 11. Title.
GV848.5.H86A3 2000   796.962'092   C00-911106-9

# CONTENTS

*Dedicated to my family—*
*To my wife, Vi,*
*our children Beverley Wenninger,*
*Terry Dodd, Brent Hunter,*
*Donna Van Kessell, Gwen Dodd,*
*Bart Hunter and Brent Dodd.*
*To my grandchildren*
*Michelle and Nicole Van Kessell,*
*Travis, Shelby and Carrie Peters,*
*and Chase Dodd.*
*Also in loving memory of our son*
*Gregory William Hunter.*

*Acknowledgments*

The authors and publisher gratefully acknowlege the following
for their generous support of this publication:
The *Edmonton Sun*—photographs and research
The *Edmonton Journal*—photographs and research
Jim Korchinski—photographs
Instant Memories Photography—photographs
Mr. Print—photographs
Ned Powers—research
The University of Saskatoon Department of History—research
Gordon Yake and Bart Hunter—for unwavering
commitment and loyalty to this project

# FOREWORD

I KNOW IT SOUNDS ODD, BUT I'VE BEEN friends with Bill Hunter for almost a quarter century and I still can't call him by his first name. "Wayne, Wayne, call me Bill," he's invited many times, but I just can't do it. To me he'll always be Mr. Hunter. Until I sat down to write this foreword, I've never really thought about why that is. But when I did it became pretty clear. It's just a measure of the respect I feel toward this great gentleman of our game.

The first time I met Mr. Hunter—all right then, Bill—it had nothing to do with hockey. It was a business deal that brought us together, and the nearest ice was in the water glasses on the conference table. He and my agent had worked out a deal with a couple of major department stores for a series of T-shirts and caps with my picture on them. Bill and I got together at a local studio to get the pictures taken.

And with anyone else, that would have been it. With Bill that wasn't it at all.

I was still a teenager back then. Bill had sold the Oilers by the time I came along, and he was mostly a legend to me, a fiery, red-headed, locker-room orator that the older players on the team told me about. I was just at the start of my hockey career. Bill was approaching the end of his—although at that time he still had one more grand campaign up his sleeve. You wouldn't have guessed that we'd have much in common to build a relationship on. But somehow we did. Later that summer he and his wife, Vi, visited my parents and I in Ontario. My whole family and I—especially my father—have considered him a friend ever since.

For one thing he helped me have the kind of career I had by broadening hockey's horizons. I never actually worked with Bill Hunter the hockey man, but the world I played in was one he had a big hand in creating. It was Bill who founded the league that forced the NHL to start opening in new markets and brought pro hockey to people in cities like Edmonton, where the game was already deep in people's hearts. It was Bill and the WHA who did the players a huge favor by breaking the old option clause, allowing us all to finally earn what we were worth and have a voice in whom we played for. I never played junior in Western Canada, but who knows how many young players benefited from their apprenticeships in the tough, competitive Western Hockey League that Bill and his friends put together? And on a personal note, I have to point out that it was Bill who founded the Edmonton Oilers. I think I would have had a good career wherever I played, but that team at that time was special. The Oilers gave me my greatest triumphs and some of my deepest and longest friendships, and it was Bill who dreamed them into existence. I'm grateful to him for that alone.

But I don't think so highly of this man just because he was a visionary.

Bill and I share a lot of values. He has always taught the value of discipline and commitment. He knows the importance and joy of working together as a team. Bill is well known for expressing himself forcefully when he sees something needs to get done or a point needs to be driven home, but he's always used his considerable gift for words to motivate, not denigrate. His locker-room pep talks are the stuff of myth. He's generous with his praise, and you'll never catch him making easy criticisms or taking cheap shots. He's just not that way. He doesn't tear people down. He's been a builder—of leagues and teams and individual careers.

I remember running into Bill at the Boys on the Bus Reunion in Edmonton, a get-together for all the Oilers alumni. By this time Bill was ill and was moving slowly, so I went to his table and sat with him for a while and visited. We'd been talking for a while when Bill looked at me (he may not be well, but those eyes are still arrestingly blue) and said, "Wayne, I'm so proud of you." Praise from a man like Bill is worth having.

I'm proud to say Bill Hunter has managed to remain resolutely his own man and play by his own code in a business that doesn't always reward such behavior. He's fiercely independent and cannot be bought. I'm lucky enough to be in a position where I can sometimes do favors for people and help them out. I've asked Bill many times if I can do anything for him, and he always graciously declines. In all the years I've known him, he's never asked me for a single thing. I finally got him, though. At the Boys on the Bus gathering, I grabbed the Oilers jersey he was wearing and signed it. At least I gave him that.

I've often thought that if anyone should write a book, it's Bill. For one thing, he's a wonderful storyteller, as anyone who's had the pleasure of his dinner-table conversation will tell you and as you're about to find out. But there's a bigger reason I'm glad to see him in print.

The world of hockey has changed dramatically since Bill bought his first team after returning from the Second World War. Almost every time it's changed, Bill's been in the thick of it. As often as not, the change was his idea. And if he wasn't there, he knows the ones who were and what they were like and what they said and how they dealt with people. He knows the players, too—from guys like Max Bentley, whom I know only by their legends, to greats like Gordie Howe, whom I grew up idolizing, to a lot of guys I played or worked with. If you want to know what Glen Sather was like as a player, ask Bill. He drafted him. I've been lucky enough to hear a lot of Bill's stories about the changes he's seen, the hockey people he's worked with and the life he's led. Down to his very bones, Bill understands where this game came from and why people continue to play and love it. That understanding of our roots is going to be increasingly important to keep in front of us as the hockey world continues to evolve. That understanding is in this story, and that understanding is why I think this is an important book. And if you get a few chuckles out of it along the way (and you probably will) so much the better.

I'm pleased to be able to introduce him to those who don't already know him by writing these few words. And I know you'll enjoy the time together as much as I have. Ladies and gentlemen, I'd like you to meet my friend, Mr. Hunter.

–Wayne Gretzky
JULY 2000

# PROLOGUE

*... this upstart team that first took to the ice in an upstart league playing in an upstart town became the class of the venerable old NHL. How they came to be is part of my story.*

EDMONTON, OCTOBER 13, 1979. ANY diehard Oilers fan remembers that date, and anyone who follows hockey can guess what it meant. That was the night the Edmonton Oilers made the jump on home ice from the now-defunct World Hockey Association into the promised land of the National Hockey League. You bet I was there. I had founded the team, and I had been one of the founders of the league in which the Oilers began. And the club's new owner, Peter Pocklington, had invited my wife, Vi, my old WHA colleague Ben Hatskin and me to Edmonton to watch the game.

I had attended a special reception earlier that night, before the puck was dropped. The president of the NHL was there along with some team owners. They had made a bit of a fuss over me and I have to admit that felt good. I was glad Detroit Red Wings owner Bruce Norris had come. My first hockey job in Edmonton had been with his organization, and it felt appropriate to shake his hand and reminisce on this night, a night that was all about the future.

Before the drop of the puck came the speeches you'd expect on such an occasion. Alberta Premier Peter Lougheed and Edmonton Mayor Cec Purves addressed the crowd. But what happened next came from the stands, from the hearts of the fans. It was the affirmation of a lifetime of dreams, and it brought my heart to my throat. Gradually, I became aware of a chant starting in the crowd. "We want Bill!" I heard. Then again and louder, "We want Bill!" I was about to experience perhaps my proudest moment in sports.

The Oilers weren't my team anymore. I'd sold out a few years before. They weren't playing in the league I'd co-founded, either. The WHA was no longer, its teams having either folded or merged with the NHL. But the Oilers were my dream, the culmination of my goal to bring the greatest hockey on earth to the greatest fans on earth. At that moment the dream was there, big as life and wearing blue and orange. Those fans that night shared my dream, and that's why the moment is so precious to me. For one magic moment, we were all Oilers.

My life has always been about such moments. Nothing beats the magic of people inspired by a common goal. I've felt that power at school and in business, but sports are where it's always been strongest and that's what's kept me coming back.

I've paid the price and a few times I've fallen short. I've made some bad calls and I've had calls go against me that should have gone my way. But I hope no one can ever say that I did things small. Like I always said, "It only costs a few dollars more to go first class." And only a few short years after the puck was dropped in October 1979, this upstart team that first took to the ice in an upstart league playing in an upstart town became the class of the venerable old NHL. How they came to be is part of my story.

This is how it went. . . .

# 1

# HOMETOWN

**In our minds we were all Eddie Shore closing in on net while the quiet houses around became bleachers filled with cheering fans.**

**M**Y NEIGHBORHOOD THESE DAYS ISN'T much different from the one where I grew up in Saskatoon, Saskatchewan. It has the same green canopy of sheltering trees and the same kind of modest, tidy houses and well-kept yards. On some days even the sounds of children playing games in the street are the same. Those sounds carry me back to where my story begins—the backyards, playing fields, alleys and streets of my hometown.

In early summer there'd be the sweet perfume of lilacs from yards along Seventh Street, a scent that soon gave way to the pungent aroma of baked asphalt-and-tar as the days grew hot. It seemed we could play all night in the long June twilight, and it felt like a cheat to have to go to bed when it was still so bright. Fall brought a sharpening wind, and the odor of dead leaves was replaced in winter by the smoky tang of fireplaces while we played under streetlights in the early dark. Spring came with the smell of wet earth, which muddied our boots as we mucked about in the gathering green.

Sounds, too, changed with the seasons. The scrape of hockey sticks on pavement gave way to baseball chatter from the vacant lots which gave way in turn to the counted cadences of football. There were, however, constants: high-pitched shouts, cheers, traffic warnings. Eventually, mothers calling in the players from porches, maybe two or three times before they actually obeyed. Then quiet.

That was over 70 years ago, but the memories remain sharp as a freshly honed skate.

I was born May 5, 1920, in Saskatoon. It was a wonderful time and place to be a boy as my city and I were both young together. As I grew from a baby to a 10-year-old ranging through the parks and rambling river valley, Saskatoon almost doubled in size. I watched new neighborhoods being built. The Canadian National Railway brought its yards into town, a magnet of lumbering, smoking, fascinating machinery made all the more so because we weren't supposed to be there. There were stockyards, a new Robin Hood Flour mill and a brewery. The John East Ironworks across the river was expanding. I watched gangs of stonemasons and bricklayers push up the Gothic spires of the Bessborough Hotel along the downtown riverbank. They were an instant landmark. When the Saskatoon Quakers won the 1928 world hockey championship in Milan, Italy, I watched the team lined up for a civic reception on the hotel's balcony even though the building wasn't yet finished. Horses were giving way to cars (I still remember how proud my dad was when he brought home our new Buick), and auto dealerships were replacing the old livery stables. You could feel excitement in the streets. Everything seemed to be on the move—getting bigger, going faster.

*At age four I was already anxious to climb to the top.*

Of course, there were many reminders of Saskatoon's pioneer past still around. In our travels through the busy streets, we saw plenty of houses that had privies out back instead of indoor plumbing. And in our own neighborhood we'd see horses at least twice a day when the milkman and the bread delivery man came through with their teams. There were the garbageman's horses, too. And yes, the calling cards those big draft animals left behind furnished the pucks for more than a few sessions of road hockey. But those throwbacks were fading quickly, and we never heard the grown-ups mourning the old days. They were forward-looking and believed in progress.

Sports seemed to focus the energy of everyone I knew. My parents and their friends still talked about the Saskatoon Sheiks, one of the best hockey teams anywhere. They were owned by Joe Ganguish, a hotelier and friend of my father's. They would tell me stories about crowds of 3,000 people cheering on George Hainsworth in goal or the great Newsy Lalonde, hired away after nine seasons with the Montreal Canadiens, four of them as the NHL's leading scorer. Everyone had a favorite Newsy goal to recount—or favorite fight. They'd shake their heads when describing how the team broke up in 1925, the Toronto St. Patricks taking five players, the New York Rangers taking four, including Bill and Bun Cook. Newsy went back to Montreal. But everybody remembered how Saskatoon had once been the smallest city in North America to boast a professional hockey team. And one of the best, to boot.

My hockey memories begin here. The man who managed the Saskatoon Arena was a family friend, and he used to let me climb up into the loft high above the ice, where the organ tender sat. From there I had a bird's-eye view of the entire white sheet. I was mesmerized by the colorful patterns of the game and the excitement of the crowd. The great player organ huffed music behind, and sometimes I'd help the organist change the rolls.

Curling was every bit as important as hockey in my family. My dad started taking me to the curling rink when I was about four years old. In those days the curlers brought their own rocks in wooden crates. Dad would stack the crates along the curling sheet and leave the top one open. He'd pick me up and stick me in the open crate and wrap me up in a good thick blanket with just my eyes and nose peeping out. I could hardly move and could see only in front of me, but I was warm and snug. There I'd sit and take it all in: the shouts, the slapping of the brooms against the ice, the rumble and clack of the rocks, the clouds of steam that came off the men as they panted and shouted.

Dad always seemed to be organizing something, and sports were the center of attention all the time. He was president of the Saskatchewan Curling Association, founder of the Nutana and Hub City curling clubs and one of the founders of the Saskatoon Arena. He also was vice president, general manager and treasurer of the

Saskatoon Quakers hockey club and the president of the old Saskatoon Quakers football club, which played in the senior league with the Regina Roughriders.

Growing up in such a family in such a place and time, it was only natural that my attention should become fixed on sports. Eleven boys within a couple years of me in age lived in the surrounding few blocks, and it was never a problem to round up enough players for a little shinny, a little pickup baseball or any other game that you need a pack of boys for. We made hockey nets out of gunnysacks, and when we weren't stickhandling around with a frozen road apple, we'd use a tennis ball for a puck. In the summer our neighborhood had its own softball team. When we weren't doing that, we'd have track meets on a nearby field. We measured everything out. A mile race was around two square blocks. We even gave each other ribbons for first, second and third place. And somehow, just like my dad, I was always in the middle of things, bringing people together, trying to get something going. I loved doing that. I had the biggest delivery route in the city for the old *Liberty* magazine. I'd hire other kids to help me, subcontracting out parts of the route.

Our house was in the Nutana district at 226 Seventh Street. In the giant construction lot that was Saskatoon, Nutana was a vision of an old and established neighborhood. Some of the homes were up to 20 years old and had mature and spreading trees. Our house, a brown and white two-story with a glassed-in porch, sat at the center of three lots. My dad filled up the empty space around us with his gardens. He lovingly tended islands of snapdragons, pansies and other flowers in the middle of an immaculate green sea of lawn. You could have balanced a carpenter's level on his hedges. The trees were carefully trimmed and the prairie orchard in the back had apples, chokecherries and strawberries. In the summer my parents hung up

Chinese lanterns, and the neighbors would gather and visit.

But before the gardens were completed, one side of our yard sat empty. One winter day Dad came to me and my friends and said, "All right, I'll tell you what I'm going to do. I'm going to allow you fellows to have the vacant lot next door and you can have a hockey rink there." We were thrilled. In those days you could phone the Saskatoon Fire Department and they'd come out and flood your rink for you, providing you had the banks all made up and the snow scraped off. So that's what we did. We ran a little hose out a window to maintain the ice, and we skated and played there for hour upon hour. In our minds we were all Eddie Shore closing in on net while the quiet houses around became bleachers filled with cheering fans.

But never past nine o'clock. That's when the curfew horn would blow and everybody had to be at home. The police would see to it. Soon after the horn, Officer Ward would come by in his car and empty the ice. In summer he'd pedal his bicycle, ringing his bell alongside Buena Vista Park, saying, "Okay boys, time to go home now." We'd head off down the peaceful streets to our lighted porches.

That's where my mother waited for me, watching out the window of our home, her face framed by her thick, silvery hair. Even when she was young, her hair was pure white. Her friends called her the White Lady. My mother's striking hair was the result of having contracted influenza during one of the great epidemics after the First World War, and that was the mark the fever left on her, although to me, it was just a mark of how special my mother was. In fact, I was lucky to have her at all. She had compounded the flu with double pneumonia and diphtheria and was so sick that she wasn't expected live. She pulled through, but her oldest daughter, Orpha, succumbed when she was about five. Mother took a long

*My mother and I on a California beach, 1924.*

time to recover from her illness. For a couple years after, we spent three or four months every winter with one of Dad's sisters in California so Mother could get some sunshine and warmth to help rebuild her wasted body. I watched her on many mornings, pulling a comb carefully through the thick, deep waves in that pure white hair.

Mother had come from Moosomin, Saskatchewan, where her dad was a big farmer. When she grew up, she went to business college and came to Saskatoon to work as a secretary. That's how she met my dad. She worked for him.

All the ladies in our neighborhood loved her, and she was the center of their social circle. Not that she had much time to socialize. Dad was often away on business or out at a meeting, so there were many days and nights when Mother had to run the show on her own. We were her life, and she was very protective of us. In return I and my three sisters—Eileen, Bev and Gwen—worshiped her and never talked back. We knew that was an absolute sin. Dad would let us know. If he heard us acting smart, all he'd need was the newspaper to set things right. He'd be relaxing on the chesterfield in the living room, and we'd hear the rustle of his newspaper, as if to say, "I can hear you out here. Listen to your mother. Don't make me get up and sort you out." That was all it took. We jumped to whatever Mother had asked us to do.

My job was to get up at five o'clock in the winter and six in the summer to stoke the furnace, take out the ashes and put on the porridge. My sisters made breakfast. We ate the breakfast Mother wanted us to have, and we dressed in the clothes she wanted us to go to school in. She knew how to get us on her side so it sounded like a good idea, like something we'd come up with ourselves. I'd say "Mother, I want to play," and she'd say, "I know Billy, but you know, we just have to have this done here, and I don't want you to miss your play, so if you'll just get it done, then you can go." And off I'd go to do whatever it was she wanted me to.

We always looked up to Mother. We never saw her drink, smoke or swear. She was proud but treated people gently. And every Sunday she trooped us off to the Grace United Church. Not Dad, though. He was heavily involved in the running of the church and in paying off the mortgage, but that was it. He used to come with us, but then he'd come home and complain about our Scottish minister's dull sermons. One Sunday after church he announced, "I'm not going to listen to him one more time." And he never did.

That was my dad, all right.

Jack Hunter was an awesome figure to me. He was an important man with an important job—district director of the postal service in northern Saskatchewan and Manitoba and senior director of western Canada. He was in charge of all the post offices in the west back when the post office was still the Royal Mail, so it was almost as if he were a representative of the King. For my dad, missing work was unthinkable, and he would be at the office every day, even when he was sick, always in a suit and tie. He was strict with his staff, too. They had to be at work 10 minutes early, and their desks had to be clean and tidy by the time they left. What was even more impres-

sive to my friends and me was Dad's close association with Saskatoon's hockey heroes. He knew all the Quakers by their first names
and could get game tickets whenever he wanted. And then there
were his own exploits.

Jack Hunter wasn't an especially big man, about six feet tall and
190 pounds. He'd lost an eye playing bow and arrow as a child. But
he could sure play hockey. He had played defense in the old Winnipeg senior league, which was nearly as good as the National
League back then and sometimes paid the players better. And every
year he won the long drive championship at the Saskatoon Golf and
Country Club. He could just kill a ball. I swear that 320 yards was
no big deal to him.

I was Dad's only son, and he let me know he expected great
things from me. He wanted me to excel. Anything else wasn't good
enough, but when I did excel, he took it for granted. He rarely came
to watch me play baseball or hockey or football. He always seemed
to have a meeting or something important to do. I thirsted for his
praise, but later about all I'd hear was, "Did you win?" He had kind
words for my sisters, yes, but not me. Still, I learned it was worth
keeping him happy. If I did something to upset him, he would give
me a sound tongue-lashing, ground me or take away my privileges,
and he never spared the rod. He was sure tough on me.

I suppose my dad was only passing down what he had been
taught by his father, who had owned a livery stable in Swan River,
Manitoba. My dad used to tell me how when he was just 15, his
father made him take a customer from Swan River to Yorkton,
Saskatchewan, driving cross-country with a team of horses and a
wagon. There was no path and no one had ever done the trip before.
The journey took about two and a half days of trail-breaking and
route-finding across the open prairie.

Now and then I'd see my dad's soft side, especially when he was talking about Orpha. She had been a brilliant little girl. Dad would tell us how she used to go downtown with him on Saturday mornings to the Great Western Furniture Company store, where they'd put her up on a little stage and she'd sing and dance. Even as a boy I could tell how much losing her must have hurt him.

My sisters used to say that Dad was unfair and harsh with me, but I still loved him. I wanted to be like him, to work hard, move forward, make things happen and be admired and respected for the success I'd made of life. But how I wished for some recognition and praise from him. The few crumbs I got I used to hoard and treasure like a starving man, for starving I was.

Because Dad was away so much and was so often busy, I got much of the attention I craved as a boy from my maternal grandfather. Grandpa Dickenson Hewgill was a successful farmer from the Moosomin area. He was tall, slim, good-looking and intelligent. My middle name comes from him.

During the boom years of the 1920s, Grandpa and a friend of his named Kaiser (another big farmer whose first name I never learned) used to play the stock market. Eventually, of course, the market collapsed, and their banker called and asked to see them. Grandpa and Mr. Kaiser sat in that man's office while he told them they were both broke. They left the bank badly shaken. They each had some errands to do, and they agreed to meet at the livery stable at four o'clock to return home. But when Grandpa showed up, Mr. Kaiser wasn't there. When they searched around the livery stable, they found him around the back, dead. He had shot himself. Mr. Kaiser's suicide seemed to take some of the steam out of my grandfather. He could have kept on farming, but somehow he just couldn't bear it anymore. After the crash and his friend's suicide, Grandpa sold his farms to his sons and came to live with us. He was in his seventies.

Having Grandpa in the house was a wonderful thing for me.

He would sit me and my sisters down for hours and tell stories about the past. They were the real Canadian stories—pioneering, homesteading, the building of the railroad, the Louis Riel Rebellion. He had lived through these events, and he could make those times come alive for us. When he talked I could hear the clang of the navvies pounding in spikes for the Canadian Pacific Railway and feel the clatter of the gattling gun at Batoche. Those stories made me proud of where I was from. They made Saskatchewan as interesting a place as any other, a place with its own dramatic events and fascinating people. It only seemed right for the kind of place Saskatoon was becoming.

Grandpa also liked to take me driving in his car. He loved to drive (all dressed up in his suit and tie—I come from a line of natty dressers), and he stayed perched ramrod straight behind the wheel of his old Model T right up until he was about 90, which was a little too long. He scared us all terribly one winter day when he backed out of the garage and ran over my sister Gwen. The wheels passed right over her body. Fortunately, there was so much snow that the tires just pressed her stomach down into it and a neighbor was able to pull her out. She wasn't even hurt. But then he drove over a child on Broadway Avenue. Again, thank goodness, the child wasn't hurt, but Dad had the police take Grandpa's license away. Grandpa was furious.

I used to go down to the curling rink with Grandpa, too. He had a competitive fire just as strong as Dad's. At the age of 78, with Dad playing second, he won the Grand Challenge in the Saskatoon Bonspiel, and that was no small feat. In those days the bonspiel attracted more than 500 rinks, and play lasted for two weeks, with the farmers playing their draws on weekends so they could go back to the farm during the week. After that win, Grandpa threw the bonspiel's first rock every year until he was 92. Finally, he put a stop

*The family home in Nutana, Saskatoon. My dad was not only a noted sportsman but a passionate gardener.*

to it. "Nobody should be curling at this age," he said.

We buried my grandfather at 99, 13 days before he would have turned 100. As he lay dying, he called all the family in, all the grandsons and the granddaughters. I was the last one he called in. "Bill, you have tremendous leadership ability," he said. "Work at it." Those were his last words to me.

Two other members filled out our busy household. Mike, our gardener, tended Dad's beautiful flower garden. Mike was tall and very straight and somehow always looked tidy despite the salt and pepper stubble on his face. He dressed in Dad's castoffs or clothes Mother bought him. He spoke hardly any English at all. He always called my parents Mr. and Mrs., but nobody ever knew his last name. He lived in a trim little shack on the riverbank with his own carefully tended flowers.

Dad loved to garden with Mike. Every evening he could, Dad would come home after work, change into his plaid flannel shirt and work pants and step outside to join Mike, who'd usually been hoeing, raking and digging since early morning. And every summer the judges from the Saskatoon *StarPhoenix*'s Beautiful Grounds Contest would come around and return a little while later with a ribbon. Mike was with us for years, and he was just like a member of the family. When he died, my parents made sure he was looked after properly.

Finally, we usually had a maid living with us. A lot of my friends' families had girls from the country come in and help out. There was never any lack of work. Those girls always seemed to have soapsuds up to their elbows from dishes, dirty clothes or floors. They would come and go as they earned enough money to head to secretarial school or fell in love and got married. We lived and ate together and got quite close to some of our hired girls. Mother and Dad even paid for one girl's wedding.

Near our house lived the Griffiths family. I knew Mr. Griffiths as the father of my friend Bob, but he was also the head of athletics at the University of Saskatchewan. Griffiths Stadium, where University of Saskatchewan Huskies still play, is named after him. When I was about seven, Joe Griffiths began showing up in our neighborhood with a gifted young athlete named Ethel Catherwood.

Not too many people remember Ethel Catherwood these days, and that's a shame because she was probably one of the best female track and field stars Canada has ever produced. In 1927, at the first-ever Canadian Women's Track and Field Championships, Ethel placed first in the high jump, third in discus and set a new javelin record with a throw of 114' 7". The next year, at the Olympic Games trials, she made a world record high jump of 5' 3" and went on to win Olympic gold that year in Amsterdam. When she won the gold, the city rang the curfew bell and people ran out in the streets shouting, "She did it! She did it!"

My friends and I got to watch this amazing athlete in action because Mr. Griffiths trained her on one of Dad's side lots. Every day she'd walk to Nutana carrying her discus and javelin, and Mr. Griffiths would get to work. We were her unofficial assistants. We would set up the bar on her high jump and pick it out of the sand when she missed. Mr. Griffiths would say, "Stand back from the poles," and Ethel would come running. Even using the old-fashioned scissors style she sailed up and over like a bird. Then Mr. Griffiths would say, "Okay, I want you to raise it another quarter of an inch," and we'd think, Oh boy, look at her go. We were amazed at how high she could jump.

Then it was time for javelin and discus, and we raced each other for the honor of retrieving them for Ethel. We would have done anything she asked, for we held her in awe. She was tall and slender with bobbed brown hair and a lovely smile. She was very quiet and didn't have much to say to us, but we didn't care. She was so pretty and she worked so hard. When she looked at us and said, "You boys are doing a wonderful job," that was all the reward we needed.

We were, however, a little afraid of Mr. Griffiths, for he was a tough taskmaster. He'd look at his young charge and say, "Now Ethel, you're going to win this. And here's what you have to do. And unless you're prepared to do it, I'm not going to waste my time on you." He was thorough, too. Mr. Griffiths would have Ethel start her high jump approach at different spots until it was perfect and rehearsed step by step. He'd give her warm-up routines and sprinting exercises and drills, and she'd do them all faithfully. He wasn't mean, but he was firm. Sometimes, we'd screw up our courage and come to Ethel's defense, saying, "Gee, Mr. Griffiths, don't you think she's working too hard?"

Watching Ethel was something of a revelation to us. Sure, we played hockey and ball and ran races, but we were just fooling around and having fun. Ethel's discipline and rigorous approach was different. My friends and I would talk all this over after Ethel's training sessions as we gathered up her stuff to take it over to Mr. Griffiths' garage.

The Great Depression of the 1930s devastated so much of Saskatchewan, but its impact wasn't felt so deeply in our family. Dad had a good job all through the Dirty Thirties. So did all the other fathers on our block. But it was impossible not to recognize that something had changed, even if we children didn't know the cause. Parents were saying pensively, "We've got to work hard. We've got to save." My mother would talk to my dad about people we knew who had lost their jobs. "Are they hungry?" she'd ask.

The bustle on the streets slowed. Men loitered on street corners they had rushed by a few years before. Ragged, hungry men used to come to our back door, where Mother would fix them a sandwich. Bennett Buggies (a car drawn by horses after the owner could no longer afford gasoline) became a common sight on the streets. All the fathers of my little gang made it clear to us that others didn't have it as good as we did and that we were not to lord our good fortune over anyone. Although my family was better off than many at my school, my dad made sure I never had one dime more than the other boys, something all the fathers seemed to agree upon. All the kids were made to feel equal.

Every week my dad would go over Eaton's warehouse store on the south side to buy groceries. Dad would have items bagged in different lots, and he'd have me take a bag of groceries to the home of friends who were having a tough time. I was instructed to leave the bag on the back step so as not to embarrass them.

The Depression left other, grimmer memories. Those dark times killed the dreams of many young men and forced them onto the road. Most of them were just regular guys made desperate by bad times.

And most of the drifters through Saskatoon on their long trip to nowhere in particular set up camp at the exhibition grounds. My mother and a group of ladies sometimes went there to set up kitchens and make meal for them. Some of them must have heard about Mother's soft heart and habit of feeding the drifters who came through. One afternoon about 10 of them showed up at our home. Mike didn't trust them. I watched him stand there with his big pitchfork, protecting my mother and all of us while she made the men sandwiches.

On May 8, 1933, we kids decided we wanted to have a look at these fellows ourselves, and we headed to the exhibition grounds. Our timing was very bad. When we got there, some trouble started. There was some yelling and shoving between the drifters and the police. We didn't understand what was going on at all. Then someone started throwing stones at a young mounted policeman's horse, and it bolted. He fell from the saddle, but his foot was caught in the stirrup, and he was dragged helplessly behind as the horse ran. That poor young man died right in front of our eyes. The police told us to get the hell home, and we sure did.

People still found ways to have fun despite the Depression. Dance clubs were popular, and Mother and Dad belonged to one with about 50 other couples. Every now and then they'd hire a hall and a band, get all dressed up and go out dancing. I think I looked forward to those nights almost as much as they did. Mother and Dad would be excited, looking forward to the evening. We kids would eat on our own, as Mother was too busy getting ready. Dad would be getting into his best suit or, on truly special occasions, his tuxedo, and Mother would take what seemed like forever in the bathroom. It was always worth it. She looked beautiful, slim and graceful, her white hair shining against her black and white evening gown. And she smelled wonderful. Dad used to have a couple drinks at those dances, and when they got home, he would sit outside in the car until he was sure all the effects of the alcohol were gone, winter or summer.

In the summers my mother would visit a friend of hers who had married a big rancher in southern Alberta. She always came back with great stories of life on the range. Two years in a row, Edward, Prince of Wales, who later became Edward VII until he abdicated the throne, visited that rancher. Edward would ride horses and chase cattle and generally play cowboy. My mother got to know the charming, handsome, well-dressed young heir and grew quite fond of him. Edward made quite the impression on the local girls, too, said Mother.

Dad's hobby, on top of everything else he was involved in, was the Rotary Club. Each year the Rotarians would put on a minstrel show, complete with white gloves and blackface and tuxes. They would practice for six months before the show. Dad was one of the end men who made wisecracks off to the side of the stage—just about the only time Dad ever told jokes. Back then, those minstrel shows were popular. They were staged in the old Capitol Theatre, and they were sold out every time.

As I got a bit older, my world grew wider. We had a pretty good baseball team in our neighborhood, which played in a mercantile league. In the summer, when virtually every country town hosted ball tournaments, we traveled around on weekends and played in a lot of them. Often the entry fee was $10 and first-prize money was $50. We'd try to make the playoffs to earn back our entry fee and maybe turn a little profit. In the winter there were hockey tournaments run along the same lines.

Those hockey tournaments once got me in pretty good trouble with my dad. One night when he was away traveling, we "borrowed" his car and took off to a tournament in Prince Albert, about two and a half hours to the north. Of course, Dad could tell by the tracks in the snow leading from the garage that we'd taken his car.

*The Nutana Collegiate curling team, 1937.*

Dad knew all the chiefs of police because, as head of the postal service, he had to lay charges for any robberies involving mail. He called up one of his RCMP buddies and said, "I want you to go after these kids, especially my son, Bill." So the next day we had to go down to the RCMP detachment. We were four frightened kids. When the officer gave us a lecture and told us that we could be charged, we promised we'd never do that again.

Saskatoon was a hockey hotbed. The Saskatoon public schools had their own hockey league. So did the high schools. We also had church-league hockey. There was a high school curling league, too, and when I got to high school I skipped the Nutana Collegiate rink, which won the 1938 provincial championship. I also loved track and field. I was Nutana's mile and half-mile champion.

When I entered Grade 10 in Nutana Collegiate, I discovered football. I made the team in my first year, playing center. I was small, but I did all right. Just as in all our neighborhood sports, I ended up being a kind of leader of this team, too. When school let

*The Nutana Collegiate curling team of 1938 went on to win the provincial championship.*

out for the summer, I said, "Hey, let's stay together and practice and win the championship next year." All summer we practiced diligently every day in a park down by the river. And after the Saskatoon Public School Board made a special ruling to clear the way, I coached the team. I would have to have a teacher with me on the sidelines during the games, but I would be the coach. When we went back to school that fall, I was the first student coach in the history of the city. Our hard work paid off when we went undefeated and won the championship.

Winning a championship made me hungry for an even bigger prize. I decided I would organize a new junior football team to go after the national title. The Regina Dales had gone down east and won it the previous year, and I thought if they could do it, so could we. I decided to name the team the Saskatoon Dukes. I talked some older friends into forming the executive. I chose the colors, blue and gold. I knew we'd need money to buy equipment, and I got an idea from something I'd been doing at school.

The previous year I had helped produce a show at school. We called it our annual Lit Night, and it was like a big variety show with band and skits. The teachers were supposed to approve of what went into them, but we always used to rehearse a couple of satirical bits in secret and then spring them on the teachers. It was all in good fun. I figured if I could produce a show, I could produce a dance. I went to go see Mr. Tate, who owned the Avenue Ballroom downtown, a beautiful ballroom near the Bessborough, with an oak dance floor sprung underneath with rubber tires. I told him I would put on the finest high school dances he'd ever seen, and he could make his money from concession sales. I'd put a couple bouncers by the door to make sure there was no trouble. He gave me the ballroom for practically nothing. I hired a couple of bands, scheduled my first dance and we jammed the place with over 800 people. It was great affair. Everybody had fun.

I held several of these dances, and I raised more than $8,000 in the middle of the Depression. I took that cash over to Jimmy Madden's sporting goods store, where lots of athletes hung out, and I ordered a complete set of football gear for 36 players, including training equipment such as dummy bags for blocking drills. I hired star quarterback Bud Weaver from the University of Saskatchewan to be my coach, and he got teachers from all over town to be his assistants. I was writing letters to players all over Canada, drafting contracts for them to play for me. My plan was to pay no salaries but to divide up the proceeds from the gate at the end of the season. I even had an indoor training camp at Exhibition Stadium.

Things were going great. But between playing sports, doing my chores and schoolwork, promoting and running the dances and organizing the Dukes, I was on the go round the clock. I was too busy to eat regularly and sometimes didn't eat at all. I had so many things to plan and was so wound up that I didn't sleep at night no

*In 1937 I played center on the Nutana Collegiate senior rugby team.*

*The following year I became the first and only student coach of the Nutana squad.*

matter how exhausted I was. The pressure became too much for a kid in Grade 11. My mother tried to calm me down several times. She'd try to keep me in, but I'd always find a reason why I had to go out. "Bill, you can't go at a pace like this," she'd warn. She was right.

I started experiencing dizzy spells but nothing that really warned me of what was coming. All of a sudden, one day in June I just collapsed. I really can't remember exactly what happened. Dr. Armitage said I just ran out of gas. I had kidney failure and for a few days went completely blind. I lay in darkness in my bedroom, tired to my bones, feeling sick and not understanding what was happening to me. I don't think Mother left my side. My parents and our doctor did their best to reassure me, but I was very frightened. Slowly, I came around. My sight came back like a gray fog lifting. When it did, the first thing I saw was my mother's face. I'd never seen anything so beautiful. "Billy, you're going to be fine," she said. And before too long, I was. The only mark that breakdown left on me was a slight tremor in my left hand, which I have to this day.

Still, I was in no shape to finish my Grade 11. The Dukes were history, too. My executive took that gear and formed a new team, the Saskatoon Hilltops, which is still playing. They kept the colors, though. That's why the Hilltops are blue and gold.

Mother and Dad were very concerned for my health. Our doctor suggested getting me out of Saskatoon because he knew that once I was up and around, I'd just want to get everything going again. My parents decided to send me to my uncle's farm in Moosomin, where I could calm down, relax and restore my health. Moosomin did slow me down, and I enjoyed it. I milked cows and stooked hay. In our spare time, my cousin Gordon Hewgill and I would ride bareback across the prairie, and he'd do acrobatics. He could stand on the horse and do all kinds of stunts that you wouldn't see outside a circus. When fall came, I restarted Grade 11

*The Grace United Church Boys Club. Standing second from the right, I'm sporting my first fedora.*

in Moosomin. My uncle gave me my own Bennett buggy to drive to school. By Christmas we all felt it was time for me to come home.

Still, I wasn't able to get back into the swing of things. I had been proud of my work for the Dukes, and I was crushed the team wasn't ever going to take the field. Everything seemed like a letdown and nothing interested me. I wasn't going to school, just staying at home resting, and I've never been much good at that. I needed to move forward. I began to think about Notre Dame College in Wilcox, Saskatchewan.

Notre Dame is a great Canadian institution of scholarship and athletics. Founded in the 1920s by Athol Murray, a Catholic priest renowned for his leadership and learning, Notre Dame has always been famous for its sports teams. No matter what the sport, the Notre Dame Hounds were at the top of it. In fact, the Hounds earned much-needed revenue for the school by heading out on the road and taking on all comers across the prairies. The Hounds had often played exhibition hockey and baseball games in Saskatoon, and I loved those teams. They seemed to have such great spirit, and somehow I felt that team spirit was what I needed to get back to my old self. I began to think more and more about Notre Dame and the Hounds. As I lay in bed, dissatisfied, restless and bored, Notre Dame came to seem more and more like the answer to the funk I was in. It drew me like a magnet.

One weekend I decided I was simply going to run off to Notre Dame. I told my sisters, but I didn't tell my parents. I packed my kit bag with some clothes, and one of my sisters made me a sandwich. I hit the road, riding my thumb. It took me all day and three rides to reach Wilcox. I walked in to Father Murray's office and told him, "Father, I want to come to school here at Notre Dame." He said, "What's your name, son?" I told him who I was and where I was from. When I told him who my father and mother were, he said, "Your father and I are good friends." They'd gotten to know each other through my dad's involvement with the Quakers.

Father Murray, who I later learned was called Père by everybody, looked thoughtful for a moment. I pleaded with him. "Father, can't I stay here? I want to be a Hound." Père gazed back at me, paused a moment and said, "Well, you're here, so you're a Hound."

And so I was.

# 2

# THE HOUNDS

**We spent our last few nickels at a Chinese restaurant across the street, and now we had to win the Togo tournament in order to pay our hotel bill.**

AND IT REALLY WAS ALMOST THAT SIMPLE.

The first thing Père did was to call my mother and dad to let them know where I was. Dad wasn't a bit surprised to hear from him. " Père, I know why you're calling," he said. "You've got our son Bill there." That's right, Père answered. "Well, I hope he does well," said Dad. And as far as he was concerned the matter was settled.

Mother wasn't about to send me off so easily. This wasn't like going off to Moosomin to live with her brother and go to school there. At Notre Dame I'd be surrounded by kids she didn't know and be taught by teachers she couldn't just walk down the street and talk to. But most of all, here was her poor little Billy, who only a few months ago was bedridden from a breakdown, running off to some hick town in the middle of the prairie dust bowl. She was devastated when she realized I'd run off. She remained unhappy about me leaving home until she met Father Murray and understood the kind of man he was. After that she was more than willing to leave me in his care.

Of course Père, in his usual way, didn't make that introduction any easier. Soon after I entered Notre Dame, the Hounds were at the Saskatoon Arena to play hockey, and my mother went there to meet the man who was educating her son. I'll never forget how Père greeted my elegant, gracious mother. "Marion, you've got not a bad little bastard at all for a son here," he said. To him that was an expression of love. I can only imagine what my mother must have thought.

But that came a bit later. After my parents had agreed to let me stay at Notre Dame, Père asked me to leave the office. He and Dad had a brief conversation, probably about money and about how things were going at the school. I couldn't have been happier. I was in. I would be a Hound, and Athol Murray would be my mentor.

Athol Murray was born to a wealthy Toronto Rosedale family. His father was keen to see him comfortable in both English and French, so young Athol was sent to university in Quebec. He kicked around a little bit after graduating, working as a reporter and flirting with the idea of attending law school. One day he walked by a secondhand bookstore and saw a copy of St. Augustine's *The Confessions* in the window. Something moved him to buy that little volume, and it changed his life. Père became a Catholic priest and was sent to Saskatchewan, an English-speaking province with many French-speaking Catholics.

Père was a dynamic, energetic man, full of enthusiasm and always interested in other people. Those qualities especially endeared him to boys. He founded a boys club in Regina, and in 1927 he brought a group of those boys with him to Wilcox to start a new school. By the 1930s Notre Dame was well known as sometimes the only place where a farm boy could go to get a decent, affordable education. Tuition was negotiable, sometimes in terms of chickens or sides of beef. Notre Dame offered both a high school, which I attended, and a college, which was organized along the lines of Père's alma mater, Laval University. Readings from Moliere to Socrates were assigned and then discussed in class in a kind of simple Socratic dialogue. But Père's reading list and his great learning won the college an endorsement from the University of Ottawa.

Père believed the body should be cultivated along with the mind, and sports always accompanied books. Père was often the coach and manager of the hockey and baseball teams although maybe he was better at motivating his players than explaining the subtleties of the game. People tell the story of one road game when the hockey team was tired from travel and sapped by a nasty strain of fever raging through the line-up. The Hounds were getting pasted by the Regina Pats, and after the second period Père roared, "Goddamnit boys, if you can't beat them at least give them the measles!"

That was Père, all right. One writer described him as "a Catholic priest with the soul of a saint, the mind of a Greek philosopher and the vocabulary of a dock worker." He was a deep scholar and a extraordinary teacher. He spoke fluent Latin, was well-versed in history and started the collection of rare and ancient books that is now one of the college's prides. In cold weather Père covered his thick black hair with a World War One-vintage leather flying helmet and his stocky frame with a huge buffalo coat, which did double duty as a blanket for the couch in his office, which in turn did double-duty as his bed. You'd never catch him in a suit and tie, and he often tore off his clerical collar when he got going on some rhetorical flight, which was often. Mismatched plaid shirts and work pants were more Père's style. We'd see him stomping up and

*Monsignor Athol Murray, founder of Notre Dame College and a great Canadian.*

down campus, all 5' 7" and 200 pounds of him, his coat flying, a cigarette dangling from his lips and shedding ashes all over his shirt. In fact, he chain-smoked four packs a day and drank, too. He kept a bottle of Scotch in his office, from which he would pour the occasional evening nip for some of the older boys.

Père could build people up, and he could also yank them back to earth if they started to float off. He challenged everybody but was proud to know successful people and was a stranger to envy. Most of all, he believed in the individual. Monsignor Athol Murray was a special man and he was our leader.

Moving to Notre Dame, however, was quite a culture shock for a middle-class boy from the city. Wilcox really was in the middle of nowhere. It had one main street with two stores and a hotel on one corner. Lane Hall, where the arts students studied, was at the end of the street. It was named after the owner of the San Diego Padres, who donated money to the school and kept the Hounds in uniforms. Wilcox was dirty, too. The street was unpaved, and when it was hot, it was dusty. On those rare days when it did rain, just walking across the street would leave a layer of prairie gumbo inches deep on your shoes.

We lived in shacks, usually old bunkhouses Père had gotten from the railroad. They were rebuilt and adapted by the students, and we continually patched them up, using whatever materials we could get our hands on. We lined the walls with cardboard boxes to keep the draft out, boxes we lifted from the backyards of Wilcox's stores. The shacks had no running water and were heated with stoves. Most of the shacks housed seven or eight kids, sleeping on bunk beds with mattresses that weren't much more than wire strung across the frames. All the shacks were named. I shared the Annie Shack with Gus and Bill Kyle, Al Hardie and Stoney Ganshorn.

For the first month I was homesick. I was used to my comfortable home in the city with bathrooms and bedrooms and good meals cooked by my mother. There was none of that at Notre Dame. I wanted to go home, and I might have, too, if it hadn't been for Mother Edith.

Mother Edith was the principal of the high school. She was a tiny, dynamic woman who flitted about the campus in her nun's habit like an amiable but determined bat. She could be very stern, and we all quickly learned to respect her, but she understood her young students, too. She could tell when a new boy was missing his mom. She'd seek him out in the quiet corner where he was having a bit of a cry and have a gentle talk with him. A few times that boy was me. We all loved Mother Edith.

It didn't take me long to find a place for myself among the other boys at school. They were all saying, "Well, who's this kid from Saskatoon?" but it got around pretty quickly that my dad was manager of the Quakers. Sometimes we'd go to Regina for a game, and I'd get a bunch of free tickets. But it wasn't a few seats at the arena that helped me ease my way in the door with my new schoolmates. It took a race. There was a boy at Notre Dame named Barry Campbell. Barry was an Indian and all the guys called him the Chief. The Chief was an excellent runner. I'd been a running champ at Nutana back in Saskatoon, so when word of that got out, naturally the challenge was on. The boys set up a race, just me and the Chief. We went out on a dusty section road north of town where we wouldn't be disturbed. It felt like the whole school had come out to watch. The Chief and I were to run out to a corner in the road, back into town and finish at the church. I won by a good 50 yards, and after that I was in. I felt like a Hound—and that felt great.

These were the closing years of the Depression, and Notre Dame hadn't been exempted from tough times. Stories about how the ditches were filled with dust and how the grasshoppers would eat the handle right off the hoe have entered Saskatchewan myth, but I swear we could hear those hoppers coming from miles away in a huge black roaring cloud. We'd hustle off to our little bunkhouse shacks to batten down the hatches, but nothing could shut out the clatter and drone of millions of insects. I wasn't to hear another sound like that until I heard German buzz bombs falling during the war. You couldn't have drawn a breath in the middle of those swarms. They'd leave not one blade of grass or flower petal. One time after such a swarm had passed, the whole school had to go down to the train station and push the train to get it going. The wheels were slipping on the bodies of thousands and thousands of grasshoppers.

It's too bad we couldn't eat grasshoppers because it was often a struggle for Père to keep food on the table for his ravenous young flock.

A lot of our food was donated from by farmers and ranchers. A lot more was actual tuition from those who could only afford to pay in bushels of wheat or a supply of fresh eggs. But this was the Dust Bowl, and many people were going hungry. Still, it was amazing how we'd go for two or three days with nothing in the larder and then have something turn up. Someone would donate a side of beef. A carload or two of potatoes and carrots and other vegetables would come from people in the East. We'd eat fine for a week, but the carloads always ran out, leaving us hungry again.

One stretch was particularly bad. We'd been living on toast and coffee for what felt like two weeks. Nobody complained. We were Hounds; we'd be ashamed to complain. That morning we were in the meal hall downstairs at the church, all in our places at the long wooden tables, when Père stood up before us. "Gang," he said, "this has gone far enough. We're going to pray. I want you to stand up, all of you. We're going to pray."

He lifted his face toward the heavens and closed his eyes as we sneaked looks at one another. It was a powerful moment. We were mesmerized. Père looked up and he said, "Dear Lord, you gotta forgive me, but my poor little bastards are starving. You just gotta help us."

The next day a cheque arrived in the mail on the stationery of Maple Leaf Gardens. I knew that Conn Smythe, the owner of the Toronto Maple Leafs and Maple Leaf Gardens, was a good friend of Père's and that a couple of ex-Hounds were playing for the Leafs. So I said, "Hey, that may be from Conn Smythe. We better open that." We opened it and out slipped a $500 cheque, a fortune in 1939.

I took the cheque, forged Père's signature, and with a couple of cronies took the money to Fuhrmann's Butcher Shop in Regina. I said, "Mr. Fuhrmann, we want to buy some groceries. And I know we owe you a lot of money, so here's a payment on our account."

Mr. Fuhrmann thought that was just wonderful, but by the time we left I'm sure we had $700 in groceries. Our Chinese cook was just beaming when we walked in. We had chickens, we had beef, we had bacon and eggs for breakfast. We ate like kings. Père, who of course knew exactly what had happened, said, "This just didn't happen by accident. I wouldn't be surprised if that little bastard of a Billy Hunter didn't get into the mail." But soon the food from that epic shopping trip ran out, too. And then we were looking again.

I was sometimes hungry and sometimes cold, but there was nowhere else I wanted to be. Whether we played hockey or baseball or no sports at all, we were the Hounds, and we were all in it together. We were all on one big team, all pulling for one another. The feeling was one I'd never experienced in my life, and it was everything I'd hoped it would be. I forgot all about the feeling of futility that had been depressing me in Saskatoon. I felt alive again, and it wasn't just me that was electrified by Notre Dame's sense of pride and belonging. A lot of tough kids were sent to Notre Dame in the hope that life as a Hound would straighten them out, and most of the time it worked. At Notre Dame discipline wasn't just imposed on us—it was instilled in us. That meant the students wouldn't put up with nonsense any more than the teachers. If something was stolen, we would hold our own court and we would deal with the problem. It was something we did without telling the teachers, and our court assigned penalties like cleaning up in the kitchen for a month. Each shack had its own discipline, too. One or two kids would have to get expelled every year, but 90 percent of the real toughies would fall into line and become great Hounds. And that powerful sense of pride in being a Hound all radiated from the personality of Athol Murray.

Because we were so isolated, there was little to distract us from our studies. We had classes at night, and students from Notre Dame routinely achieved above-average grades on provincial exams. For entertainment the Hounds listened to Foster Hewitt's hockey broadcasts on Saturday night and that was about all we had. We'd hear, "He shoots, he scores!" crackle out of somebody's crystal radio set in one of the shacks, or sometimes we'd drape ourselves over the broken-down furniture in Père's living room and listen to the game on his big radio.

We high school students were taught by nuns. But the main attraction in the classrooms of Notre Dame was, of course, Père. He could talk for hours off the top of head about classical authors like Socrates, and he was spellbinding. He'd shut his eyes and talk and make lessons so real you'd believe Socrates was right there in the room with you. I loved to hear him talk so much that I joined the choir just so I could listen to Père preach.

And what did Père teach? Just this: There's nothing you can't do if you want it enough and you will not accept mediocrity. Mediocre is the dirtiest word in English language. That lesson may sound corny these days, but I don't care. That's what I still believe. Every Hound knew Père's "Notre Dame Man," and every Hound believed in it

### The Notre Dame Man

*The world today is looking for men and women who are not for sale.*

*Who are honest, sound from centre to circumference, true to the heart's core with consciences as steady as the needle to the pole.*

*Who will stand for the right if the heavens totter and the earth reels.*

*Who can tell the truth and look the world right in the eye.*

*Who neither brag nor run.*

*Who neither flag nor flinch.*

*Who can have courage without shouting it.*

*In whom the courage of everlasting life runs still, deep and strong.*

*Who know their message and tell it.*

*Who know their place and fill it.*

*Who know their business and attend to it.*

*Who will not lie, shirk or dodge.*

*Who are not too lazy to work, nor too proud to be poor.*

*Who are willing to eat what they have earned and wear what they have paid for.*

*Who are not ashamed to say "No" with emphasis.*

*God is looking for them. He wants those who can unite together around a common faith—who can join hands in a common task—and who have come to the Kingdom for such a time as this. God give us such as them.*

*Not only will they be better prepared to fulfill their duties as a citizen, they should make a better friend, a better husband, a better father, a better wife because free people do. They will, in short, be better prepared to live, and when their hour comes, they will know better how to die because free people do.*

Père had many interesting friends who dropped by the college. One was a scrappy little Baptist minister named Tommy Douglas. The two of them would get together and argue like hell over politics and such, but they loved each other in spite of their philosophical differences. I think they remained friends even when Tommy became premier of Saskatchewan and enacted Canada's first Medicare program. Père was dead set against Medicare, as he was against anything he thought was socialism. Across the province he was one of the most influential opponents of this new health-care idea, and he almost won, too. When I used to see Tommy, though, he was just getting entering politics and was a minister over at Weyburn. Père would get him to speak to the students whenever he visited, and Tommy was quite a speaker, too.

Archie McNabb, the province's Lieutenant-Governor, was another of Père's bosom pals. He'd give the students a little lecture, and then he and Père would get together over a bottle of Scotch and tie on one, laughing and trading stories long into the night in Père's dilapidated living room. The older boys, the ones in the university program, were allowed to listen in on those sessions. As a high school student, I wasn't supposed to be there, but I snuck in a few times anyway.

Every now and then, Père's antics would get out of hand, and he'd be called into the archbishop's office in Regina. We'd drive Père into town to the rectory, and the archbishop would have his staff serve us milk and cookies in the waiting room while he dealt with Père, usually over some outrageous thing he'd said. The archbishop would leave the door open, though, and we'd hear him say, "Athol, here's a list of things I'm not going to accept," and then he'd go up one side of Père and down the other. But the archbishop knew Père was a special man and made allowances for him.

Mother Edith was just about the only person who could put the brakes on Père. Père was scared stiff of her. She may have been a wee thing, but she was fierce. When she told us, "You tell Athol I want to see him," Père would dodge into some campus cubbyhole and plead, "Don't tell her I'm here." I learned not to cross her the time I cut a few classes to go help hammer a few nails on the new arts building. She scooted me back to my books in a hurry.

Another one of my amusements at Notre Dame was sportswriting. I made a connection with Dave Dryberg, the sports editor of the Regina *Leader-Post* and I'd string little stories to them. Mostly I'd cover the Hounds, but sometimes I'd get tabbed to cover a junior hockey series on the weekend. I'd make five bucks or thereabouts, which was not bad money in those days.

But whenever I wasn't studying, my biggest occupation at Notre Dame was running sports teams. Just like at Nutana Collegiate, I'd gravitated to the position of manager. One summer I took the ball team on a tour of western Canada. I'd been manager of the ball team during the school year and when it ended, I said, "Let's not break up the team. Let's hit the road and go out on tour." The guys all agreed.

We had an ancient Dodge panel van with benches in the back. We made up banners that read, Father Murray's Famous Notre Dame Hounds On Tour, which we hung on the side. We headed out with all of about $17 in our pockets. I don't think we ever did tell Père.

I had booked us a couple games in Carlyle, Saskatchewan, and on our way we passed through Regina. We stopped at the station where we always gassed up, and Mr. Reeves, the owner, asked us what we were doing. "We're going to tour western Canada," I told him. "Not on those tires, you're not," he responded. He sent us off to the old Balmoral Cafe, where the Hounds always ate, for a round of Nick and Albert Pappas' famous hot beef sandwiches. We told Nick what we were doing, and he thought it was great. We couldn't pay him, but he'd known that before we sat down. "I know, Nick, that somehow God'll take of you for this meal," I told him. Nick loved the Hounds. When we got back, Mr. Reeves had given us four new tires and a new spare, gassed us up and changed the oil. He never asked for a dime. People used to do things like that for Notre Dame. That's how important the school was to the people of Saskatchewan.

So off we went. Finding a place to play was never a problem

*The Notre Dame Hounds baseball team hit the road in 1939 on a Saskatchewan and Manitoba tour. As manager I tried to stay one step ahead of the bills.*

because baseball was huge in Saskatchewan. We played something like 78 games that summer all over the province and into Manitoba. Baseball was cheap family entertainment, and during the Depression that was a precious commodity. So minor-league baseball in Saskatchewan could draw major-league crowds. Thousands would come out to watch a couple of good teams. Ours was just one of many touring ball teams and by no means the best known. A lot of barnstorming teams would come up from the States. Satchel Paige, the great pitcher whose race kept him out of the major leagues until the end of his career, pitched many times in Saskatchewan with the Kansas City Monarchs and his own team, the Satchel Paige All-Stars. The House of David team, used by many major-league teams to rehabilitate injured players, was a regular visitor. We played a few of those barnstorming teams. They were outstanding.

But even with all those games and all those fans, touring was not a lucrative proposition. I'd stay one step ahead of the team, booking games by telephone a few days down the road. Most of the time, we didn't make anything unless we won. Sometimes we'd take up a silver collection, which would usually net 10 to 15 bucks. We bought big loaves of sandwich bread and tubes of baloney, and that would be our meal—baloney sandwiches by the side of the road two or three times a day. As soon as we got money, maybe after winning first prize at some small-town sports day, we'd go out to the nearest Chinese cafe and stand ourselves to a good meal.

We played a few games in Saskatoon, and the whole team stayed at our house. There I was, returning home as the manager of the famous Notre Dame Hounds. I guess I felt a little proud. My dad just looked up and said, "Well, they're here." But I could sense that he really was proud of me. He just didn't want to admit it. We sure caused a stir in my old neighborhood, though. All the girls and guys came by when we pulled up in our old van.

The next morning we all sat down at our dining room table. My mother had cooked us an old-fashioned Saskatchewan break-fast: porridge, bacon and eggs and ham, toast and jam and mar-malade, jugs of milk. It looked and smelled great, but we couldn't eat it. None of us were used to eating big breakfasts anymore. As soon as we had our porridge and a glass of milk and piece of toast, we were finished. Poor Mother was so disappointed.

We were pushing pretty close to the financial edge all summer, but the closest we got to falling over it was in Kamsack, Saskatchewan. We were entered in a ball tournament nearby in a tiny little place called Togo. It was a one-elevator town even back then, but it had a big ball tournament with $125 for first place. We were staying in the Kamsack Hotel, but we had no money to pay our bill. I said, "Fellas, we have to go out the fire escapes," and out we crept, bags in hand. We spent our last few nickels at a Chinese restaurant across the street, and now we had to win the Togo tournament in order to pay our hotel bill. Off we went to play.

We wound up in the final game. And by the bottom of the ninth inning, the score was tied at one. We had two out, two men on and Fred Wiest, our big hitter, was up to bat. The first two pitches came in right down the middle, but Fred just looked at both of them as they whizzed by. I called time out and ran in from third base. "Fred, what are you doing?" I pleaded. "You gotta get a hit." Fred, always so calm, just waved me off. "Don't worry, don't worry. I'll get one." I went back to my spot. Fred took a couple of balls, then nailed one, just laced it over second base for a beautiful line drive. I think Fred left those first two pineapples deliberately, just to make it more interesting. With his hit, we won the game, pocketed the money and went back to Kamsack to pay our bills.

My time at Notre Dame seemed to fly by. I arrived in the summer of 1938 to finish my Grade 11 and graduated from Grade 12 in 1940.

But in a very real way, I never left Notre Dame. Yes, I've put in a lot of work on the alumni association and fund raising and serving on the college's Senate, but that's not what I'm talking about. That feeling of being a Hound, of belonging to a band of brothers under an exceptional leader, is still with me today. Père was like a second father to me. He used to say to me, "Bill, you're going to be a leader. You can do it. Don't even listen to the nayers. What has negativism ever built? You've got to be positive and enthusiastic." I'm sure Père told that to many boys at Notre Dame, but his words made a huge impression on me. I guess I'm probably not alone in that, either. If you look around, you'll find Notre Dame graduates all over the world, many of them at the top of their field. Père's gift was the ability to inspire. I like to think that's one of my gifts, too.

And I believe it was Père who showed me how to use that gift and how powerful it can be.

Some years later, when I owned the Medicine Hat Tigers and later the Edmonton Oil Kings, I'd take every opportunity when we were on a road trip to bring my players to Notre Dame. I'd give a talk to the student body, and then Père would get together with my boys. Every time they were enthralled.

That, however, was years down the road. It was 1940 when I graduated, and it seemed to me and most of my friends that there was work to be done overseas. I thought I'd see what I could do to pitch in.

# 3

# FIGHTER PILOT

**One day as we were about to take off,
Harley reached up into my cockpit,
jammed the throttle forward and said,
"Good luck!" He stepped onto the ground.**

I HADN'T TOLD MY MOTHER I WAS GOING
away to school at Notre Dame, and I didn't tell her I was going away
to fight the Nazis, either. I enlisted almost immediately after I graduated from Notre Dame.

The war seemed like an adventure that everyone was getting in
on. All my chums on the street had gone, and fighting for your
country seemed like something you had to do. Night after night,
Winston Churchill was on the radio talking about fighting spirit
and courage, and day after day the newspaper ran drum-beating
articles praising Saskatoon's war effort and the boys who were heading overseas. I wanted to be a part of this massive effort. I felt I owed
it to the community around me.

Debate was a big part of Notre Dame's teaching program, and
I was used to people having differing opinions. I knew it was nor-

mal to open the newspaper and have columnists and letter-writers arguing over an issue. But when talk came to the war, there was near complete unanimity. Hitler and the Nazis had to be fought. The patriotism was coming from everywhere, and you could feel it bubbling up in yourself, too. It was in the air, and I caught myself a good dose of it.

My buddies and I had been talking about joining up for a while, tossing around which branch of the service we'd choose. Like a lot of prairie boys, many of my friends joined the navy. So many Saskatoon boys became sailors that they named a destroyer *The City of Saskatoon*. I'm not sure why, but I opted for the army. In the fall of 1939, I walked down to the recruiting station at the exhibition grounds and signed up with the Saskatoon Light Infantry.

The recruiting was done in one of the big buildings normally used for the exhibition shows. But instead of livestock or displays of homemade preserves, it was full of officers sitting behind tables piled high with sheets of paper in front of which stood long lines of would-be soldiers. The officers gave us a quick medical exam and jotted down our particulars. They wanted soldiers to be 21, but I was only 19, so I lied about my age. The recruiter was a friend of our family, a Captain Kramer, and he knew perfectly well how old I was. He was a handsome man, very imposing in his immaculate uniform, and I quailed a little when he looked at me hard and asked, "Bill, are you sure you want to do this?" I swallowed hard and said, "Yes, sir." I signed up. I was told I'd hear in a couple of day if I had made the grade, as if only the select few would be allowed to fight for King and Country. Of course, that's how they wanted you to feel, and I suppose I fell for it. I was scared stiff I'd be rejected. I was so proud when the phone call came and I was informed I had met His Majesty's lofty standards and I would muster at the Saskatoon exhibition grounds.

I'd broken the news to my parents when I came back from the recruiting station. Dad's blind eye had kept him out of the previous war, but he'd seen and heard enough to sit me down and do his best to burst my bubble. He made it clear that I was doing a serious thing. War was no lark and it wasn't about glory. People were going to try to kill me, and they might well do it. He wasn't trying to talk me out of going. He just wanted to make sure I had joined because I was proud of my country and wanted to keep it safe. He was really proud of me and he told me so. That felt good. Of course, my sisters and mother cried, and that didn't feel so good. "Oh Billy," sighed Mother, "I don't think this is necessary. You're so young." Still, nobody really tried to talk me out of enlisting. Mother knew that once I got my heart set on something, nothing could keep me from it. It was Notre Dame all over again but for much higher stakes.

About a week after our first muster, we were taken to the army camp at Dundurn, just south of Saskatoon, for training. At first army life suited me. In many ways it wasn't that much different from being a Hound. The army was like being on the biggest hockey team you could imagine. You were wearing a snappy uniform and felt you were doing something positive. I felt right at home. I even enjoyed the discipline and the regimentation.

And a good thing, too, because there was plenty of regimentation. The Sergeant-Major in charge of our training was from the famous Princess Patricia's Canadian Light Infantry. He was a stickler who carefully waxed his handlebar mustache every morning and strutted around the camp with a swagger stick under his arm. If your rifle didn't absolutely gleam and if you didn't make your bed so a bullet could bounce off, you were in trouble. He drilled us hard, but part of his job was to give us heart and pride, and he did that, too. Like my grandfather and Père, he could inspire with words.

He'd fought in India and in the First World War, and he could talk army for hours. He was proud to be a soldier, and he passed that on to us. But my God, he was tough.

We stayed in long wooden buildings with bunk beds for up to 60 soldiers. A sergeant at the end of the barracks kept up discipline. Lights were out and silence reigned at 11:00 P.M. sharp. We marched our feet sore across the parade square, out in the sand hills and over the bald, tabletop prairie. Our machine-gun unit drilled for hours on heavy old Lewis guns. We could strip down those tripod-mounted beasts and build them back up again blindfolded. Once we were good enough, we had mock battles using live ammunition. We'd go on the firing range and practice spraying our bullets back and forth so that the fields of fire would cross and nobody could get through.

Dundurn wasn't much bigger than Wilcox, but its social life was a big improvement. We had a decent hockey team, for which I played goal although my dad snorted when he found out that was my position. I moved myself to center after that. But the best part was getting dressed up in our brand-new uniforms and going to check out the local dances. In Dundurn, of course, there were a hundred of us young bravos for every girl, so we had to go a bit farther afield until the odds evened out. We were pretty cocky. We were young, fit and full of purpose. We felt good.

But all of a sudden it was taken away from me. One day our unit got the word we were going overseas—all except me and a few others. We were to stay back in Dundurn and help train the next recruits. Sure, I'd gotten pretty good on the Lewis gun. But I think the real reason I wasn't shipped overseas was I was still under age. They didn't want any 19-year-olds on the front lines, not just yet.

I was brokenhearted. I couldn't believe I was going to be torn away from my new friends. I thought these guys were going to be my comrades through blood and thunder and my pals for the rest of our lives. I felt like my team was leaving without me. I stood in the parade square watching the boys load into the truck convoys to head off to battle. I was thinking, You lucky stiffs.

For three weeks I stayed in Dundurn trying to whip a new bunch of raw recruits into shape. I did the drills and the marches and the inspections, but I had no heart for it. I was promoted to lance-corporal, but I didn't care. I kept comparing the new guys to my old pals, and they just didn't seem to measure up. I dogged the admin office, pestering them for any word about going overseas to rejoin my team, but none ever came. Nor could I seem to get over my loss. The thought kept stirring inside me: My gang is gone; they left me behind. One day I couldn't stand it anymore. I said to myself, I'm going AWOL. I'm getting out of this goddamn thing. I packed up, went back to Saskatoon, checked into the King George Hotel and waited for the military police to arrest me. I didn't dare go home.

The MPs hauled me back to Dundurn and tossed me in the brig. I called my dad and told him what I had done. I told him I wanted to get the hell out of the army. I said I wanted to fly and that I wanted a transfer to the air force. If I couldn't be with my old team, I'd find a new one. Besides, I'd seen planes soaring overhead while we were training at Dundurn, and it seemed flying would sure beat marching. Dad just said, "Mm-hmm" or something like that. For over a week I sat in military prison. It felt like a lot longer. I wasn't allowed visitors, the drill was even tougher than basic training and worst of all I didn't know what was going to happen to me.

Though I didn't learn the facts until later, every day my dad was pulling strings and talking to his friends who were high-ranking officers, but the army wouldn't let him contact me. Finally, Dad's old post office colleague Lieutenant-Colonel Pallie Pascoe wangled me a transfer. One morning a pair of officers marched down to my cell and said, "Hunter, you're going into the air force." They marched me smart out of my cell and an MP took me to Saskatoon and into the office of Dr. Barney McPhail. I took a few tests. One involved standing a nail on its head in the middle of a metal plate and having me raise and lower the plate without tipping the nail over. They wanted to see how steady my hands were. I could do it with my right hand, but I couldn't with my left because of my tremor. Dr. McPhail looked at me, paused a second and said, "I didn't see that." He called me fit to fly and welcomed me into the air force.

My flight training began in Vancouver, where the air force had set up a flying school on Sea Island at the airport. Canada would soon develop a huge pilot training program, but at this point things were just getting started. We didn't even have proper uniforms yet. Instead, we just pinned blue wings on our air force khaki. We were something of a novelty, and our Sunday training exercises got to be a bit of a show. The local girls would come down to watch, and we played up the air of mystery our ambiguous uniforms gave us. We'd tell them we were with General Chenault's famous Flying Tigers and in Vancouver on secret assignment. The girls seemed impressed.

Life in the air force was much more relaxed. We were living in civilian quarters, not barracks. We didn't do much marching. The life felt different, too. In the army you were always surrounded by other men, and you hardly ever acted individually. But a fighter pilot is on his own. The air force was trying to get recruits used to making their own decisions. We'd listen to speakers sent out to inspire us with stories of the great Canadian pilots of the First World War. At first I missed being on a team. But soon I grew to love the freedom and excitement of flying as much as I had loved pulling together in a group with my infantry buddies.

But first we had to learn how to fly. We flew Tiger Moths, an old two-seat open-cockpit biplane. We looked like something right

*My little sister Bev posed with me for this photo just before I left for flight training. It felt great to be in an airforce uniform.*

out of the last world war with our flying jackets, leather helmets and goggles. Our instructors were bush pilots the air force had hauled down from the North. My bush pilot was a grizzled old curmudgeon named Harley Godwin.

For a few flights, I kept my hands on the linked controls as Harley flew the plane. Shouting over the roar of the engine through the speaking tube between us, Harley explained what he was doing as I felt his maneuvers on the linked controls. We spent about three and a half hours in the air like that. One day as we were about to take off, Harley reached up into my cockpit, jammed the throttle forward and said, "Good luck!" He stepped onto the ground. Before I knew it I was rumbling faster and faster down the runway, pulling back on the controls and suddenly I was in the air. God, it was wonderful to be flying for the first time by myself with the wind and the

*The day before leaving for Halifax to await orders to embark for overseas. Beside me is Captain Bob Porter.*

engine in my ears and nothing but sky all around. Wonderful, that is, until I started to think about landing. The airstrip looked about the size of a playing card in the middle of a football field. My landing was anything but perfect, but I got the Tiger Moth down.

We spent about three months at Sea Island before being sent to Macleod, deep in the southern Alberta foothills country to finish our training. I took to flying pretty naturally, and Macleod was where I got my wings, chasing cattle while practicing low-level flying. I couldn't believe how much force the wind picked up coming down off the Rockies. We could point our Avro Anson twin-engined trainers directly into the wind, throttle back and just hang motionless in midair. One day it blew so hard that a couple of planes were torn loose from their moorings and flipped over like a kid's balsa-wood glider. The roof was blown right off one of the hangers, and we had to lie on the floor along the windward wall for our safety.

After three or four months in Macleod, where I received the rank of Sergeant Pilot, our group got the call to head overseas. We all got a week's home leave before being herded aboard an Australian troopship called the *Andes,* on which we steamed into the Atlantic and toward Britain.

The crossing was no fun. The *Andes* had a flat bottom, and she swayed like a drunken man. Everybody got seasick. Some of us were so miserable we would have handed Hitler the keys to the Commonwealth if he could have made that ship sit still. And when we weren't concentrating on keeping our meals below decks, we were thinking about U-boats. We were a tempting target. Our convoy was so huge it had taken five days for all the ships to embark from Halifax in two long lines. With tens of thousands of soldiers and airmen in our convoy, the destroyers around our perimeter had a job keeping lookout for German submarines.

Two or three days out of Halifax, our convoy did tangle with a U-boat wolf pack. The sirens started to howl, and we all scrambled onto deck to man our battle stations. The night sky was lit up with flares and the dark, choppy water was aglow with floodlights sweeping back and forth, searching for the enemy. Guns were firing and engines were roaring and our escort ships were tearing around trying to fight off the attack. Once or twice the floodlights lit up a U-boat that had surfaced right in the middle of our convoy, but they were too close to fire their torpedoes. While the U-boat tried to move into firing position, our destroyers would try to ram them and drop depth charges. We watched sailors roll depth charges off the end of our ship, too, and the underwater explosions sent up huge geysers with a muffled whump. At one point another troop ship pulled within a few hundred feet of us. It was the *Acquitania* with 17,000 men aboard. It was about midnight, but everything was so lit up that the staring eyes of the soldiers on the decks opposite were as clear as at high noon.

Eventually, our Canadian destroyers beat the German subs off without losing a ship. It had been my first taste of action. I felt not a bit afraid, and I don't think any of my comrades did, either. We were still too dumb to understand that the bombs were real, and that they could actually sink us. So we watched the spectacle like a crowd at a hockey game, cheering our side on, for that's all it seemed.

Our innocence didn't last long. We landed in England after about a week at sea and were sent to the embarkation point at Bournemouth, along the English Channel. From Bournemouth young pilots were assigned to various squadrons. Bournemouth was also the target of low-level bombing raids by the Luftwaffe. You could hear the planes before you could see them, five or six Messerschmitts skimming over the water in broad daylight beneath the Allied radar. Eventually, the whine of their engines would be joined by the boom of the shore batteries trying to knock as many down as they could. The raiders that dodged the flak would send their planes hurling over the embankment at the last moment and roar over the city, leaving crashing bomb blasts in their wake.

For some reason the park in the center of Bournemouth took many hits, and it was where the reality of war began to sink in. Here, there'd be green, manicured grass, paths and park benches, just what you imagine in a peaceful English park. But over there would be a gaping crater full of blasted earth with huge trees uprooted and tossed about like twigs. I got my final lesson in the reality of war the day one of those raids hit a hotel. A bomb went through the roof into the pub. Among the other patrons that day were about five Canadian boys playing pool and having a pint. They all died and took the last shreds of my sense of invulnerability with them.

I had trained on twin-engine aircraft and was assigned to a squadron flying Blenheims and Beauforts, which were small fighter-bombers with a navigator and a tail gunner. My first assignment was flying raids much like what the Germans had done over Bournemouth. We'd get our orders, skim the ocean over to France and try to take out our target before the Germans could scramble fighters against us. It was in and out, and we could usually avoid the Luftwaffe, but the flak from the ground was like flying through a tunnel of fire. All around would be explosions, smoke, fires, planes holding formation and planes going down. Your ears would be roaring with the sound of your engine, the crackle of your radio and the hell that was breaking outside the cockpit. Sometimes we flew at night, and you couldn't tell where the ground was. Your mind would be focussed on two things: dropping an accurate bomb and staying alive. There was just fear, adrenaline, snapshots of sight and sound, and mingled triumph and relief as we headed back over the channel to England.

I'd been flying those missions for about six months when my plane got shot up on a night flight. Fear melted away in my desperation to get my crew and my plane home, which I did despite the bullets in the engine. The landing, however, was harder on me than the mission. The wheel snapped back and slammed me in the mouth. I broke my arm and wrist.

After recuperating I was reassigned to a fighter squadron, piloting Spitfires and Hurricanes with the RAF's International Squadron. I loved both those planes. The Hurricane was a beautifully balanced, agile little machine that was forgiving and a delight to fly. But the Spitfire was like riding a wild beast with wings. It was fast and powerful to start with and just got faster and more powerful as the war went on. When that muscular Rolls-Royce engine fired up, you could feel the vibration all the way down your backbone. The Spitfire was touchy to handle but thrilling.

Our days quickly fell into a routine. We each had a little bedroom, and if there had been no early scramble to respond to an enemy attack we'd be rousted from them at 6:00 or 7:00 A.M. We'd meet with our flight commander and plan our next mission. Sometimes plans were sprung on us to foil any intelligence the Germans had gathered. We flew a lot of bomber escort duty. We also patrolled the channel, looking for those daylight raiders that had terrorized Bournemouth. You couldn't just swoop down and attack those guys. They were too low. You generally had to shadow them until they gained a little altitude. Then you could make your move.

After eight months in Spits, the RAF pulled me back from the front. With my experience flying both fighters and bombers, I became a test pilot. Eventually, I flew four-engine Halifax and Wellington bombers but never into combat. I also flew a lot of dispatches and dignitaries around England. This was fairly hush-hush work. Much of the time I didn't even know who was on board.

The RAF gave its pilots 17 days leave every six weeks, time that I usually spent in London. It often wasn't much of a respite. At the height of the blitz, the Germans were desperately hammering the British people, trying to break their will. Cities like Coventry were being bombed regularly, and I experienced many, many air raids in London. It was like being in our troop convoy all over again: sirens, floodlights, explosions, tired and frightened faces glimpsed in flashes of light.

Those are my war stories. By some standards I didn't see much action, and I don't talk much about the fighting I did see. Those planes breaking formation and going down were full of my friends, my teammates. It still hurts me to think of them and the sacrifice of their young lives. Still, not everything that happened was tragic. We had some fun and a few laughs. We only in our early twenties, and the war didn't knock all the spirit out of us.

One night there was a big dance at one of the towns where we were stationed. A bunch of Canadian and American officers in attendance had a few drinks. Okay, more than a few drinks, and we were acting like it. At one point the town mayor, a proper tea-taking Englishman, came over and surveyed the whole disorderly lot of us. "Well," he announced to the colonials, "I'm disgusted."

"Pleased to meetcha, Disgusted," slurred one of my buddies. "I'm Lou."

Armed forces of any kind are notorious for administrative snafus, and at one point I ran into a beauty. For a while I was a warrant officer at an aerodrome in a place called Halton. We numbered eight pilots, a parachute officer and an administrative officer and me. However, the unit that had been housed on the base before us had numbered 120, and their rations continued to arrive. In came big flats of food and drink, and I'd sign for them. Best of all, those rations included liquor. We had cases and cases of Vat 69 scotch whiskey. We did our best to live up to the RAF's apparent expectations of our capacity, but eventually even we couldn't keep up. I struck a deal with the pubs in the neighboring villages. We slipped them our extra scotch, and in return we ate and drank on their premises for free. But even that tactic didn't much to reduce the stock of whiskey. We forced it by the caseload on fellows going home on vacations. "We gotta get rid of this stuff," we'd insist. Whiskey cases overwhelmed our storage facilities until we had to stack them out back and cover them with a tarp.

One day our group captain came by for an inspection. He lifted the tarp with his swagger stick, gave me a wry little look and said, "Hunter, you people seem to be doing all right." He never mentioned it again. The whiskey river was still flowing when I was transferred, so I don't know how long it lasted.

Of course, the military always gets you back. I had been serving with the RAF, but I was still a member of the Canadian Forces. Early in the war the Canadian Pay Corps had lost stacks of our records. They realized the mistake at the end of my fighting, when the RAF was through with me. As they sorted the mess out, we were to go to RCAF headquarters at Lincolnson Field in London and sign chits for cash as we needed it. I saw what I thought was an opportunity. I said to my friends, "They'll never catch up with this. Those records are gone forever. There's no way they're going to be able to compare these chits with what we're actually owed, so let's spend as much as we can." I convinced them, and for a while we had a ball. But much to my dismay, the original pay records turned up, and I was summoned into some dreary little paymaster's office in Warrington. I wound up owing the air force $4,800, which was duly deducted from my pay when I mustered out.

In 1943, while I was flying out of an aerodrome at Little Risington in Gloucestershire, I met an English woman named Dorothy Capelle. Dorothy was serving in the women's corps at a nearby village. We crossed paths socially, and in the course of our duties, and we fell in love. Things happened quickly, as they do in wartime, and that year we were not only married but also had our first child, Robert John. Our second, Carol Anne, came the next year. Dorothy followed me back to Canada, but she never felt at home here. I never understood what I could do to make her happy here, and she just couldn't get used to the Canadian way of life in places like Saskatoon and North Battleford. She was constantly homesick for England, and after a few years she returned home. We were divorced, and she took the children with her. Robert has since returned and now lives in Canada. I'm starting to rebuild a relationship with both him and his sister. My first marriage was the product of the times we were living through, and perhaps once those times were over, there wasn't enough left to sustain the hard work of making a life together. Dorothy was a fine woman, though, (she has since died of cancer) and she did a wonderful job with our children. I'm proud of them both.

My tour of duty ended in 1944, and the air force decided to send me back to Canada for a while. I was sent home on the *Queen Elizabeth,* an enormous luxury liner that had been outfitted as a troopship. For this voyage, however, there were only 500 of us—250 airmen and 250 American Red Cross nurses—accompanied by a USO troop featuring Jimmy Cagney. The voyage back was one long party, and one night Cagney put on a two-and-a-half-hour show. Cagney did his signature bit, his Yankee Doodle Dandy routine. He looked exactly like he did in the movies, all cocky and confident.

The only problem was that the *Queen Elizabeth* was so fast that our trip only lasted a few days. In fact, it was so fast it didn't need an escort. When we saw we were pulling out of the harbor with nothing to defend us from the U-boats we were a little concerned. But our captain reassured us over the intercom in the plummiest of upper-crust tones: "Ladies and gentlemen, fear not. Should any submarines try to disrupt our passage to America, we are quite fast enough to outrun any of them."

We heard him again when we sailed into New York Harbor. "Ladies and gentlemen, I advise you muster on deck immediately. You are never likely to see such a sight again."

It was the Statue of Liberty. The Americans started singing "The Star Spangled Banner." We answered with "O Canada." We were all weeping. And as we neared the dock, everywhere you looked were people waving and bands playing. It was as if the whole city had come out to welcome the team home and shake our hands. Walking down that gangplank was overwhelming.

Of course, I wasn't quite home. We took the train to Ottawa that night and there the reception was somewhat different. There were no bands, no banners, no welcoming committee. A few officers met us to make sure we were all right and get us on the right trains to our final destinations. It was somehow a very Canadian greeting.

Now I had some thinking to do. I had survived the war. I was grown up. What was I going to do for the rest of my life?

My first choice was to stay in the air force. I was assigned to a base in Portage la Prairie, Manitoba. I had lots of fun playing and coaching football and heading into Winnipeg for a few beers after games. I enrolled in officer's training school at Trenton, Ontario. But after two weeks, I started to have doubts.

I was sitting a bar socializing with a few veterans when I suddenly realized I was tired of thinking about the war. I wanted to move on. I didn't want to be constantly rehashing memories of that raid over Calais or how bad the food was or how good the friends were. And I knew that many people around me who hadn't served for one reason or another didn't want to listen to me till and retill that same old ground. I wanted to rejoin the world. I wanted to move forward, to prove to the world that Bill Hunter could do some things on his own.

I was 19 years old when I enlisted, motivated by a desire for adventure as much as anything else. I enjoyed the military and took a lot of valuable lessons from it. Nothing drives home the value of discipline and teamwork like times when your life literally depends on it. But I was 24 now, vastly more experienced and with a growing sense that I wanted to do something in the world to make my mark. I didn't need the military anymore.

Finally, there I was, sitting in a drowsy classroom in Trenton, listening to our instructor begin the process of turning former pilots and soldiers and sailors into military paper-pushers. I realized that if I became a permanent serviceman, my life was going to be spelled out for me. I walked over to the office that day, filled out more of those forms the military loves and received my honorable discharge.

I took the train back home to Saskatoon. My war was over.

# 4

# BACK ON CIVVY STREET

**I'd left the air force because I wanted to see what I could do, and it seemed to me that working in radio was all about describing what other people could do. I wanted to be on my own.**

GOT OFF THE TRAIN IN DOWNTOWN Saskatoon in the late spring of 1944. I had some money jingling in the pockets of my service uniform and not much else. I had a world of experience behind me and the rest of my life in front of me. It was the best feeling in the world. I stepped onto the platform and got on with it.

There were no marching bands or banners of welcome. The train had been a short-hauler from Regina, and it had carried just a couple ex-servicemen like me. But I got all the welcome I needed from my family. Mother and two of my sisters shed a few tears to see me home in one piece. Even Dad gave me a hug. "Well done, Bill. I'm so proud of you," he said, and there may have been a bit of a choke in his voice, too.

The first chance I got, I went out for a bit of a walk and had a look at my old hometown. I'd enjoyed England, but it was good to be back in Saskatoon. The river valley was fresh and green with spring. The air had that prairie smell I'd missed for four years. And the years I'd been away had been kind to the old place. That bustle I'd remembered from my childhood was back on the streets. The downtown sidewalks were crowded with businessmen and secretaries wearing sharp suits and nice skirts, and the streets were filled with cars. There were men and women in uniform, too. We smiled at each other a little sheepishly, as if we realized that we were wearing last year's fashions to the party. We'd won the war. Now everyone wanted to get on with a prosperous peace.

New industry was moving into town. Gangs of workmen were building a new bridge across the river. A new hockey arena had been constructed on the riverbank. The university was expanding with great things beginning to come from it. In the country, crops were good, and the farmers were coming into town on weekends with money to spend. It seemed as if everywhere there was a new enthusiasm. This place is on the move, I thought. That suited me. I didn't know what I was going to do, but I knew one thing: I was on the move, too. I decided Saskatoon would be a good place to knock around a bit until I figured out what that move would be.

After putting my feet up for a few days, the first knocking I did was on the door of CFQC radio. I knew sports and I'd done that bit of sportswriting back at Notre Dame, so I thought I'd see if I could get a job as a sportscaster. I made a few calls and wound up in the office of A.A. Murphy, who had started CFQC radio in 1922 as a way to sell more crystal radios out of his electronics store. Local legend had it that when he and his partner split up the electronics business, A.A. kept the station because nobody figured there would ever be any money in radio. I made my pitch. I told him about my record from Nutana Collegiate and Notre Dame. Murphy knew how prominent my family was in Saskatoon sports, for he was a longtime family friend, and I suppose that didn't hurt my job chances. Whatever I said must have worked because Murphy gave me my first civilian job at the wage of $85 a month. Dad liked the idea of his son being a broadcaster. CFQC was the only radio station in town, and to him, being sports director was a pretty prominent job to walk into fresh out of the service.

CFQC didn't waste any time putting me on air. Almost my first day at work, I found myself sweaty-palmed and nervous in the studio. It was a dimly lit cavelike room, with a saucer-sized microphone, sound-deadening padded walls and a window behind which the technician did mysterious things with switches and knobs. Stan Clifton, the station engineer, had designed and built practically everything in the station, and hardly anyone understood those control panels except him. I started out reading hospital reports, reciting the names of patients in the Saskatoon General and giving a one- or two-word description of their condition. When I got the producer's cue, the first words I croaked onto the public airwaves were probably something like: "Mrs. Mary Jones, progressing favorably."

I had so much to learn. I had to learn how to handle myself in a studio and get comfortable with being in front of an audience. I had to learn when to follow a script and when—and how—to improvise. My initial ignorance was painfully obvious to news director Godfrey Hudson. Hudson was of the old school, very meticulous and precise, especially when it came to pronouncing the English language. He was always hounding the announcers when it came to diction, and it was Hudson who taught me to speak clearly and distinctly. Eventually, I got comfortable addressing the public. It seemed to come naturally to me, and I started doing other things such as reading newscasts. I spun records. And I'd go out in the field, hauling a clunky reel-to-reel tape recorder with a microphone the size of a potato masher.

I covered a lot of court, where I saw some colorful jurisprudence. One particularly memorable lawyer named Ludwig, a man with a well-known and powerful thirst for malt beverages, used to defend bootleggers. I was covered one of his cases that all the reporters expected would end in a conviction, for it seemed pretty clear what the accused had been up to. We had all but laid bets on the sentence when Ludwig walked into court with suspicious clinks coming from his briefcase. The Crown put their star witness on the stand, an informant who claimed to have such an educated palate for beer that he could identify the maker simply by tasting the product. Ludwig began his cross-examination by opening the musical briefcase. Out came four bottles of beer, no doubt from Ludwig's personal collection. He lined them up before the witness. "Open them, sir, and have a swig," commanded Ludwig. "Can you identify which one was made by my client?" The witness couldn't, the Crown's case collapsed and Ludwig's client walked. As to whether he was paid in kind or in cash, I never discovered.

I often watched another interesting young lawyer argue cases in Saskatoon, a tall, slim, wiry-haired chap with fervor in his voice. He was John Diefenbaker and he could mesmerize a courtroom: the judge, the jury and all the witnesses. You couldn't take your eyes off him. He'd look around the courtroom and it would seem as if he was looking directly at each and every one of us. Diefenbaker was always well-prepared and confident. He never spoke from notes. He was quick and witty, and whenever the atmosphere in court got a little tense, he'd slip in a joke to get the jury on his side. He was such a speaker that I'd joke to my courtroom cronies that by the time Diefenbaker was finished, a man who knew he was guilty as sin would be saying to himself, "You know, I may be innocent after all."

Court was interesting but my passion was for sports, and in the winter of 1944 I became sports director. Right away we got involved in broadcasting an exciting intermediate championship series between Laura, a tiny town just outside Saskatoon, and my old alma mater, the Notre Dame Hounds. This was pretty good hockey. The Laura Beavers were financed by a wealthy local farmer who had brought in some good players, one of them being Doug Bentley, one of the famous Bentley brothers, who was their playing coach. Doug had been a star in the National League and led the league in scoring, but he was back home during the war on a farmer's exemption and was a powerhouse on the local team. There were quite a few National Leaguers in similar situations. The Canmore Brickateers, for example, had the Chakowski brothers from the Chicago Blackhawks. They were back home pulling shifts at one of the local coal mines.

In this series I was secretly cheering for the Hounds although I think I inadvertently had something to do undermining their chances. Bentley knew his Beavers were weak in goal, but the league rules did not allow changes in the roster. While talking hockey with him one day, I mentioned that Prince Albert had a great young goaltender named Johnny Kiskin. Johnny Kiskin later changed his name and went on to great fame in the NHL as Johnny Bower. Doug went away and thought about things and shortly after he called in his regular goalie and informed him that he was sick. "I'm not sick! I feel fine," the poor guy protested, even coming down the rink, but Doug insisted that the man was on death's door and even produced a medical certificate from a cooperative local doctor as evidence. With his regular goalie feeling so poorly, Bentley was able to go to the league and get their permission to bring in a new netminder. Doug headed to Prince Albert and came back with Kiskin. I broadcast that whole series, which had loud sellout crowds of 5,200 people and great, exciting hockey every night. Even with Doug Bentley controlling the play and Kiskin backstopping him, the Beavers needed seven hard-fought games to beat the Hounds led by Doug Toole. As for Laura's regular goalie, he spent the entire series up in the press box, just a few feet from where I was calling the game. I never did tell him who had tipped Bentley to Kiskin.

I covered everything in sports: hockey, football, baseball, curling, whatever came up. I fit right in with Saskatoon's sports world. I knew almost everyone, and we'd spend hours over a coffee or a beer arguing about who was better at what and how this coach should have handled that situation. It was great fun except for one thing.

At the end of every month, I walked down the hall to the office of Miss Murphy, a heavyset, warmhearted woman who was CFQC's controller. She held the purse strings. "Miss Murphy," I told her, "I'm starving! I can't live on $85 a month." The first time she just sighed, pursed her lips and handed me my cheque. But I wore her down, and eventually her grandmotherly soul found me another $5 a month. I persisted, and she coughed up another $20. Still, it wasn't enough. I finally walked in to her office and said, "I have to leave. I really enjoy it, but it's a luxury I can't afford."

A.A. Murphy's office was next door. He hardly ever left the room, but he kept the door open and his ears peeled for everything that went on in that station. For a big man in a tightly buttoned suit, he hopped over to his controller's office pretty quickly. Murphy wasn't known as a free-spender (CFQC's offices were notably bare of any decoration), but he offered to make me the highest-paid sportscaster in western Canada at $150 a month. That kept me around a little longer. But ultimately I decided sports journalism wasn't for me any more than the military was. I'd left the air force because I wanted to see what I could do, and it seemed to me that working in radio was all about describing what other people could do. I wanted to be on my own.

A friend of mine was a traveling salesman, and he'd been telling me how well he was doing. When I saw an ad in the *StarPhoenix* for a job selling for General Foods, I jumped at it. Harry LeBlonde, General Foods district manager, gave me an interview and hired me at $200 a month, plus expenses, plus a brand-new, four-door Dodge painted a deep midnight blue. That was decent money, and it was great to have a vehicle. But best of all, I was now on my own to see what I could make of things.

My territory was northwest Saskatchewan, so I moved to North Battleford. The job wasn't complicated. General Foods sold everything from Swansdown Cake Mix to Post Corn Flakes to Baker's Chocolate to Maxwell House coffee. I'd drive around to all the general stores and restaurants in the surrounding towns, pitch the products and take the orders. I'd make my first call at eight o'clock in the morning and hit seven to nine towns a day. I knew all those little towns so well—all with their one or two elevators, their Railway Avenues and their Chinese cafes. Meadow Lake, Lloydminster, Radisson, Dalmeny, Kerrobert, Maidstone and Biggar. Banging and clattering over roads that were barely worthy of the name, I schlepped java and Jell-O in towns that don't even exist anymore.

On one trip I thought I'd be clever and save a little time by driving cross-country from Meadow Lake to Goodsoil on an old Indian trail I had discovered. It was a great trip. I had the window down, my elbow hanging over the sill, enjoying the day and the countryside—until I got hung up axle-deep in sand without a farmhouse or even a proper road to one for miles. Fortunately, I was prepared. I hauled out the axe and shovel I always traveled with and cut down some willows to put under the wheels. I improvised a little corduroy road through the soft parts. That sort of thing was just routine. I wasn't even late for my appointment.

I got to know all the storekeepers, too. They were all different.

My challenge was to figure out how to communicate with them, and I got pretty quick. I could walk in and size up the storekeeper almost before I'd strolled over to his counter. I could tell immediately if he was one of those tough customers who are gruff toward salesmen on principle or if he was one of those easy-going guys who are always happy to have a visitor. I could figure out if he made the decisions or if his wife or eldest son held the real power. I was quick and I was good. At the end of the day, when I was compiling my orders in some small-town hotel room over the local beer parlor, there was always plenty to tote up. I won an award once for selling more Maxwell House coffee than any other salesman in the country. I had every Chinese cafe in my territory convinced it was good to the last drop.

Ironically, it was that award that led me to leave General Foods. Harry LeBlonde wanted to take me to Winnipeg, where the president of the Canadian division would present me with the award at the western Canada convention. We went, and as we were milling around at the banquet, Harry introduced me to the president, a Mr. Egli, who had come up from the United States. My old Princess Pat drill sergeant would have approved. Egli was spit-and-polish all the way. He wore a tailor-made coat with a velvet collar, white kid gloves and gleaming white spats. It's been a while since this guy has had to dig his car out to make a sales call, I thought.

My impressions didn't improve. When I was introduced, Egli said, "What's your name again?" I told him again and he asked, "Where are you from?" I said North Battleford, and he said, "Where's that?"

I thought, What the hell kind of situation is this? This guy is pretending to make a big deal of me, but he can't even be bothered to find out where I'm from. I didn't like the idea of working for a president who treated his people in the field like that. Our sales paid for his spats. I couldn't bear to be anyone's anonymous drudge, and I made up my mind to quit General Foods. George Dent, a real gentleman who was the manager for western Canada, begged me not to go. "Bill, you can be a top man," he said.

But I went back to North Battleford with my award, wrote a letter of resignation and sent it special delivery to General Foods head office in Toronto. That's that, I thought—until the next morning, when I got a letter from that same head office offering me a job as assistant advertising manager for all of Canada. At the time, General Foods spent more on advertising than the rest of the food companies in North America put together. They sponsored TV shows like Jack Benny. And I had been offered a piece of the action the day after my resignation had passed it in the mail. I breathed a few heavy sighs, but the more I thought about it the fewer regrets I had. I didn't want to be an employee anymore. And if I'd taken that job, I would have been even closer to Egli.

It was surprising how good it felt. That letter of resignation was like a get-out-of-jail-free card, and I had a few ideas about how to make use of my new liberty. I had about $4,500 left from the military, enough to set myself up nicely. My dad tipped me to a big general store in southern Saskatchewan that was for sale. I thought about that for a while, but eventually I decided against it. There was a better opportunity closer to home.

North Battleford had a small sporting goods store owned by a nice old French Canadian named Alphonse Coté. He was looking to retire and not much interested in his store. Sometimes he was open, sometimes he wasn't. Outside, the building was desperate for a coat of paint, and inside there were a lot of empty shelves. He sold a few skates and some balls and supplied all the other French Canadian farmers in the area with the leaf tobacco they liked. He had a big display cabinet full of it. Advertising? Alphonse would have asked, "What's that?" I looked around at North Battleford and thought it was a terrific place to sell sporting goods. There was great fishing, great hunting and lots of sports fans. Alphonse had a great location, right on the main street, with plenty of frontage and big show windows. I looked at the run-down old place and thought it represented a missed opportunity. So that fall I bought it, painted it white and cream with some red and black trim, hustled up some inventory and opened Hunter's Sporting Goods. That first weekend we did a land-office business with 11 people on staff and two cash registers ringing nonstop. I brought in some Christmas toys and games and sold them out in a couple of weeks.

Alphonse didn't have much in stock, but one thing he did have was bicycle parts. He easily had the biggest stock of bicycle parts in the province, bins full of them in the middle of the store. He had a great shop in the back hung with bike chains and wheels and spokes and tires and even more in a dugout basement. This, I realized, was a gold mine.

Bicycles were hard to get after the war. All the available steel had been channeled into the war effort and very little was going into bicycle frames. There were a few bikes around, and I moved quickly to lock them up. I called Jack Pape, who was CCM's western Canada sales manager, and I said, "Look, Jack, I know all your stores are clamoring for new bikes. But you can't just sell the bikes. You've got to have the parts to service them, and I'm almost the only one who does. Besides, if you sell your bikes to me, they're out of the way. You won't have the city stores badgering you about their competitors across town getting more or better stock." I worked on him, and he sold me CCM's entire stock of new bicycles—all 10 of them. Next, I borrowed a two-ton truck from the guy who owned the secondhand store across the street. Every Wednesday my bike mechanic, Nick Buziak, and I would head out into the country and scoop beat-up old bikes from farmer's yards. I'd offer a couple bucks for a frame and a fiver for a complete bike but most of the time the farmers wouldn't take any money. "Bill, you're cleaning up my yard for me," they'd say, then they'd have us in for lunch.

Nick loved to drink and I had to watch him a bit, but he was a genius with bicycles. He'd fix them up, put on new parts where necessary from Alphonse's old stock, and we'd sell them for $49.95. We had so many bikes that we filled up both the shop and the cellar. I even had to borrow warehouse space from the Bowman Brothers store across the back lane. The bikes sold like crazy, and we couldn't make them fast enough. I often had to get Nick to stay late and build more. "Nick," I'd tell him, "I've got a dozen beer and a bottle left for you if you do a great job."

Word must have spread about this bicycle guy in North Battleford because one day I received a call from a man in Winnipeg. He said, "Mr. Hunter, I have 450 brand-new bicycles. Do you want them?" Of course I wanted them. The Bowmans agreed to store the bikes for a while, which I brought for $15 each. They filled a whole train carload. I wondered where my supplier was getting the bikes, but I thought if I handled the deal carefully it could be the making of Hunter's Sporting Goods. I advertised on the radio and in the newspaper, and I sold those 450 bikes in six months. It was a sweet deal that just got sweeter. These bikes had cast-iron stems, the part of the bike that attaches the handlebar to the frame. The problem with that was that the stems snapped if the rider hit a curb too hard. Thanks to Alphonse, however, I had plenty of steel stems. Not only did I sell bikes like Popsicles at the beach, but I sold stems, too.

By this time my supplier in Winnipeg was getting anxious for his money. He kept calling and asking for payment. I said sure, just send the invoice. For some reason he didn't want to send me one, and the doubts I had at the beginning of our deal multiplied. I was

not going to put a cheque in the mail until I got some proper paper-
work. Finally, he came up with an invoice and I sent off my payment. But just a couple weeks later, an RCMP officer walked into
Hunter's Sporting Goods. "Bill, I understand you recently had a
shipment of bikes," he said. I said that's right, and I was not entirely surprised when the officer asked to see my invoice. I wasn't quite
sure what was going on, but I was damned glad I'd insisted on getting one. It turned out my supplier had been a senior employee at
CCM. For years he'd been lifting parts from the factory, taking them
home and squirreling them away. Finally, he had enough to build
the 450 bikes he sold to me. The invoice I'd insisted on getting
enabled me to prove that on my end, at least, it was an honest deal.
That supplier went to jail, but his bikes were the making of
Hunter's. After that, people said, "Go to Hunter's. If anyone's got it,
he will."

The sporting goods business was great right from the start. I
spent big on inventory and worked hard at making connections
with suppliers so they'd give me good prices and service. We used to
sell more in one weekend than Alphonse moved in six months.

By this time I'd been living in North Battleford for more than
a year and was getting pretty well known. I joined the Kinsmen and
managed and coached the North Battleford Beavers, a juvenile
hockey team. I could walk down the street and know all the other
businessmen and many of the other folks as well. People must have
looked at me as a young up-and-comer because in 1946 a committee came to me with a problem.

North Battleford had recently held a civic election. The voters
had tossed out the old mayor, but much to the horror of the local
elite, the electorate gave the nod to a shoemaker who was an avowed
Marxist. This would never do. One day Jack Abbott, a local phar-
macist and former manager of the Beavers, called me. Jack was a

*My first hockey team, the North Battleford Beavers.*

rotund man of the type who exercise considerable influence in town affairs more or less because they've worn down everyone else's resistance. Jack was always chairing committees, and this time he was heading one that was inviting me to lunch at an upstairs room at a local restaurant with 30 businessmen and church leaders, all of them aghast at the Commie cobbler resting his feet on the mayor's desk. They had figured out a way to have the election declared invalid and were determined such an electoral mistake would not be made a second time. "Bill," said Jack, "We want you to run. We'll make sure no one runs against you, and you'll be a shoe-in." I'm sure Jack didn't intend the pun. "It'll be the start of great things for you," he promised in the tones of one giving sage advice to a younger man. Jack made a strong case, but I felt I was too young to save North Battleford from the Red Menace. I had other things I wanted to do. Besides, I never did like committees. I turned them down.

My main concern in those days was the first sports team I ever owned. I was manning the till in my store one day when three women came up to see me. Thelma Murphy, Laura Kaufmann and Beryl Moore were all great ballplayers, and ball was what they wanted to talk to me about. Thelma spoke for all three. "Bill," she said, "we feel that if you would come with us as sponsor, manager and coach, we could put together a ladies' softball team that could win a Canadian championship." I looked at Thelma and her friends and I was impressed. I knew all three could play. Thelma was the head teller at the Royal Bank, a big, strong girl in her early twenties and a reliable home-run hitter. Beryl was solid hitter and a great cutoff player at second base. She was a solid, stocky girl and when she put the tag on people they felt it for days. Laura was a fleet centerfielder with a strong arm. I asked about their pitchers, and they told me they had René Anderson from Maymont, who I knew could pitch with some real heat, and Jessie Clendening, a star from Saskatoon. Behind the plate they'd lined up a young woman named Lynn, who could throw to second on a line. Tilley Lampitt, a smooth and elegant shortstop from Denholm, had also agreed to play. I told the three women I'd think about it for a week, but I knew immediately the answer would be yes.

Ladies softball sounded good to me. The sport had really taken off with so many men overseas during the war. It was competitive, good-quality ball that was entertaining to watch and regularly drew crowds in the thousands. Women's senior leagues had been formed in both Regina and Saskatoon, and the small-town ball tournaments were all starting to feature women's softball as well. This sounded like an opportunity to me.

North Battleford Bombers took to the field. I uniformed the players in real red and grey baseball uniforms, complete with cleats, instead of the shorts that all the other ladies teams were wearing. They looked great, and those uniforms informed the fans that this team was just as serious about playing ball as a men's team. And they were serious, all right. These were women, not girls. All of them had jobs or families, and all of them were older than I was. But even though a lot of them lived out of town, everyone always made it in for practice, and the team came together quickly. With René on the mound, we quickly became a real contender. The first time we got together, I caught for René as she warmed up. I used a regular ball glove, something I never did again. My hand was bruised for days. I never warmed René up again without slipping a little piece of foam padding into my glove. She could throw rockets.

We began our campaign for the Canadian championship. We didn't play in a league, so I brought in teams like the former world champion Moose Jaw Royals, the Regina Redcaps and the Saskatoon Ramblers for exhibition games. We'd draw 4,000 people to our weekend games. Because it was against the law to charge admission to entertainments on a Sunday, we took up a silver collection. But we did all right. My pal Alf Marsh, a local car dealer, was in charge of the gate and no one got past him without hearing, "Come on, put in five bucks."

The season ended in Saskatoon with a showdown against the Saskatoon Ramblers. We'd split the first two games of the three-game series, and the winner of the last game would head to the Canadian championship. It was a beautiful autumn Sunday afternoon. Six thousand people came to watch. The outfield had to roped-off for extra standing room. René pitched an amazing game. Smoke was coming off the ball. But Saskatoon had their own heroine on the mound. Muriel Koben could pitch too, and she was giving us fits. Finally, we got what we thought was a break in the ninth inning. Thelma nailed a line drive into left field and took off for first base. The Saskatoon fielder (Sylvia Fedoruk, who later became Saskatchewan's lieutenant-governor) made an amazing stabbing catch and hurled it hard to first as the winning run was coming

home from third. Thelma had crossed first safely and everyone in
the park knew it, but the first-base umpire called her out. I was furious. I ran across the diamond from third and yelled and stomped
and protested. The fans were booing—even some Saskatoon fans.
Roger Strumm, the head umpire, acknowledged to me later that the
guy on first got it wrong, but his decision stood anyway. We lost
that winning run. And eight innings later—17 innings in total—we
lost the game.

That was the end of the season for the Bombers, but it was only
the start of things for me. I'd spent three years since leaving the air
force trying this and sampling that. I'd had some success, and I'd
gradually figured out what I wanted. I wanted to work for myself,
and I wanted to work in sports. The Bombers had reminded me
how good it felt to be part of a team, and I wanted more of it. I was
soon to get my wish.

# 5

# THE REGINA CAPITALS

**And the more Whitney talked, the more excited I got. It turned out he was not only looking for a partner, but also for a coach and general manager—and all for the low, low price of $2,500.**

I WAS WORKING IN THE STORE ONE DAY shortly after the Bombers' season ended when a fellow walked through the door just before noon and introduced himself as C.B. Whitney. I knew a little bit about him. He was from Regina. He'd made millions in gold and he'd made millions in oil and he'd lost millions in both. One day he'd be rich, and the next day he'd be broke. But what intrigued me most about Whitney was that he was the owner of the Regina Capitals senior hockey team, and it turned out that was why he'd come to North Battleford.

"Bill," he said, "I'm looking for a partner. I want you to come in with me on the Caps."

Those were words I'd been longing to hear. After getting a taste of team ownership with the Bombers, I wanted to own a sports team so badly I could almost see my name in the program. And the more Whitney talked, the more excited I got. It turned out he was not only looking for a partner, but also for a coach and general manager—and all for the low, low price of $2,500. It never occurred to me to ask why. Hearing that a team wanted me was all I needed. He was an older fellow, probably in his late 50s. He had a patrician look to him—tall, handsome, immaculately dressed and groomed. He looked like he could be trusted. C.B. headed back to Regina that day with my promise to think about it, but I'm not sure I ever did. I called C.B. bright and early the next morning to tell him I was in. I was an owner, the youngest senior hockey owner in Canada. I was pretty pleased.

Once I'd hired a manager for the store, moved to Regina and set up shop, a few sobering realities began to set in. The Caps were terrible. They'd won only two games in the entire 1945–46 season, the worst record of any senior hockey team in the country. I almost didn't know where to start, but we launched right in with training camp that fall. Because the Regina Stadium wasn't ready yet, I had to hold training camp in Moose Jaw. I put the players up in a hotel and fed them in the Exchange Cafe every day. Those expenses—my expenses, now—were mounting. Still, I kept the players working until one day I got a call from the manager of the Dominion Bank, a man named Radcliffe who handled our finances.

Radcliffe, a proper pinstriped banker, took me into his office, sat me down and fixed me with a hard look. "Bill, we can't find your partner," he said. "He's vanished off the face of the earth." Whitney had left town for parts unknown. Radcliffe said that the Dominion would have Whitney's shares turned over to me, making me the sole owner of the team. That would have been wonderful, except for the small matter of $17,000 in red ink that was now my sole responsibility. Nor was there any sign of the $2,500 I'd given my onetime partner. I just about fell over. My God, $17,000 in debt! At the time, that was the price of a very luxurious home. How could I pay the money back? I was scared stiff, stunned, and Radcliffe picked up on it. "Promise me, Bill, that you won't go off and do something rash," he said. "Don't sell your store, Bill. Do you hear me? Don't sell your store." I mumbled that I wouldn't, collected my things and staggered into the street.

I went home confused and frightened. I'd trusted Whitney. I'd been impressed with him and his past business ventures. So what if he'd lost some money? That's what happened sometimes in oil and gold. I knew his friends, too. When I talked to them later they seemed to be just as confused by Whitney's disappearance as I was. Taking off and leaving me holding the bag just didn't seem to fit. But I had to admit that it looked like he'd scouted around to find some young guy so eager to get into hockey that he wouldn't ask too many questions. Then Whitney had set him up. I was angry at myself for not checking a little harder into the Cap's books, but that wouldn't do me any good now. Radcliffe had told me to let things sit and give myself time to make some proper decisions, but I felt I had to do something about that debt. I'd never owed money in my life. I thought about folding the whole operation, collapsing the Caps and going back poorer but wiser to Hunter's Sporting Goods. But I couldn't see giving up like that. I'd wanted a hockey team, I had a hockey team and by God I was going to stick with that hockey team. I just didn't know how.

To make things worse, a few days later I got another call from a business friend of mine in North Battleford. He didn't want to alarm me, but he was concerned about all the inventory from Hunter's Sporting Goods my new manager had been seen carrying out of the store. That weekend I threw a few things in a suitcase and flew up to North Battleford to investigate without telling my manager I was coming. I thought about the Caps the entire way, but I still couldn't see any way out. When I arrived I went right to the store with the friend who had called me. Sure enough, we opened some skate boxes and found them empty. There were some guns missing, too. The manager had heard I was in town and took off. He never did show up and I never did go looking for him. I should have had him charged, but I didn't.

Deeply disheartened, I went for coffee with a couple of men I knew, among them Ed Caplan. We were sitting at the counter and chatting when out of the blue Ed asked me, "Bill, would you like to sell your store?" I could hear Radcliffe's warning in my head, but by this time I'd worked myself into such a state over the debt and the problems at Hunter's that I felt I had to do something immediately to start digging out of the mess I was in. I tried to be nonchalant. "Anything's for sale, Ed," I shrugged. Ed saw his chance and jumped on it. "What do you want?" he asked. I hadn't completely lost all business sense and I responded, "No, what are you offering?" He named a figure—$10,000. I wrote it down on a napkin. I thought about the offer for a few minutes and I said, "Deal. Only it has to be as is. There may be some missing inventory." We both signed the napkin.

I stuffed the napkin into my pocket, shook hands with Ed and walked back to the store. I thought I'd done something to help both my problems at once, but I didn't feel good about it. I felt hollow. I'd sold the only real asset I had, and I was still deeply in the hole. I felt I was acting out of desperation, but I didn't know what else to do. Things didn't get any better when I returned to Hunter's.

A message was waiting for me: please call a business friend of mine in Saskatoon. He was president of a big hardware wholesaler. I made the call. "Bill, I hear your store might be for sale," my friend said. Apparently a salesman had overhead Ed and me and had rushed to give him a call. Word gets around quickly in a small town.

"Is it true you may have already sold it?" my friend asked. I said I'd had an offer. "I don't care what the offer, we'll give you double," said my friend. I replied that the least I'd take was $20,000. "Well," he said, "how does $17,000 sound?" I said I'd think it over. That sum would at least get me out of debt.

I walked across the alley to the office of Ed Conroy, a lawyer I knew. I told him what I had done, and I said, "Mr. Conroy, I want to cancel the sale. I don't want to sell my store. On top of that, it's not a fair price. I was upset and wasn't thinking straight and I don't want to go through with it." I took the crumpled napkin out of my pocket and showed it to him. Conroy looked at the figure and the two signatures, nodded, pursed his lips and called up Ed Caplan. But Ed wouldn't back down. A deal's a deal, he said. I'd signed a legitimate bill of sale, even if it was on a napkin. I was stuck.

I flew back to Regina, sick at heart. I knew I'd acted impulsively, and now I'd have to live with that, too. All I'd wanted was to own and manage a hockey team. I'd got my wish. But I had to sacrifice everything I'd built and a good chunk of my future in the bargain. And I still might lose the team. For the first time since losing the Dukes back in high school, I felt like a failure.

Radcliffe was furious. He took my $10,000 cheque in silence. He didn't bother to remind me of his warnings and my promises. But he did something else, and I've never stopped being grateful to him. First he took me to lunch at the Wascana Club, Regina's businessman's club, an old brick building with a wide veranda and an interior rich with deep carpets, leather and mahogany. As we waited for our meals, Radcliffe looked at me and said, "Bill, we're both in the same boat now. The only way out of this is to make a go of the team, so that's what we're going to do." He told me the bank would back me until I got a team on the ice. I was to come to his office on the first of every month and he'd write me a cheque for

$400, enough for living and traveling expenses. If I needed more, I'd have to justify it. If I needed to sign a player or bring one in, I could get money for that, too. I lifted my head for the first time in days. Radcliffe, in his banker's way, was telling me that he believed in me. He believed that the Caps would be a success under my direction, and he was willing to back that belief with cash. "I can put together a real team, Mr. Radcliffe," I promised. "Regina's going to see hockey like it's never seen before."

I went right to work on that promise. Last year's Caps weren't going to be good enough, so I had to sign a lot of new talent. I took Pete Slobodian, the roughest and best defenseman in the league, from the Lethbridge Maple Leafs and nabbed top scorer Bob Wiest from Windsor. I got Gopher Ashworth, Bert Olmstead and Dick Butler from the Moose Jaw Canucks and Fern Flaman, a defenseman with a tooth-rattling body check, from the Boston Olympics. But my big signing that year was the great goaltender Emile Francis. He had just finished his last junior year with the Moose Jaw Canucks and was the property of the Chicago Blackhawks, but I offered him more money than Chicago and he signed with us. That wasn't unheard of in the old senior leagues. A lot of great players spent their entire careers playing senior and would have had to take a pay cut to go to the NHL.

I was a whirlwind that summer, traveling everywhere to build the best team I could and repay my banker's faith. I read the *Hockey News* religiously, talked to scouts and traveled whenever I could to see games. My phone bills were enormous. I felt like I knew every player in the game, where he was playing and the circumstances of his current contract. I stole players from other teams. In my second year I convinced Sweeney Schriner and Mel Hill to come out of retirement, and I persuaded Gus Kyle, my old Notre Dame bunkmate from the Annie Shack, to quit the Royal Canadian Mounted

Police. It cost me $250 to buy him out. Managers and coaches around western Canada used to hate to hear that I was in town.

I'd sign a player on a handshake and never had any problems. Top players earned around $400 a month, and if they wanted other jobs, I'd find them jobs. This was quite common back then. Jobs also rooted the players in the community. I bought a big old three-storey brick house in downtown Regina, and a number of my players moved in with me. Some brought their wives, too. We had five bedrooms, but only one kitchen. It took a little organization, but it worked out fine.

But just as I had raided other teams, I was getting raided myself. The NHL scouts used to cruise the senior league rosters and poach the best players. I had 11 players turn pro that first fall, including four to the Blackhawks. They wanted Francis, too, but I wouldn't let him go. Emile didn't want to go, and he begged me not to release his contract. "I can go next year, Bill," he said. "Please don't release me." But the Blackhawks kept coming and on February 10, the deadline for signing new players, president and general manager Bill Tobin flew in from Chicago. We met at the Balmoral Cafe, where I'd been eating since I was a Hound. Bill, a short, fast-talking, bombastic man, talked me into releasing Emile for $10,000. And I got him to promise that Emile would start for the team and wouldn't be shuffled off to the minors. Sure enough, Emile started the very first game and sent me back the resulting headlines in both Chicago papers: "Francis Shuts Out the Canadiens, 2–0." Tobin lived up to that part of the deal, but I never did see the $10,000. I phoned Clarence Campbell at the NHL head office. "I'll see what I can do, Bill," he said, but nothing happened. I hadn't learned. I made the deal for Francis on a handshake and didn't get anything in writing. No paper, no money.

I was working my tail off and all the money I made was going to the bank, but I was having a ball. Regina had an old-style area with more than 5,000 wooden seats and steel support posts that blocked the view. Even in the dead of winter there was a lingering aroma from the horse shows it housed in the summer. Still, entering it every day was a thrill for me, walking into the dressing room with the smell of damp wooden benches and wet wool uniforms. I loved the inside jokes and nicknames that teammates developed. I loved the way moods shifted from the tense seriousness before a game to the horseplay afterward if you won. I even loved the somber spell after a loss as long as the team felt it together because then you knew they cared and there was hope they could win next time.

I loved discovering the power I had with words, standing in front of my players with all their eyes on me as they waited for me to say just the right thing to unlock their courage and desire and get them leaping to their feet and charging onto the ice. I may not be the greatest coach in the history of the game, but I could spot talent, and just as important, I could judge character. I coached with a lot of emotion and demanded it of my players. Many on my team were older than me, but I was never afraid to tell someone he didn't look like his heart was in it. I'd stand in front of him, look him right in the eyes and give him my little saying: "You need to take a ride on a streetcar. A streetcar named desire." Eventually, it got be a piece of verbal shorthand between me and local sportswriters. "That player needs to ride the streetcar more often," I'd say.

The Capitals came a long way in the first two years I was there. The first year we missed the playoffs by one point, and in the second we finished second in the league. And by my third year with the Caps, the nucleus of a championship team was in place. I, however, wasn't around to see it.

The problems were all about business, not about hockey. After my first season I had recruited Cliff Ehrle, a Regina hotel owner, as

*The Regina Capitals, western Canadian finalists, 1947–48.*

a 50 percent partner. Before the start of my third season, Cliff and I had sold half the club to a group of Regina businessmen, but it wasn't working out. They were businessmen, not hockey men. I just wanted to see a good club on the ice. They wanted to make some money—and run the show, too.

I had a pretty fancy payroll for those days, and the Caps were profitable, but only just. I'd managed to pay off my bank debts, but after that the team was pretty much a break-even proposition. I tried everything I could think of to boost attendance. We were drawing between 3,000 and 3,500 fans to the games, but we needed to sell out to make money. One day I went to Jack Sangster, the largest General Motors dealer in Regina and told him, "Look, Jack, I need your help. We've got a fine hockey club, but we need to get more people." I sold him on the idea of having a used car night— buy a program and you're eligible for a draw on a used car. Jack loved it and handed over a solid, clean old car. We promoted it before the game and said the only thing we'd guarantee was that the car would get the winner home. The fans got a kick out of the promotion, and they packed the place, but that was just one game.

The backroom bickering with my partners got harder and harder to take. Finally, when the Saskatoon Quakers came to me partway through the 1947–48 season, I was ready to listen. I left the Caps. The next year the team I'd built went on to the Allan Cup finals.

Saskatoon had been after me for a while by this time. Norman Couch, who sat on the Quakers board and managed the Saskatoon arena, came to me and said, "Bill, you should be managing and coaching this team. Why don't you come home?" Put like that, it made an impression on me. The Quakers, after all, had been my dad's team. Taking up the reins from Jack Hunter had a powerful appeal. I looked around at the ice and the stands, and although it was a new building with no steel posts and no barnyard smell, I could somehow feel Dad's hand there. I promised to think about it. And when I'd finally had enough in Regina, I slipped to Saskatoon on the weekend and quietly made a $500-a-month deal. I sold my share of the Capitals to my former partners for about what I'd paid old C.B. Whitney to get into the team: $2,500. I was a Quaker now.

Saskatoon was a different situation for me. Here, I wasn't an owner. The club was community owned, and I was general manager and coach, an employee. I had to report to a committee. I wasn't crazy about that, but I'd made a hands-off policy a condition of my contract and the Quakers board honored it. I never had a fraction of the trouble with my Saskatoon committee that I did with my Regina partners.

On the ice it was pretty much the same old story I'd faced in Regina. The Quakers weren't a very good team when I came on board. In fact, they finished the 1948–49 season last in the league. I didn't get much argument when I went to the board at the end of the season and told them that the club was going to need major surgery. The 1949–50 Quakers contained only three players from the previous year. I did it the same way I rebuilt the Caps: good scouting, fast talking, attractive contracts and a certain willingness to loot and pillage my rivals.

On one trip to Calgary, I persuaded Ken "Red" Hunter from the Stampeders to sign with me. Lloyd Turner, that club's manager, found out what was going on and stormed into my suite at the Palliser Hotel. I quickly stashed Red in another room and told him to keep quiet, but I didn't fool Turner. "Young Bill," he raged, "I know you've probably got Ken hidden away in the next room and you'll get away with him. But I'll tell you this: I won't ever let you steal from us again." I loved pulling off those raids.

I got Howie Milford from the Estevan Bruins and Al Staley from the Regina Pats. From the Caps I took defenseman Vic Myles and forward Chuck McCullough. Cy Rouse came up from Spokane and the old Kootenay League. Billy Maher came from the Allan Cup champion Edmonton Flyers. I took some chances. I signed Tommy Burlington, one of the greatest puck-handlers I'd ever seen and a league-leading scorer. The only reason he wasn't in the NHL was that he had only one eye. I'd watched Burlington play. I knew he could see the back of the net just fine, and he turned out to be one of the best players I ever had. Conn Smythe told me Burlington was the greatest hockey player outside of the National League. I'd gotten to know Conn a bit when I was with the Caps and now I struck a deal with him to get Cy Thomas from the Leafs. I picked up Mike Shabaga and brought over Bob Wiest from my old Caps. We had some of the best players in the league.

I lost some, too. I was interested in a fine young 17-year-old named Dickie Moore, and we were talking. Then I got a phone call from Frank Selke, who was the general manager of the Montreal Canadiens. Selke, as always, was polite. But he informed me in very clear and strong terms that the Canadiens had plans for Dickie.

*With some frenzied recruiting, the Quakers took to the ice in 1949–50
with a completely new look.*

"There has to be some misunderstanding, Bill," he said. "I want to
assure you that Dickie Moore is not leaving Montreal."

Once again I was all over the place, riding a constant string of
planes, trains and automobiles. I was talking to players from Washington to Quebec and bringing more than my share of them home
with me. Not everyone was happy about my approach to scouting
and signing talent. Most of the people around the league felt that
local teams should feature local players, and that's how the rules
were written. I knew we were allowed only two imports from out of
the province and four from within, but I wanted to build a winner
and those regulations were in my way. I brought in 17 imports. I
wasn't surprised when I got a call one day from the Canadian Hockey Association telling me I was suspended while they investigated

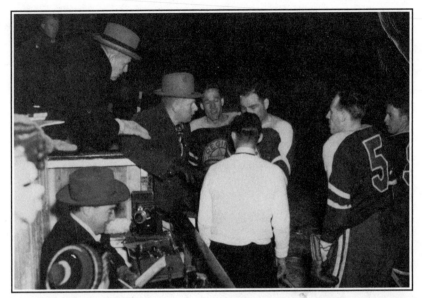

*Coaching the Quakers against the Capitals. The game erupted in a brawl much to fans' delight. They loved their hockey tough.*

my recruiting practices. So I took a leaf from Doug Bentley's book. Saskatoon was my hometown and I knew people. I got on the phone to some doctors and talked them into providing a helpful letter or two. It turned out , for example, that Cy Rouse had to come back to Saskatoon because of the illness of his father and mother. Therefore he was a local, not an import. We beat the rules and had a hell of a club that second season, finishing second in the league.

The season lasted 48 games, October to March, with the playoffs over by the middle of April. There'd be two or three games a week with the weekend games our biggest nights at the box office.

There was only room in the national league's six teams for so many players, so there were plenty of fine athletes in the senior leagues. At its best, it was fast, emotional, stickhandling hockey. There was no red line, so we encouraged our players to control the puck up the ice. We only had two refs and no linesman. Fewer zebras meant fewer whistles and more action. There was a certain code among the players, too. They were bareheaded, their pads were really just soft spots in the uniform, and as a result tactics like high-sticking were not tolerated. Any player who broke the code was likely to get a rough time from his own team because nobody wanted to face retaliation. If two players were angry with each other, they'd just drop the gloves and have a good fight. It was part of the action. Sportswriters used to pronounce over who won the fights the same way they'd analyze the winning goal. Sometimes there'd be a brawl. Coaches were supposed to stay on the bench when that happened, but I had to learn the lesson the hard way. I got so worked up during one bench-clearer that I headed into the battle myself. I got knocked on the head, slipped on the ice and wound up with seven stitches.

There wasn't a lot else to do on a winter night in Saskatoon, and hockey was king. The Saskatoon fans were thrilled to have a winning team again, and they loved the new Quakers. Our biggest nights were on the weekends when the Capitals came to town. There's nothing like a good rivalry to get fans excited and out to the game. Saskatoon–Regina was a natural, and their rivalry resulted in me earning my nickname. During one hard-fought game an absolute free-for-all erupted. While I'd learned my lesson and stayed on the bench, I was perhaps even more outspoken and emotional than usual. The next morning Dave Dryberg in the *Leader-Post* called me Wild Bill. To my chagrin, it stuck.

I did my best to play up Saskatoon–Regina rivalry with the willing help of the sportswriters at the *StarPhoenix*. I made sure they had something to write about. Cam Mackenzie was the *StarPhoenix*'s sports editor, and sometimes we'd meet for coffee at the Gem Cafe after the sports pages were done at 2:00 A.M. I'd give Cam a big story and the fans ate it up. Tickets for the next weekend's game would go on sale Monday mornings, and by 10:00 A.M. there'd often be a lineup two and a half blocks long. We'd sell out 5,200 seats and then open up the standing room. By the end of my first complete season, we'd sold the house out for 17 straight games.

Inside the arena the atmosphere was hockey with as few distractions as possible. We had a recording of "O Canada" to start the games, and sometimes we'd ask a local high school band to come in and play, but that was all. It was a big deal when we got an organ. Only a few teams had them—Regina, Calgary and Edmonton. The crowds were loud and solidly behind the Quakers. They knew their hockey and loved it.

The Western Canada Hockey League was a CPR league. We didn't go on the road so much as on the rail. Cam Mackenzie from the *StarPhoenix* would travel with us, too. My trainer, Scotty Clarke, would travel with us and we'd sip something stronger than coffee. Cam didn't drink, but Scotty did and sometimes we'd sit all night in my room over a bottle. We traveled, slept and sometimes ate in that private coach. Once we arrived in town we'd eat at a restaurant, but if mealtime came in transit I'd have the cooks prepare food specially for us. When we got to Lethbridge or Calgary or wherever we were going, the railway would find a quiet siding to park the coach, and we'd stay there over night. I set up my bedroom and office in the stateroom, and the players slept on the fold-out bunks in the coach. After a game we'd bring a few beers on board so the fellows could socialize, play a few hands of crib or poker and relax. I could always sweat a beer or two out of them at the next day's practice. The train coach was close quarters, but it was fine, providing it didn't get too cold out and freeze the plumbing. We'd have our own porter assigned to us for the whole trip and it was fun.

For the playoffs, we'd always check into a hotel. That was when you needed all your resources and the players had to be rested, comfortable and in top shape.

The caption above the drawing read "Hunter's Happy Hours," and happy hours they were.

With the Quakers the hockey world was opening up to me. I'd established a solid record with two senior teams, and I thought it was time to make a move toward the majors. In 1950 I got my chance. Charlie McCool, a Saskatoon lawyer who had lost an arm in war, owned Saskatoon's junior team and asked for my help in getting an NHL affiliation for it. I pitched it to Conn Smythe, with whom I'd had a couple of dealings over some players. Smythe, who had been wounded himself, knew McCool and agreed to help. I asked for $7,000. "No, Bill, I think $5,000 is fair," he said, and we shook hands on the deal. He cut me the cheque right there. That was the real beginning of my relationship with Conn Smythe.

Smythe eventually came to call me the Kid, and I became a part of his whole circus. I called him Major when people were around and Mr. Smythe when we were alone. I'd go to Leafs practices whenever I was in Toronto and Smythe would have me sit in a specific place, two rows down from wherever he was sitting. The reporters sat in the row between us. Smythe would shout comments down to me: "Kennedy's looking good," or "Barilko needs to pick it up a bit, don't you think?" and the reporters would write it all down, just as he'd intended and just as they knew he'd intended. Everything was done for a reason with Smythe.

He was a real stickler, too. The wooden seats in Maple Leaf Gardens were waxed until they shone. He'd walk up into the stands, rub his finger along one of the backs, and if he found any dust at all he'd start another one of his favorite set-pieces. "Broda!" he'd holler. Goaltender Turk Broda's brother was on the cleaning staff, and out he'd come wearing a tattered Maple Leafs cardigan. "Get this god-damned place cleaned up!" Smythe would yell, and Broda would start back in on him. They both knew the seats were spotless. They just liked to put on the show.

I began to visit Toronto as often as I could. I'd do a little scout-ing and recruiting and hang out with the Leafs and sportswriters like Milt Dunnell and Jim Proudfoot at the *Star*. We'd sit for hours after practice in the coffee shop in the Gardens, taking over two or three tables, swapping yarns and talking hockey and trying to make one another laugh.

Bill Barilko was a regular at those sessions—a straightforward, honest, hard-working man from northern Ontario who showed up to play every shift. Ted "Teeter" Kennedy would be there, too—a great, tenacious hockey player who never quit. A fan in the Gardens used to wait for a quiet moment, then holler in a great, booming voice, "Come on, Teeter," and the whole arena would erupt in applause.

They were fun bunch. Players spent years together on the same team, and they became a very close-knit group. Smythe would always be building them up, saying, "You're the luckiest people on earth—you're a Maple Leaf!" And the players believed it. They were always doing things together, having barbecues or a couple beers after a game. Turk Broda, who had a significant thirst, was always around for those sessions. He was a bit of a cut-up, too, and always up to something. At practice the guys would shoot pucks at him, and Turk would hold his stick like a baseball bat and knock them right back. Smythe and his coach Hap Day (they called him "Hap" because he never smiled) tried everything to keep an eye on Turk. One off-season, Smythe put Turk to work driving a gravel truck for a company he owned. Turk would make one delivery in the morning, then retire to his favorite watering hole to wash the dust out of his throat. During the season Smythe would threaten to bench him unless he lost some weight. But it was all fodder for the sports pages. Smythe loved Turk.

Max Bentley was nervous and high-strung, and we used to tease him unmercifully. We used to get into his car, move it a block or two and then come back to the coffee shop and say, "Max, I think someone's stolen your car!" He'd go for it every time. He was very sensitive, and if his line mates scored more than he did he'd be liable to break out in tears, so Ab Welch and Red Gobel used to feed him puck every chance they got. Not that Max Bentley needed help scoring goals. Those three line mates finished one, two and three in scoring that year. Max was the greatest stickhandler I'd ever seen, then or since. They called him the "Dipsy Doodle Dandy of Delisle," a nickname that always made him blush. He was a very humble man.

I was able to help Smythe with Max. One year Max stayed home on the family farm in Delisle, Saskatchewan, instead of reporting to the Leafs camp. Max would come into Saskatoon to watch the Quakers, and I always had a couple tickets for him. Finally, I climbed up the seats to where Max was sitting by himself and said, "Max, come on. What are you doing this for? You know you should be in Toronto. Your team needs you." He just shrugged and said something softly I didn't catch, but the next day he packed his bags and headed east. The Leafs won the Stanley Cup that year.

One of my dealings with Smythe didn't work out so well. My last year in Saskatoon I hired Nick Metz from the Leafs as my coach. Nick was a good friend of mine. We'd been at Notre Dame together, and Nick's dad farmed right on the outskirts of Wilcox. He'd been an important player for the Leafs, the kind who kills penalties night after night and scores clutch goals, especially during the playoffs. He'd always be assigned to check the other team's best player. One night he was trying everything to stop Maurice Richard of the Canadiens. Finally, he just jumped on Richard's back, but Richard carried him in from the blue line and still scored. I thought hiring Nick as coach would be a big signing for us, and Nick was excited about coming home to Saskatchewan. But Conn begged me not to do it. He loved Nick, but he knew what was likely to happen if Nick got behind the bench.

Nick was a lot like Max. Neither saw himself as anything more than a shy, small-town farm boy and neither could communicate. Nick couldn't inspire the players. He'd blush and stammer. My players used to beg him to lace up the skates and become a playing coach. "Come on, Nick, we need you," Tommy Burlington would plead. "We can win this thing." I talked to him about it, too. But Nick never left the bench. He'd made his decision. Nick had too much respect for other people and not enough for himself. When Conn Smythe called from Toronto, Nick would stand at attention to take the call. It'd be "Yes, Major. No, Major," until he'd hand the phone over to me.

Finally, one day I was standing outside the dressing room in the Saskatoon Arena talking to a couple of newspapermen before a game when Nick opened the door and motioned me over. He had a desperate look on his face. "Bill," he said, "you gotta come in. You gotta come and talk to the players. I just can't do it." I told him I couldn't do that. "If I go in, I'm cutting the feet out from under you."

"I just can't talk to them, Bill."

"Nick, you have to."

Nick went in and did his best. But after the game, Nick and I sat down. "Nick," I asked, "are you going to be able to coach this team or not?"

"Well, I want to," Nick said. I don't think I'd ever seen anyone look so unhappy and frustrated. "But I don't know whether I can."

I looked back at the close friend I'd brought all the way from Toronto. "Then I don't know if I can afford to keep you." I had to let him go. It was the toughest firing I'd ever done. That was the end of Nick's career and he went back to his dad's farm. Nick and I remained friends. A few years later, I went to visit him in Wilcox. We were sitting over coffee in the local cafe when Nick looked at me and said, "Bill, I want you to know that you had to let me go." It meant a lot to me to hear that.

Just as it had been with the Capitals, money was tight with the Quakers. We were filling the building, but good hockey and a first-class operation costs money. I was spending a lot on the players, and that left me always looking for a new angle and a new promotion. During my last year in Saskatoon, I heard about a man named Scotty Moir in Nipawin in the north of the province who staged a small natural-ice curling bonspiel with four new cars as prizes. This was revolutionary. Curling had always been a game for gentlemanly amateurs who competed for honor and a trophy. A new car—well, that was perilously close to curling for pay. I thought that man in Nipawin was perilously close to a first-rate moneymaker. I did a little a figuring—128 rinks at $200 a rink. Not bad. A gross of $25,000 and change. Plus ticket and concessions sales. I thought I should be able to run things at a profit. I went to the Quakers board and they said, "It'll never work. You can't do it." I said, "Oh please, let me try," and I sweet-talked them into the idea. I shamelessly stole

Moir's idea, brought it to artificial ice in the Saskatoon Arena and made it big.

Curling for cash caused lots of controversy. Some of the clubs wouldn't let their members enter. A few of the best rinks in western Canada refused to come. Even my minister, who was a curler himself, told me what I was doing was wrong. I was cheapening a noble sport by tainting it with professionalism.

I went ahead anyway and got 128 rinks. For the first three days of the bonspiel, we curled 24 hours a day to get all the draws in. At four o'clock one morning I was standing in the rink with Cam Mackenzie and we counted 500 people in the stands. Taxi drivers, shift workers, farmers making a weekend of it—all sitting there watching curling. Each member of the winning rink received a car, and the Quakers made a pile of cash. I didn't have any trouble talking the board into letting me do it again in the spring.

Still, the Quakers were run by a board, and I was having the same old problem I always ran into with boards and committees. There'd be 20 people sitting around the table, and I'd get questions I didn't want to answer. Over and over, I'd have to explain, "I'm not going to tell you what we say to a player. I'm not going to reveal that and have you blab it all around town." It was time to get out on my own again, and I quit the Quakers after the 1951 season.

I found myself a good deal in Medicine Hat. The Tigers, a junior hockey team affiliated with the Chicago Blackhawks, were owned by a wonderful old man named Fred Gibbs, a contractor who was tired of running the team but loved the game and wanted to see the franchise do well. He simply gave me the team. The arena was run down and needed some work, so I got the lease cheap. All I needed was a little working capital, and I thought I knew where I could find that.

I got in my car and headed down the Trans-Canada to Calgary.

I'd heard that the general manager of the Sick's Brewing Company was a great sportsman. I had a deal for him. I walked into Tommy Dancer's palatial office and made my pitch. I said, "Mr. Dancer, I'll sell you the sign on the outside of my arena. It'll be the only sign out there and it'll be wonderful for your sales." Nobody had thought of doing that before, and Dancer thought it was worth a try. I got a cheque for $4,000 right there, and that was my working capital. They made the cheque out to me, personally. "It'll be easier to shift around that way," Dancer advised. I was all set up, and the team had cost me almost nothing.

The Tigers had a dismal record, so I needed to generate some buzz. My first move was to spruce up the arena with some bright colors. I chose green and orange. You couldn't miss our building. I warmed up Pete Mossey, the sports editor at the *Medicine Hat News*, and Orville Cope at the radio station. We became very good friends, and before long the Tigers were front page and top of the sportscast. For the first year money was so tight that I actually recruited a couple of dedicated fans to drive the team when we went on the road. But the club started to win and that drew the fans. We led the league in attendance that year with the smallest building, and the next year I bought two Ford station wagons for the team and two trailers for the equipment. We looked sharp when we pulled into town.

I wanted to start our second season with a little excitement, and nothing creates that like a big signing. I had my sights on a stellar young junior playing for the Toronto Marlboros named Gerry James. Gerry was an amazing athlete. Not only did he star for the Marlies, but he played fullback for the Winnipeg Blue Bombers and was one of the leading rushers in the CFL. I met with Gerry in Calgary after a game at Meewata Stadium and we cut a deal. I was going to pay him the then-unheard of sum of $15,000 a year, plus a home, plus a car. All this was under the table. I didn't want my other players to know what Gerry was getting. Gerry, however, was playing in the Toronto Maple Leaf system, and when he reported to Leaf training camp that fall, Conn Smythe found out about our deal. He called me, and his response was to the point: "No way, Hunter." We didn't get Gerry James that year—or ever. It worked out well, though. When I announced we'd signed him, we sold a mess of season tickets. And I didn't have to spend the money on his salary, either.

Even without Gerry, we managed a thrilling season. We took the Regina Pats to eight games in the league final. The Pats were affiliated with the Montreal Canadiens, but when Frank Selke came out for the final, it was my boys he took out to dinner in a private room in the Assiniboia Hotel. He told my boys that they were Canada's Cinderella team. Did their eyes ever get big when they heard that.

Medicine Hat was the first time I'd controlled the arena as well as the team, so I thought I'd try to make a little money in the off-season and have a little fun at the same time. I'd been promoting sports for years by then and had gotten pretty good at it. How hard could it be to promote entertainment?

I started with music and I went to the top. I lined up a triple bill you couldn't have put together anywhere else. There was Jerry Murad and the Harmonicats, the Hollywood singing group the Gaylords and best of all, the great Duke Ellington and his wonderful orchestra. Any one of those groups could have headlined, but it just worked out I was able to get them all in on one bill. The Duke, who was at the start of a world tour, had played the finest halls in the world, so I'm not sure what he made of my green-and-orange hockey arena. But in his early years he'd played some dives, too, and if he was dismayed with the venue he never let on. He was beautifully dressed and had manners to match. He had a lordly way of speaking that made you feel as if he were lifting you up to his level rather than stooping down to yours. A classy, classy man. Unfortunately, Medicine Hat was not Duke Ellington country. We sold maybe two-thirds of the seats. But when Duke came backstage and got a look at the receipts, he sat down across from me and said, "Bill, there has to be something in this for you, too. We can't leave you with nothing for your hard work." So we redivided the gate so that it worked—just barely—for both of us. They only made one Duke Ellington.

Medicine Hat was cowboy country and I did a lot better with Wilf Carter and Webb Pierce. I brought in Gene Autry and the Grand Ole Opry, and Gene pulled up to my arena in a custom-built Cadillac outfitted with a complete bar. But what those ranchers really loved was wrestling. Stu Hart was touring wrestling shows out of Calgary, and his response to my offer was, "Bill, I'd only be too delighted to come." I brought in many of his wrestlers, and I got a big kick out of them. They'd pull up to the side door of the arena in big, black Cadillacs and they'd jump in the ring and go at each other ferociously all night long, yelling and taunting each other over the microphone and pulling all kinds of dirty tricks in the ring. You'd think they were blood enemies, and the ranchers and farmers in the audience, all men, would go wild. Then after the show the wrestlers would slap each other on the back, crack a case of beer in the dressing room, squeeze back into those Caddies and head back to Calgary. It was all part of the show, like Conn Smythe with Turk Broda. Stu Hart was sweetheart, too. I'd give him his share of the gate and half the time he'd give some of it back.

Medicine Hat was a great little city, and for three years I had a wonderful time. But I couldn't settle down, and in 1955 I thought I'd give Moose Jaw a try. Moose Jaw was bigger, and I thought I could build a champion there. Besides the Canucks hockey squad, I was also going to manage the Mallards baseball team. I owned the Mallards with five other partners, and they were playing in a solid league that included Saskatoon, Lloydminster, North Battleford and Regina. John Ducey owned a team in Edmonton and Emile Francis was the playing coach of the North Battleford entry. Fate, however, intervened. Moose Jaw's arena burned down that summer. With no ice I had to move the club, and the nearest place I could settle the franchise was in Yorkton. We had a pretty good year as the Yorkton Terriers, finishing third in the Northern Saskatchewan Junior League. But I was starting to feel that maybe the burning of the rink was an omen. Maybe it was time to try something new. Maybe it was time to get out of sports and into a solid business.

# 6

# BIRTH OF A SALESMAN

**Up and down the street I drove, back and forth, trying to screw up my nerve. Finally, I forced myself to park. I watched my hand shake as I lifted it up to knock.**

SOMETHING ELSE WAS PUSHING ME TO look for a different way to earn my living, something more powerful than any omen. In the summer of 1954, when I was still with the Tigers, I had met Bernadette Marin in Trail, British Columbia. She was a wonderful, lively woman full of high spirits and a fine athlete and curler. Bernie and I fell in love, and that summer we drove down the coast to California and got married. Our first child, Beverly, was born that year and suddenly I was a family man again. The hockey life can be exciting and satisfying, but it doesn't offer much stability. I began to look around.

I knew that my next move would have to involve sales. Selling had gotten into my blood when I worked for General Foods, and one way or another I'd been in sales ever since. Merv White, a friend of mine, sold vacuum cleaners door to door, and he tried to convince me to join him. "They're top of the line, Bill," he said. "They sell themselves." I wasn't so sure. Finally, Merv shrugged and admitted defeat. Like any good salesman, he knew how to spot a customer who just wasn't interested. However, he did know of something that might suit me a bit better, a new company starting up in Edmonton called First Investors.

First Investors was a financial services company that helped people save money. I was intrigued. I figured if most people were anything like me, this product really would sell itself. I'd never saved anything. If I had a dollar I'd either pump it back into a hockey club or use it to pay off debt. I never had a nickel in the bank that I didn't have immediate plans for, and I knew that with the way my life was changing, my ways with money would have to change as well. I figured there were lots of people in the same boat. The more I thought about it, sitting at home with Bernie, Bev, and our brand-new son Brent, the more it sounded like a market opportunity. I also liked the idea of joining a new company on the way up.

In May 1956 I drove to Edmonton to meet with the principals. I basically recruited myself. I walked into First Investors small downtown office and met Don Cormie and Stan Melton. They impressed me, and Cormie and Melton liked my prospects, too. I'd had much more selling experience than the rest of their sales force, and my hockey days had given me contacts all over western Canada. I drove home to Medicine Hat with an agreement in my pocket and headed right back north again for a training session in Ken Marlin's Calgary office.

But that session had hardly begun when I had to pull the plug on it. I got a call from our family doctor, Matt Davis, that Brent, only about three months old, had suddenly taken ill. No one knew exactly what was happening, but that poor, tiny infant was having trouble breathing. He couldn't get any oxygen, and Dr. Davis told me he was not expected to live. "Bill, you should be here," Dr. Davis said. I burned up the Trans-Canada almost sick with worry and fear. Thank God, Brent pulled through. He didn't suffer any ill effects and never experienced a relapse, either. But it was a close. If my new responsibilities hadn't been clear before, they were now. I was even more determined to succeed in my new venture.

Briefly, this is how First Investors worked. Customers bought into a 5-, 10-, 15- or 20-year plan. They could pay in a lump sum a year or in 12 monthly installments. We paid 4 percent compound interest, and the salesman made his money on the commission. We sold a planned, scheduled way to save money, and people liked it because it almost forced them to put something aside. The plans were entirely guaranteed. Banks accepted them as loan collateral.

Our family returned to Medicine Hat, and I sold my first savings plans to people who knew me through the Tigers. Those contacts gave me an entrée to most of the local business people, but they weren't going to be enough. I was going to have to get out of my office, hit the streets and knock on some doors. I couldn't believe how nervous I was the first time I went out. I drove to the home of a prospect I'd been given. I could see him sitting in his front window reading the newspaper, but I couldn't make myself get out of the car and walk up to the door. Up and down the street I drove, back and forth, trying to screw up my nerve. Finally, I forced myself to park. I watched my hand shake as I lifted it up to knock. Selling for General Foods had never been like this. With General Foods the stores were there, they needed my products and my visits were a necessary part of business. Sales were a given, and I was really a glorified order-taker. But selling something that people didn't yet know they needed was entirely different.

I learned quickly, though. I sold that man a plan, and he was the first of many. Even back in those early days I once sold $87,500 worth of plans in one night. I learned that perseverance was the key. "When they say no the first time, they're getting warm," I used to tell Bernie. My employers in Edmonton were pleased, but a bit puzzled. Why were all my sales for yearly plans? They weren't complaining because it got them their money and me my commission up front, but weren't any of my customers interested in monthly payments? Now I was the puzzled one. What monthly plan? It turned out that because I missed the training session in Calgary, I'd begun my selling career working solely from the company's manuals. There was a chart in one of them that listed the various payments under the monthly or yearly options. I misunderstood it. I just looked at the last column where the yearly payments were listed and figured, "Well, that's what I have to get." That misunderstanding helped me break First Investor sales records. I took a little ribbing, but I just shrugged and said, "Simplicity is power." Finding out that there was a monthly payment option actually hurt my commissions.

First Investors and I were a perfect fit. I believed in the product. I bought a plan myself. And because I believed in it, I could sell it. I was the first man in the company to sell more than $100,000 in plans a month for three consecutive months. Ken Marlin called me in to Calgary, gave me the first gold watch they'd ever awarded, and made me the manager of one of their Calgary branches. We set sales records there, and then I was sent to Saskatoon to open up northern Saskatchewan, where we soon set more sales records.

By this time I wasn't pounding the pavement so much. I was in management. It wasn't so much different than running a hockey team, where I was coach, general manager and head scout. I liked having former athletes on our sales team. They were used to self-discipline and were easy to motivate. Mike Shabaga was only one of several ex-Quakers I recruited.

Every morning we'd have a sales meeting, and I'd get up in front of my sales team and give them a little talk. I'd go through our game plan. We had drafted a sales pitch, and I was very strict about my people following it because it worked. The whole idea was to take ourselves out of the picture and put the customer into it. We wanted prospects to imagine themselves and their families in the secure, happy future that our product could deliver. The savings plan had to be their idea. I probably said it a thousand times: "We don't sell. They buy."

It was good to be back in Saskatoon—good for business, too. It was home and my family was well known. And a lot of doors were open to me because of hockey. In 1958, however, First Investors packed me and my family off to Vancouver. I was to open the company's first branch in British Columbia, a huge, untapped territory that was to be all mine. I couldn't wait.

I moved my family into a small home in Vancouver's east end and then started thinking about the job I'd been sent to do. I had a ground-floor office on West Hastings Street, and when I showed up for my first day, the workers were still finishing. I sat in the reception area on a keg of nails, watching a man put the gold leaf lettering on the door, and I wondered how to begin. British Columbia was a big province, where nobody had ever heard of First Investors or Bill Hunter. I had no staff and few contacts. For the first time in long while, I didn't know what to do next. As I sat there holding my sales kit, a fellow walked by, glanced at the name being lettered on the door and stopped. Curious, he walked through the door and we started chatting. His name was Vern Greensword. I booked an appointment with him and his wife, sold them a $20,000 savings plan, and then hired Vern as my first recruit. I was off. Within 18 months I had 157 full-time sales staff, 27 offices and was doing $78 million in business.

I had branch offices all over province, and I visited them all regularly. I'd travel throughout the interior and out to Vancouver Island.

I spent days and weeks and months on those twisting little roads fighting holiday traffic and mountain weather. One night Mike Shabaga and I were out in Coquitlam, and the fog got so thick we couldn't see the road. Mike walked in front of the car while I drove behind him with one wheel on the shoulder. We drove like that all the way to our appointment. As division manager I could have sat behind a desk, but I believed that to be successful you had to demonstrate to everyone that you were giving everything you had.

I loved meeting new people, and I took a personal hand in training as many new recruits as I could. I'd drop in on a branch and tell the manager, "I'll work as a trainer for you today and take a man out for a few cold calls." Sometimes they'd have appointments booked, sometimes we'd go door to door. I taught them the ropes. We'd take two square blocks and knock on one door to start. Then we'd go around the block and knock on another door, weaving back and forth in a figure eight. That way people didn't look out the window and see us coming. I taught my recruits how to size people up quickly and determine whether they were good prospects. I 'd ask a few leading questions: "Would you be prepared to tell me your current income? Do you find you're able to save money? Do you have insurance? Do you have a savings plan?" I'd remind my trainees that just as they were sizing up a prospect, the prospect was taking their measure as well. People can know when you're truly interested in them, and they can tell when you believe in what you're saying. We had only a couple minutes to win their confidence and respect. Over and over I told those trainees that they had to organize their time. I'd show them my diary, which I'd kept for every day of my life since my earliest hockey days. Every day I wrote out a schedule, and I stuck to it. My trainees and I always came back with sales.

Those were valuable sessions for the sales staff, but I was also trying to give a nudge to my branch managers as well. If I was still eager to get into the field and sell, they were expected to do more than push paper behind a desk.

I'd never worked so hard in my life. I went day and night, starting with breakfast meetings during which I'd wind everyone up with a sales talk. Even our social life revolved around work. I'd do things like rent a cruise boat and sail the harbor, winding up the evening with banquet for over 400 of my staff. Holidays? Hardly ever.

I was having the time of my life, but I knew who was paying the price. I'd signed with First Investors because I thought it would provide a better life for my family, and financially we were doing well. We moved out of our little east-end home into a bigger one on Cambie Street. But like my own father before me, I wasn't there much. After Bart was born in 1959, our family was up to three, and I knew I was missing out. Young children change so quickly, and I simply wasn't around for much of it. I told myself that being a leader requires a sacrifice. If you commit 100 percent to something, something else has to suffer. Usually, that something is family. I was fortunate that Bernie was a wonderful mother. She devoted herself to raising our children so that I could devote myself to my work. She made the life I led possible.

In 1960 First Investors sent me off again to open new territory. We went to Seattle, where we became the first Canadian savings company go enter the American market, but we returned to Vancouver after about a year and a half. I wanted to try starting my own company, People's Investors. It offered similar products to First Investors, but I felt it was run better and gave much better service. My partner, Stan Kendall, and I quickly built the company up to a sales force of 125 in Alberta, Saskatchewan and British Columbia. In our second year we moved the company's head office to Edmonton and became associated with Dr. Charles Allard in managing and distributing Dominion Funds, a mutual fund based in Victoria.

But I had another idea I wanted to try. I knew I could sell any product as long as I believed in it. I knew that I understood sales well enough to explain it to others. I also had learned how to make people feel good about themselves and what they were doing, and how to use that to fire them up. I decided that instead of selling a product, I would try selling my knowledge and enthusiasm. I would sell selling. I knew there was great demand for someone who could coach sales staff, who could not only give them some useful direction but could give them a good old locker room pep talk and send them out to take on the world.

I developed three seminars: one for managers, one for sales staff and one for personal motivation. They went over great, and I traveled all over western Canada like an old-time traveling evangelist thumping the gospel of salesmanship. I had some beautiful brochures printed up, and then I'd book a big hall such as the Jubilee Auditorium in Edmonton. About a month before the date, I'd visit the major companies in town and tell them who I was and what I was doing. I'd get them to send their managers and sales staff. It worked great. I'd give technical tips on selling, such as the importance of organization. I'd throw out little rhymes.

*There may be nothing wrong with you,*
*The way you live, the work you do.*
*But I can very plainly see*
*Exactly what is wrong with me.*
*It's not that I am indolent*
*Or dodging duty by intent.*
*I work as hard as anyone*
*And yet I get so little done.*
*The morning goes, the noon is here*
*And before I know the night is near.*

*President and CEO of People's Investors, 1960.*

> *And all around me, I regret,*
> *Are things I haven't started yet.*
> *If I could just get organized—*
> *I suddenly have realized*
> *That all that matters is not the man.*
> *The man must also have a plan.*

I quoted Walter P. Chrysler: "I'll pay more for enthusiasm than any other known quality, such as capacity, energy, or ability. When my salesmen get excited, they get customers excited and they buy."

Henry Ford said, "Behind all success lies the power of enthusiasm. Enthusiasm is the spark that kindles the world." I had one for the managers, too: "Praise is oxygen to the soul."

To everybody I would emphasize the importance of believing in yourself. "When you get up in the morning," I'd tell the crowds, "look at yourself in the mirror and say 'I like you. I believe in you. You're going to have a great day.' Never degrade yourself! Never put yourself down!" Those personal motivational seminars took five hours and people would come out of them flying.

I poured over books and journals on salesmanship, looking for ideas or phrases I could bring into my seminars. Steal one idea and you're a thief. Steal a bunch and you're doing research. Where those sayings and rhymes a bit hokey? Maybe. But my goal was to change people's behavior. And those slogans and bits of doggerel could stick in people's memories long enough to do them some good.

Those seminars were all me, all the time. I was up on the stage by myself, holding the audience with my words and ideas. It was exciting and rewarding. And lucrative. I'd get 2,500 people in an auditorium at $50 a pop.

But there were drawbacks. Again, I was on the road and away from my family all the time. And eventually it just got too hard on my body. Every day I was on my feet for hours at a time. Prowling and prancing across the stage with the energy and verve you need to keep people's attention simply wore me out. My knees began to hurt too much to keep up the pace.

Plus, that old hockey bug was starting to resurface. Nine years had passed since I owned a team. I'd worked with plenty of teams since, but I was getting hungry to return to one on ice. In 1965 I got an interesting call from the Detroit Red Wings that promised to do just that.

# 7

# THE EDMONTON OIL KINGS

**A western team hadn't won the Memorial Cup on eastern ice in 22 years. The Oil Kings, they all agreed, weren't going to be ones who broke the Eastern domination.**

IN THE SUMMER OF 1965, THE DETROIT Red Wings found themselves in a bit of a spot. Their farm club was the Edmonton Oil Kings, and Bruce Norris back in Detroit wanted to keep it that way. The problem, however, was that Detroit owned only half the club. The Edmonton exhibition board owned the rest, and it was receiving a suspicious number of visitors from San Francisco, where a group of businessmen were starting up the California Seals. The Seals were known to be shopping around for a farm club. Their general manager, Bud Poile, a former forward for the Leafs and the Wings, had been the manager of the Edmonton Flyers, the city's old entry in the Western Hockey League. Poile knew what great hockey country Edmonton was and what a good property the city's junior club would be. But the Red Wings' chief western scout, Clarence Moher, who recruited players for the Oil

Kings, got wind of what was going on. He immediately saw that if the exhibition board decided to sell out to the Californians, the Red Wings would lose control of the Oil Kings. Clarence was on the phone to Norris every day that summer, warning him that he was about to lose a farm club he'd put a lot of effort into developing.

Finally, Norris asked Clarence what he should do about the threat, and Clarence had a plan. For years Clarence and I been seeing each at arenas, restaurants, locker rooms and pretty much everywhere that hockey men congregated. Clarence was an old-time hockey man, short and solid, with his seamed face always shaded by his favorite fedora. You could always spot Clarence in any arena way up in the corner, puffing furiously on cigarette after cigarette. We went way back and were good friends. He knew I had recently moved my business to Edmonton, where I'd hooked up with a couple related businesses called Pacific Western Securities and Northwest Trust, which was owned by Dr. Charles Allard. Clarence knew I was thinking about returning to hockey, and he knew I could run a club. Clarence's reply to Norris was simple: "Get Bill Hunter."

Bruce Norris called me the next day. We weren't exactly strangers. We'd met at NHL meetings, and Bruce had even dealt with my father back in the days when the Red Wings held training camps in Saskatoon. I could picture tall, athletic Bruce on the phone, leaning back in his chair, probably not far from a glass of something. "Bill, I'd like you to handle negotiations to buy out the exhibition board, and then we want you to run the club," said Norris, thinking I would jump at the opportunity. I wasn't too excited. I'd run clubs for someone else before. I wasn't about to leave a successful business to become someone's hired hand, even if it brought me back into hockey. "Like hell I'll run the club," I told him. Bruce was smart and didn't argue with me. "Sleep on it and get back to me tomorrow," he said. I did but the answer didn't change.

Clarence kept after me. Finally, I said yes. Norris was a little surprised at my terms: I refused to take any money from Detroit. I still owned People's Investors, so I didn't need hockey for a living. Working with the Oil Kings for free, I felt I'd be my own man. I wouldn't owe anything to anybody at the Red Wings head office, and I could quit with a clear conscience if I didn't like the way things were going. Norris was only too happy to have me working completely *gratis*. He signed me and told me to go ahead and buy out the exhibition board.

"How much are you willing to pay?" I asked.

"We'll go up to $20,000," said Norris.

I almost choked. No wonder they needed me. The Oil Kings were solid on the ice but they were a financial disaster. They were losing thousands of dollars every year. They played in an antiquated arena where they didn't even charge admission. They just took a silver collection.

"That's way too much," I said. "Leave it to me."

We ended up paying $10,000. I became president and general manager of the Edmonton Oil Kings, and to satisfy legalities, I joined the board of directors of the Detroit Hockey Club, which owned the Red Wings. I was back in hockey.

I have to admit there was more than business and hockey that drew me to Edmonton. I've always spent a lot of time on the road and the years with People's Investors and giving seminars all over western Canada were no exception. Edmonton was a common stop for me, and in 1962 I met someone who ensured I'd keep coming back.

My Edmonton office was in the Empire Building on Jasper Avenue downtown, but I used to stay in the west end at the Mayfair Hotel. One evening I noticed the hostess of the restaurant downstairs, a slender woman with striking blonde hair and penetrating green eyes. She was beautiful. I asked one of the staff members to introduce us. Her name was Vi McKort. For the next six months, every time I was in Edmonton, I couldn't keep myself from that restaurant. The attraction got stronger and harder to resist. Finally, late one night I could see she was about to get off shift. This was my chance. I'm not a shy man, and I can usually think of the right thing to say, but my opening line that night gives some idea of how badly this young woman had shaken my composure.

"You're so skinny, you better eat something," I said. "How would you like to go to out for a bite to eat?"

Vi consented, despite my awkward invitation. Apparently, she was interested in me, too. For three years I had jumped at every opportunity to come to Edmonton and see her. Now we could live in the same city. I was married the entire time, and Bernie and our three children joined me when I moved People's Investors. It was complicated. I don't defend my actions, but I don't apologize for them, either. Bernie and I had spent some wonderful years together, but they were coming to an end. We were to divorce in 1968. The split was amicable. We remained in contact through family functions. Vi and I attended Bernie's funeral in Saskatoon when she died of a heart attack.

There may have been turmoil in my personal life, but what I needed to do with the Oil Kings was perfectly clear and straightforward. The team was strong on the ice and had made several recent Memorial Cup appearances. But in some ways the team had lacked strong leadership and was in disarray.

That summer I had all the players over to our house for a team meeting. I told those boys there was new management and things were going to change. I noted that about half of them were living in high-rise apartment buildings downtown. That would have been fine for a senior team, but I wasn't going to have it for juniors. Some of the kids on the team were only 17 years old—far too young to be in that kind of environment. And even for players a year or two older, the temptation would be too great to start cutting school, running around and partying if they were all living in apartments. "That's not good for you and it's not good for the Oil Kings," I told them. "You will find homes or we will find them for you. We need commitment and discipline if we're going to build a championship club, and by God that's what we're going to have." I said they had to be out of their apartments within two weeks. I also told them we were going to make a run for the Memorial Cup, Canada's junior hockey championship, and that's all we were going to talk about. That was to be our only goal the season.

The very next week, our team suffered its first loss, a much deeper loss than anything that could happen on ice. Our captain, Greg Tomalty, a fine young man and a gifted center, was killed in a automobile accident. He was only 18. I hired a bus and the whole team drove to Red Deer for the funeral. It was a terrible tragedy, but it brought the team together. The mood at training camp that autumn was serious. Everyone wanted to get down to work and achieve something. I knew the raw material was there.

The first coach I hired was Bill Warwick. He did a great job, but coaching isn't easy, and it soon took a toll on Billy. After two months the strain was so great that his doctors told him he should look for other employment. He said, "Bill, I just can't take this. I have to step down."

I replaced him with Ray Kinasewich, who was a popular choice with the players. Ray was an affable, good-natured man with a great sense of humor, but he had plenty of steel where it counted. His parents had been killed in a car accident when he was only 18. Ray and his 20-year-old brother refused to allow the authorities to split the family up, and they raised their three younger brothers themselves.

Ray had been a Pacific Coast League star in Seattle, where he played on a line with Gyle Fielder and Val Fonteyne. He'd coached a little in the minors and had benefitted from working with the Red Wings staff, too. Ray had a deep understanding of the game and how to teach it to kids. He'd attended a number of the Red Wing's coaching camps and had a real professional approach. He had solid, strong systems that were effective enough to win and simple enough for everybody to stick with in the heat of a tough game. He had the technical understanding that I appreciated and he knew how to use a system to get his players pulling together. Ray's players always looked like they knew what they were supposed to be doing out there. But what I really liked about Ray's style was that he never bogged the players down with niggling details or criticism.

Every day at 5:00 P.M., Ray ran fast-moving, highly structured practices that covered all the fundamentals. The players were always moving. There was a flow to his practices, and they were exhilarating and upbeat to watch.

Ray was probably the best coach I ever worked with in junior hockey. I stayed out of Ray's way and watched his well-coached team, but I was his second pair of eyes, and we certainly talked privately about what was happening on ice. The one thing I could do better than Ray was motivate the players, and that became my role. I knew how to fire them up.

The players looked good. The days of Johnny Bucyk and Normie Ullman were a fading memory, but there was plenty of talent around. We probably had the league's best defenseman in tall, rangy Al Hamilton, a tremendous rusher and goal scorer. Our captain, Bob Falkenberg, wasn't the greatest player, but the others respected his smarts and the way he always played his heart out. Those two were among 14 Oil Kings from that season who eventually turned pro. Others included defenseman Kerry Ketter, who played in Atlanta, and his line mate Doug Barrie who went to Buffalo and Los Angeles. Ross Perkins, Craig Cameron and Ron Anderson all went to Detroit and Garnet "Ace" Bailey played for years with the Bruins.

Sometimes a team simply melds. Some of these young men had been together for three or four years already, and that fall, the sense of individuals jelling into a unit was palpable. Watching from the bleachers in the old Edmonton Gardens arena, I could see my players begin to skate as something unified and purposeful, like a flock of birds moving as one. The scrape and swoosh of blades on ice was like an orchestra tuning up. I could hardly wait for the season to begin.

When it did, of course, we took a beating. I expected it. Although the Oil Kings were a junior team made up of boys no older than their early twenties, we played against men. There was no junior hockey league in Alberta, and we were members of the Alberta Senior Hockey League, which included the Drumheller Miners, the Lacombe Rockets, the Red Deer Rustlers and the Ponoka Stampeders. All of those teams were bigger, stronger and more experienced. Some of them had former NHL pros playing out their careers. Our average age was about 18. Our opponents averaged about 27. So for the first half of the season, we got pounded—physically, mentally and on the scoreboard.

But we had some advantages. Our rivals were all grown men with grown men's responsibilities. Our players were basically school kids. We had few distractions, and we practiced every day after school, drilling and working Ray's systems to perfection. We were together every day and we became a real team. As well, our players weren't shrinking violets. They quickly got accustomed to the seniors' rough and tumble, and they toughened up to meet its challenge almost without realizing it. One Sunday afternoon in late November, we were playing Lacombe before a sellout crowd in the Gardens. It was a thriller—hard-skating and hard-checking, the kind of game you win only if you don't let up for a second. And we were the team that didn't. After that we started to take off. By Christmas we were a group of men racking up regular victories. The Oil Kings started to believe they could win, and once you've got a team believing in itself you've got a contender.

The season ended in a series against the Drumheller Miners for the league title. Drumheller was a powerhouse with the great Al Rollins, formerly of Maple Leafs, in goal. The series went to seven games with the final played in Drumheller in front of a packed and rowdy crowd. We were tied 2–2 after regulation and still tied after one overtime period. I thought we'd won it in the middle of second overtime when we sunk one right in the middle of the net, but the goal judge didn't see it. I thought I'd rupture something yelling at the ref, but the goal was still disallowed. When the score was still 2-2 after the second overtime period, I went to the Miners' general manager. "Hey, let's get smart," I told him. "This is an opportunity for both of us. We're both hard up for cash, so let's play an eighth game instead of another overtime period. The players will be fresh, the fans will be at a fever pitch and we'll split the gate from another sellout crowd. Everybody'll be happy." I never knew a hockey owner who couldn't use a little extra revenue, and he went for it. We called the game a tie and announced a rematch in Edmonton.

I thought I'd hit on a great idea. The Canadian Amateur Hockey Association, however, did not. The CAHA governed minor league hockey in Canada, and they ruled that there would be no eighth game. So the Alberta Senior League had two champions that year: the Oil Kings and the Miners. The Miners went on to play for the Allan Cup, the Canadian senior crown, which they eventually won. We took the next step toward the Memorial Cup, the prize I'd been holding in front of our boys since the fall.

First we met the southern Alberta champs, the Calgary Buffaloes, who played in a commercial league. They had Garry Unger,
but other than that they couldn't keep up to us, and we beat them
easily in two games. Next were the British Columbia champions,
the New Westminster Royals. They had the Shmyr brothers (Paul
Shmyr went on to a great career in the NHL) and a barrelful of
heart, but they couldn't beat us either. The Oil Kings outscored
them 28–3 over four games.

The Estevan Bruins from Saskatchewan were next, but they
were a different story. The Bruins were owned and managed by my
great friend Scotty Munro, and he had put together a powerful club.
Don Caley was in goal with Stan Fuller and Dale Hoganson anchor-
ing their defense. Forwards like Ross Lonsberry and Jimmy Harrison, who later played for the Leafs and starred with the Edmonton
Oilers, were out front. The games were all 1–0 and 2–1 squeakers
with the Oil Kings up three games to two after five games. But the
next two games were to be played in Estevan, and I didn't want the
series to go to game seven. Not after coming this far.

We were in the dressing room before the start of game six. Ray
carefully prepared the players, going over the game plan and thoroughly outlining each player's assignments. Every player knew what
he had to do. Now it was up to me to give them the heart to do it,
and I took my place at the head of the dressing room. "Fellows," I
said, "we've got to end this. We cannot take the chance of this going
to a seventh game. I know you can do it tonight. My confidence in
you is absolute. And to prove how much faith I have in you, I went
down to the travel agent today and bought our airplane tickets for the
Memorial Cup final in Toronto. Here they are." I reached into my
pocket, and there wasn't a sound when I pulled out a big fistful of
tickets. Everybody's eyes were on them. All of a sudden the dream of
playing for the Memorial Cup and Canadian junior hockey suprema-

cy was as real as the handful of paper I fanned out before them. The Oil Kings went out and played as if possessed. We had probably our best game of the season, and we beat the Bruins handily.

After the game I picked up three Bruins to take to the final. I took Harrison, Lonsberry and Ted Hodgson with me back to our hotel, where the Oil Kings were having a team meeting. I had Bob Falkenberg introduce our new teammates and everyone lined up to shake their hands. "Don't ever mention the Estevan Bruins again," I told them as they slipped on their new team's sweaters. "You're Oil Kings now."

Our opponents would be the Oshawa Generals. Everybody picked the Generals to take us in five games at the most. The Generals, after all, had a young defenseman named Bobby Orr, who everybody said was the finest junior in Canada. And they had tough guys like Wayne Cashman, who would wipe the corners of the rink with us. Even our writers and broadcasters from Edmonton like Al McCann, Wes Montgomery, Gordon Fisher, Ernie Afganis and John Short didn't give us a chance. A western team hadn't won the Memorial Cup on eastern ice in 22 years. The Oil Kings, they all agreed, weren't going to be ones who broke the eastern domination.

We arrived in Toronto a couple days after beating the Bruins. I made sure we made an entrance. The whole team was kitted out in matching blazers and pants as we walked into the lobby of the Royal York Hotel, which was to be our headquarters and my personal media theatre over the next few weeks. The series was to be played in Maple Leaf Gardens, where I'd spent so many hours watching other men's teams. Now that my boys were playing there, I wanted that arena packed to the rafters, and I knew we'd need a little controversy to get things stirred up.

I set to work, holding court in the lobby every morning. Any scribe looking for a quote or a story got one. "Al Hamilton is the best junior hockey player in this country, not this Bobby Orr," I'd opine. I was in the papers so much that the Oshawa fans took to calling me "Hunter the Mouth." Sometimes, I'd get burned. One smart guy from the *Toronto Telegram* wrote that I'd called my goaltender Don "Smokey" McLeod "excess baggage." I'd said the words, but that wasn't what I'd meant, and the writer knew it, too. No matter. Don just got mad and played even better.

Finally, the series began. At the pre-game meal I had Bert Marshall come in to talk to the boys. Bert was playing defense with the Red Wings, but he'd been on the Oil Kings team when they won the 1963 Memorial Cup in Edmonton. He told the players what a wonderful opportunity it was to play in the junior championship and how every NHL player with both Memorial and Stanley Cup wins in their career values both memories equally. After hearing that we jumped out of the gate and before 4,500 fans we stunned the Generals 7–2, outshooting them 52–20 . Orr, however, was amazing. He got half the Generals' shots himself. Our players had never seen a defenseman do what he did, making rushes, moving in from the point, being just as dangerous on offense as any forward. The first shot he took was a blazing slapshot from the blue line that whistled just past Don McLeod's ear. If it had hit him, it would have killed him. Everyone in the crowed blinked. And even on a weak knee, Orr could move. Sometimes it was if he was on skates and everyone else was wearing shoes. He was willing to get rough, too. He took a fighting major in the third after a dust up with Jimmy Harrison.

"Kings Shock Everybody" blared the headline in the next day's *Edmonton Journal.* Well, everybody except us. We'd scouted Oshawa pretty thoroughly, and I really believed we had a better team. With Lonsberry, Hodgson and Harrison, I felt we had the depth to win.

The second game, however, went differently. The easterners were feeling a whole lot more comfortable after we got trounced

7–1. Orr had a groin injury, but Cashman picked up the slack with a goal and three assists. And after the Generals thumped us 6–2 in the third game, even without Orr, all the sports pundits felt the universe was pretty much unfolding as it should. Don let in four goals on the first seven shots. He even steered the first one in with his skate. And Wayne Cashman was giving us fits with his spears and pokes and elbows. It was chippy play, but it was knocking us off our stride and frustrating us. Frustrated hockey players make mistakes and take foolish chances. Ray told the sportswriters that the referees were losing control of the game. "The blood will flow," he told them. Back in Edmonton, the *Journal* headline read "Oil Kings' Collapse Continues."

I'd had enough. I kicked the reporters out of the dressing room, barred the door and had a meeting with my team: players, coaches, trainers, everyone. They all sat there in silence, their heads hanging low. They were full of doubt, wondering if they were good enough. They needed some shock treatment, and I was prepared to give it to them. "Pick up your heads," I began. "I've got a few things to say, and I want every one of you to look at me as I'm talking to you. We didn't come down here to lose. We came down here to win. That's the only thing we're going to do. We're going to win this series. We're the best hockey club. And if any one of you in this room who doesn't believe, I want you to let me know because you're going home. Nobody is going to leave this room unless we totally believe we're going to win." For half an hour I gave them all a speech that blew the cobwebs and dust of self-doubt out of their heads. I dissected the Generals and pointed out where we were better. I gave them a reason to believe, and when I was finished they sat there in silence.

I stared at them a moment to let it sink in, and then I walked out of the Edmonton dressing room to deal with the hometown sportswriters: Ernie Afganis, Al McAnn, Wes Montgomery and a few others. I had words for them, too: "We came down here to win and we're going to win this series. And if any of you don't think we can, get the hell back to Edmonton because I don't want your negativism around our club." I got the same stunned silence from them as I had from the players. But later, back at the hospitality suite we kept at the Royal York, the tone was different. This was a place for socializing and things said there were off the record. The writers clustered around, asking if I really thought we could beat the Generals. "I know we can," I said.

Ray later told a sportswriter, "Bill held a meeting with the team and they came out believing they could walk on water." I had grabbed the entire team by the throat, and for the rest of the series I did not intend to let it go. From that point on, we did everything as a team. We ate every meal together in a private dining room at the Royal York. We went to movies together. We held constant team meetings, many times a day. We'd all be walking down Yonge Street, and I'd stop in the middle of the sidewalk. "Okay guys, team meeting!" I'd cry, and we'd all huddle up as the businessmen and a passersby stared at us. We must have looked like some kind of cult in our matching blazers, and in a way I guess we were. We had to brainwash ourselves that we could beat the Generals.

We had some time to do it, too. During game three, Harold Ballard, owner of both the Leafs and the Gardens, came to me with a proposal. His American Hockey League team in Rochester was about to play Cleveland for the league title, and there was a circus booked into the arena in Rochester. Would I be interested in cutting a little deal and taking a break so he could squeeze in a couple games? "Everything has a price, Harold," I said. We got a big chunk of cash from Harold that the CAHA couldn't get its hands on, plus Ray and I had a couple extra days to work with the team.

I did my best to keep the media interest high, too, and there was always some nugget in the papers about the Oil Kings and the Memorial Cup. The Generals got a little tired of me. During the break a dinner was held for both teams. Baldy Cotton, Oshawa's general manger, came up to me complaining about how I was monopolizing the attentions of the press. I just smiled. "Tough luck, Baldy," I said.

In game four the Oil Kings were a changed club. We'd had enough bullying, and we were determined not to take it anymore. I won't say we instigated what came next, but we were hoping that something like it would come along. Ray and I had discussed Cashman's tactics, and we were prepared. Soon after the opening face-off an incident emptied the benches. After the smoke cleared, Generals were flattened all over the ice, and our players were standing over them saying, "Come on. Who's next?" The message had been delivered. We were not going to be intimidated, and if the easterners wanted to beat us they would have to do it playing hockey.

We came from behind three times in that game and finally won 5–3. I watched from the passageway to the dressing room. Ray wanted the total attention of his players, and he wanted me out of sight. I couldn't watch the game in the stands, in the press box or anywhere else. I was so charged with emotion that I had to be by myself. I paced up and down the hall, peering over the boards and yelling and cheering like any fan. After the game I announced, "We've just had revival. God help Oshawa." The *Journal's* headline read "Oil Kings Bounce Back."

The next game we were even more dominant. Our long, tough season back in Alberta playing against senior teams was becoming an advantage. We were stronger, grittier and had more endurance. We wore our opponents down. We manhandled the mighty Generals 7–4, outshooting them 52–33.

The Oil Kings were playing great hockey. Punch Imlach came up to me in the passageway and watched part of the game with me. He looked up at me from under that hat he always wore and said, "This is the best hockey I've seen in years, Bill." Fans all over the country were riveted to the series, following it in their local newspaper and radio sportscasts. The games were even broadcast on TV in Ontario although most of the revenue from that went to the CAHA. Nobody followed the series with more passion than the folks back in Edmonton. After his sievelike performance in game three, poor Don was getting poison-pen letters from back home. Others spun conspiracy theories. One woman wrote to the *Journal* to suggest that the Generals were drugging Don's food: "For them any measure is honorable and right if it will save face for them and avoid a humiliating defeat from the west." When a *Journal* scribe asked me to comment on that, I played along. I invited the Generals to join us for supper. "Everybody but Oshawa manager Wren Blair," I said. "Dope would be wasted on him." Reporters were all over us, and I was always available in the Royal York lobby. You have to have media attention, whether it's ridicule or praise or humor. That's what brings the fans out, and I never saw a notebook I didn't like. You have to be a bit of a showman, and I love a parade.

Game six was played on a Sunday afternoon. The Generals were desperate, and they came at us furiously. Both teams had 37 shots, 14 a side in the third period. The action swung back and forth for 60 minutes with outstanding goaltending from both sides. Oil Kings' goalie Don McLeod got full revenge for being called "excess baggage." Jimmy Harrison had two goals disallowed, but we didn't let that get to us. Finally, Ted Hodgson won it for us 2–1 in the third period when he ripped one by Generals netminder Wendell Young. We were Memorial Cup champions. The next day the *Journal's* top story was "Oil Kings Crowned In East."

*The Edmonton Oil Kings, Memorial Cup Champions, 1965–66. Nobody had given us a chance, but we won.*

Unbelievably, nobody had thought to organize a celebration for the Memorial Cup champion—no luncheon, no dinner, nothing. Our NHL sponsors in Detroit were conspicuous by their absence. General manager Sid Abel chose not to interrupt his Florida holiday to watch his juniors win, and as for Bruce Norris, well, he just wasn't around. I went up to Harold Ballard and said, "Harold, this is bush league. We have to do something for these boys." Harold agreed. He closed down the Hot Stove Lounge at Maple Leaf Gardens, and we had a celebratory banquet. We ordered in cases of bubbly, locked the doors and had the greatest party that any team ever had. I gave a speech, and we celebrated with champagne, hugs and tears. Nobody had given us a chance, but the underdogs had bitten back and had come out on top. Nothing could be sweeter. It was sheer ecstasy.

# 8

# NORTHWEST REBELLION

When he was finished he looked at the
table full of owners and the one or two
cheques in his hand. Someone said,
"Well, I guess we haven't got a meeting."

**N**OBODY WAS HAPPIER WITH OUR
storybook run for the Memorial Cup than I was. But it wasn't long
after our celebration in the Hot Stove Lounge that my frustration
with the powers that ruled minor hockey returned.

That frustration stemmed back to when the Canadian Amateur
Hockey Association suspended me as I'd been trying to build a winning team in Saskatoon, but it boiled over during the Oil Kings' series
with the Drumheller Miners when we were ordered to scrap plans an
eighth game. The CAHA had their rules, and they were going to
damn make sure we lived by them. They were happy enough to take
their cut of the gate from our playoff games, though. And then when
we got to Toronto for the finals, we discovered that the CAHA had
sold television broadcast rights without even informing the Oil Kings
or the Generals. We didn't see much of the television revenue, either.

Nor was I the only junior team manager who was getting fed up with the hockey bureaucracy. People like Scotty Munro in Estevan and Jim Piggott in Saskatoon were tired of sending off a chunk of every playoff ticket they sold. We owned teams, buildings, equipment, contracts and took a huge financial risk every time our players hit the ice. The guys who stickhandled paper back at the CAHA office didn't own so much as a puck, and our dues ensured they got their pay cheques on time.

Everyone knew trouble was brewing, even the CAHA. After we won the cup, I received a letter from the league office. It informed me that the Oil Kings would have to find a junior league to play in next season or be ruled eligible to defend the championship. Never mind that there was no junior league in Alberta. That was our problem. I thought back to my grandpa's old stories about Louis Riel. Maybe it was time for another Northwest Rebellion.

I got on the phone to a few of the likeminded owners. There was Jim Piggott and Del Wilson in Regina. And of course, there were my old pals Scotty and Ben.

Scotty was a short, stocky man, shaped like one of those old stubby beer bottles. He'd been a great catcher in his day, but he'd gotten bit by the hockey bug early, just as I had. He'd owned teams from a young age, and we had met when I was with the Regina Caps. I'd send him players from my training camp to his Gravelbourg Black Cats in Saskatchewan's intermediate league. He was full of enthusiasm that sometimes tipped over into bombast. Scotty never left you in any doubt about his opinion. Sometimes he'd let his temperament get the better of him. At one league meeting, Scotty got upset over something, stood up, slammed his notebook shut, declared, "I'm leaving!" and stormed out. The other owners looked at me. "Shouldn't we go after him, Bill?" they asked. But I knew Scotty pretty well by this time. "He'll be back, he'll be back," I said.

It took him until the evening, but back he came, quiet and contrite.

Scotty and I ran similar teams with lots of discipline and emotion, and we loved to get together. We'd hold court with whoever was around, talking hockey and swapping jokes and having a few drinks until well into the early morning. Scotty and I brought out the raconteur in each other. We grew very close over the years. Scotty thought you could work your way out of anything if you applied yourself enough, and he never complained about anything. Many years later, Scotty and his wife, Rose, joined Vi and I for a holiday in California. We'd meet for supper at six o'clock every evening, and half an hour later, Scotty would say, "We have to leave now. Rose is tired." One night Rose needed to borrow something from Vi and we walked over to drop it off. Scotty was in bed. "What's this?" we asked, and Rose answered, "He's like this every night." It was his leg. It was all scarred and full of sores. He had no strength left in it. No, he hadn't seen a doctor. He thought he could tough it out, or maybe he was just frightened of what a doctor might say. We had him diagnosed as soon as we got back to Calgary, but it was too late. Scotty was full of cancer and he died a week later.

Ben Hatskin was the other member of what became known as the triumvirate of hockey in the west. Ben, Winnipeg born and raised, wasn't a tall man, but he was big and heavyset. He was a great football player and became one of the first Canadians to get a football scholarship from an American university when he attended Ohio State. He later came back and played center for the Blue Bombers. He got into real estate and made a lot of money at everything from putting up industrial warehouses in his hometown to operating Wurlitzer jukebox concessions across the Prairies. He was a gruff man whose conversation consisted of short, sharp barks, and many people were frightened of him. But once you got past the gruff exterior, he had one of the softest hearts I ever knew. When

*Scotty Munro, a close friend and a great hockey man.*

our son Greg died, Ben was on the phone to us steadily. He was in hospital in Palm Springs, injured for a car accident, and yet he called. It broke his heart that he couldn't come for the funeral.

Ben sometimes liked to take the fastest route to solving a problem. When I was chairman of the Western Hockey League, I fined Ben $5,000 for trying to steal someone else's player. Ben didn't even have a team at that point. He was just getting ready and here he was, already tampering with another team's lineup. "You son of a bitch, Hunter" he grumbled, but he paid. Another time we were trying to raise money for our league by holding a car raffle. Every owner was given a minimum of 5,000 tickets to sell. Guys like Scotty and me had to get out and hustle those tickets, but Ben was rich and decided it would save him a whole lot of valuable time if he just bought them all himself. He got his office staff to put his name and address on every one of them. We had no idea what Ben had done. He sent us the stubs and the cash, and we went ahead with the draw. There I was, chairman of the league at the WHL all-star game in Estevan, at center ice with a barrel of entries in front of a microphone and a packed house, most of them holding raffle tickets. We rolled the barrel around, and Miss Estevan reached in and pulled out the winner. My heart sank. Sure enough, Ben held the winning ticket. Oh Lord, I thought, I have to announce that one of the raffle sponsors is the

*Ben Hatskin, a great friend and powerful businessman.*

winner. But I did, and Ben got the car. "Damned right," he growled. "There's no way you're not giving it to me, Hunter."

But that was in the future. At this point, in the early summer of 1966, no one knew where junior hockey was going although everyone knew changes were coming. I got Scotty on the phone in Estevan, and I said, "I want you to meet me. I've got a plan." Scotty came to Edmonton and we hopped in a car together and drove to Saskatoon. On the five-hour trip past rolling parkland, river valleys and wheat fields, I talked to him about forming a new junior hockey league embracing Alberta, Saskatchewan and Manitoba. We'd start with the two westernmost provinces and expand from there. The separate provincial leagues weren't good enough anymore, I told him. An interprovincial league would be more competitive and improve the hockey for everyone. We needed to run more professional operations, pay better attention to the press, get our fans excited with on-ice promotions and a little showmanship. And because we were the ones spending our money and taking the risks, we needed to make our own rules. Finally, Scotty turned to me. "You know, you're right."

Our rebellion was on. We checked into the Bessborough that night and made a couple calls. Jim Piggott decided he'd come with us, and Del Wilson was interested. We drove to Regina that night through a pelting rainstorm. The next day after church we signed Del up over breakfast at the Regina Inn.

Over the next few days, Scotty and I talked to most of the junior hockey owners in western Canada. We made a pretty good pitch.

We knew the new interprovincial league would raise everybody's travel costs, so in return we pointed out that bringing together all three provinces would let the fans see the best players from across western Canada. We were also going to improve the hockey by allowing each team to ice four overage players. With better quality hockey on the ice, we'd be able to charge more at the gate. That got their attention because almost every team was in financial trouble. We also said the new league would be much better run. Every team would have to be a full-time, year-round operation and give a lot more attention to promotion. That was popular with the owners who were tired of the amateur-hour practices of some of the clubs.

At that time we thought we would have teams in Edmonton, Estevan, Regina, Weyburn, Moose Jaw, Brandon and Calgary, with Winnipeg in line for next season. We rebels were ready to fire our first shot.

On June 21, 1966, the Saskatchewan Junior Hockey League held its annual meeting in Clear Lake. Most of our new teams came from that league, and some writers refer to that meeting as the Clear Lake Massacre.

I wasn't there. It was too dangerous. We didn't want to tip our hand, and if I'd shown up at the meeting of a league to which I didn't belong everyone would have known something was going on. We wanted this to go exactly according to plan, and it did. League chairman Frank Boucher called the meeting to order and went on with the first order of business, which turned out to be the last. The league's rules stated that owners couldn't vote unless they paid their annual dues. Frank asked Scotty for his cheque. "I can't afford to pay it," Scotty said. "You can't vote, then," Boucher warned him, but Scotty just shrugged. Frank went around the table and got the same response from nearly everyone. When he was finished he looked at the table full of owners and the one or two cheques in his hand.

Someone said, "Well, I guess we haven't got a meeting." Frank said, "I guess we haven't." And those who hadn't paid got up and walked out. Three days of planned meetings were over in one morning.

Soon after, the rebel owners got together in Regina and drew up our bylaws, elected our officers, wrote our mission statement and announced the formation of the Canadian Major Junior Hockey League, today known as the Western Hockey League. Our first commissioner became none other than Frank Boucher. After more than 27 years in the NHL as player, coach and general manager with the New York Rangers and several more years in amateur hockey, it was Frank's first job with a pension plan.

But the CAHA wanted separate provincial junior leagues that they could ride herd over and within days they fired back. They didn't want to see us joining forces, and they informed us in a letter that they would refuse to acknowledge our league. It was as if they were telling us, "You can't quit, you're fired." On October 1, we received a letter of suspension. We knew they just wanted to feel that they were still in control. Still, it was a blow. Losing CAHA affiliation meant losing NHL affiliation, too, since the NHL had agreed not to sponsor teams that operated outside the national association. This was one way the CAHA kept control of hockey out west. NHL affiliations meant money, and I had more to lose than anyone—$20,000 a year from the Red Wings.

We took blasts from the people who ran the old junior leagues in Saskatchewan and Manitoba, too. For a while the papers and sportscasts were full of complaints from towns like Melville and Swift Current that some dirty play was going on in the corners and that they were getting bumped out of hockey. Scotty and Del were deputized to deal with those complaints. We had been expecting them. Not only had we stolen most of the teams from the old leagues, but we even took some of their officials.

And we ran into inevitable opposition from the NHL. Most of the pro teams were quite happy with how junior hockey was managed in the west. With several junior leagues, the pros could sponsor several teams and play them off against one another if one got uppity. Because the leagues were small and didn't have any bargaining power, sponsorships were cheap. Through sponsorships an NHL club could lock up a pretty good selection of junior prospects without spending much cash. The NHL knew that if we formed one big junior league its costs would rise.

We did, however, receive some support. Weston Adams, the owner of the Boston Bruins, was sympathetic. Boston sponsored their Estevan namesake, and Weston had actually been out to the farm team and had ridden the bus with his juniors.

But at NHL head office, Clarence Campbell simply wanted us to take off our skates and go away. We talked about our league on the phone many times, and Clarence was confident we could never pull it off. "Bill, it won't work," he told me. "You people will go broke. You'll never be able to handle the travel costs without our help, and we just can't participate while you people are out of the CAHA." Clarence was waiting for us to run out of money and come crawling back. He'd grown up in Edmonton, but he assumed that the game of hockey should be controlled from Ontario and couldn't understand why we were so upset. Wasn't that the way things were always done?

Even our own NHL affiliate, the Detroit Red Wings, wasn't happy with our move. They liked us playing in the old Alberta senior league. That way they got players who were already used to lining up against stronger, older and more experienced veterans. It gave Detroit's rookies a leg up on everyone else's. And they were on side with the other pro teams when it came to who should control the game. They wanted us playing under the CAHA banner for the

Memorial Cup. In fact, Bruce Norris at the Wings' head office tried to renege on $20,000 in sponsorship he'd already promised me. I had to get Campbell on the phone and threaten to go public with the news. "If I don't get a cheque deposited to my account within 48 hours, I'll walk out the door and tell the first reporter I see how the NHL lives up to its commitments," I threatened. I meant it, too. I'd had enough broken big-league promises. "Leave it with me," Clarence said. A cheque arrived at my office 48 hours later.

That wasn't the only financial battle we had with the NHL. All the teams tried to stop paying us our sponsorship money. They tried to cut our travel funding, too. We were to get less than the teams in the Ontario Hockey League even though our distances were much greater. We took the NHL to court in Calgary and we won easily. With meetings and phone calls and lawsuits flying around, it was a busy summer.

Threats and criticism could not stop us. We knew the time was right to take control of our own affairs. We all kicked in enough money to hire referees and run a front office, and we set to work. When the puck was dropped that fall for the 1966–67 season, our league boasted seven teams: the Calgary Buffaloes (later the Centennials), the Estevan Bruins, the Weyburn Red Wings, the Saskatoon Blades, the Regina Pats, the Moose Jaw Canucks and the Edmonton Oil Kings. Ben Hatskin was sitting in on meetings and getting ready to bring in a Winnipeg team next season.

We had plenty of support where it counted. The same sales pitch that had convinced junior team owners to come with us worked on the public and the press. The reporters called us The Outlaw League and the public loved it. I staged a photo for the *Edmonton Journal* of three of our players wearing cowboy hats and Lone Ranger masks as they held their sticks like rifles. We did a lot more promotion and we were able to establish rivalries because we were playing each other more consistently. We set out quite consciously to create rivalries between towns like Estevan and Weyburn, Regina and Saskatoon, Calgary and Edmonton. We didn't have to work too hard. We just had to exploit the feelings already there. Our attendance went way up. The Oil Kings drew 13,000 fans in its first nine home games that season. Our entire previous year's attendance had been 7,000.

Efforts to make peace with the CAHA were really halfhearted on our part. Scotty said it best at a meeting in Regina in the spring of 1967 when the CAHA officials walked into the room wearing matching blazers. "What team do you fellows play for?" he asked. They didn't have a dime invested in a team, but we were to buy them uniforms and pay their way. I was the chairman of that meeting, and I looked at those guys in their blazers and said, "You know, fellows, I really don't think we've got anything to talk to you about. You're not on the same page with us. We believe that the people who finance the teams have to control their own destiny and we're not prepared to give you a free ride on our backs any longer. So have a good day." And we walked out of the meeting.

Eventually, both the NHL and CAHA had to concede defeat. Our second season was going to expand to 11 teams with the addition of the Flin Flon Bombers, the Winnipeg Jets, the Swift Current Broncos and the Brandon Wheat Kings. It was clear we were here to stay, and the eastern hockey establishment couldn't ignore us any longer. It was just a matter of coming to terms.

Later that spring, Frank Boucher, Ben, Scotty and I met with three representatives of the NHL in Calgary. Shortly after, the full board of governors of the NHL met with us in Montreal. It was the first time the NHL had deigned to meet with an amateur league. Frank, our commissioner, got up to speak for us. It was his chance to stare down and dictate terms to the men who'd run his life for nearly 30 years, but he couldn't stand the strain. "My name is Frank Boucher and you all know me," he said, and he couldn't get any far-ther. His knees were literally knocking. I stepped in. "As you can see, Frank is very emotional about this," I said, and took over as spokesman. We agreed that the CAHA should get no part of our gate receipts and that we'd control our own playoff format. We agreed to negotiate the number of overage players each team was allowed so our bylaws were consistent with the major junior leagues in Ontario and Quebec. The NHL agreed to restore both our spon-sorship money and our travel allowance, which they increased in recognition of the greater distances western teams have to travel. At that time we also recommended an open draft system. That would mean no team was directly sponsored, but that junior teams would be paid by NHL teams when their players were drafted. Eventually, that's the way our league went. We knew we were taking a risk because if we didn't produce hockey players, we wouldn't get any NHL money. But we were confident the pro scouts would like what they saw in our teams. One year I got about $180,000 from various NHL clubs when five Oil Kings were drafted in the first round.

By May 1967 we were back in the CAHA, too. The hockey bureaucrats surrendered after 12 hours of debate at a meeting in Regina. They would get their money from the draft picks, and that was all we were willing to give them. They had no choice but to accept. Our western rebellion was victorious.

# 9

# THE KINGS OF EDMONTON

**Over 5,000 fans met us at the airport and followed us to our hotel, the Chateau Frontenac, with a parade of cars. They carried banners proclaiming, "Vive le Oil Kings!" We were heroes just for showing up.**

I'D SPENT A LOT OF TIME IN EDMONTON over the years, but running the Oil Kings for a season really gave me a good chance to look around. I decided I liked what I saw. It was an energetic city of 300,000 with streets full of young people on the move. Businesses were expanding. The great petrochemical facilities east of town were growing. Downtown, a dynamic impresario named Joe Schoctor had built the Citadel Théatre. The Jubilee Auditorium was bringing some big shows to town. In a way, and on a much larger scale, Edmonton's dynamism reminded me of the Saskatoon of my youth. Edmonton even had a green, leafy river valley curving through the city, just like my old hometown. I felt right at home and decided to dig in. Besides, after that Memorial Cup win, I had the hockey bug again, but good.

The first thing that had to change was my situation with the

Oil Kings. I had no intention of remaining an employee of the Detroit Red Wings, and certainly not an unpaid one. I resolved to convince Bruce Norris to sell me the team, lock, stock and uniforms. Norris turned out to be receptive. The Red Wings weren't keen on sponsoring a team in the new junior league. The whole structure of the new league didn't fit into their plans. They liked to have total control of a club and exclusive rights to its players. They wanted it run by a loyal minion, whom they could trust to do things their way. The Oil Kings and the whole fledgling western junior league were shaping up as something quite different, and Bruce Norris knew it. I met with Bruce at the Red Wings training camp, and after considerable time on the phone he finally sent a couple representatives to Edmonton to close the sale though I'm not sure you can call it a sale. The Oil Kings had been losing money for years, and Bruce didn't charge me a dime for them. He simply signed them over.

Once I had the team, I wanted to make a splash. We had a new league with a whole new manner of doing business and I wanted to put Edmonton on notice. I didn't want some office tucked away in the Jasper Place arena. I wanted the head office of the Edmonton Oil Kings to demonstrate that we intended to go first class. It so happened that the gentleman who managed the Canadian National Railway in the Canada was an old friend of my dad's. He oversaw the railway's hotels as well, so I called him with a proposition: rent me a suite of offices at the Hotel Macdonald, the premier address in downtown Edmonton, and I'd make sure the hotel saw lots of traffic from visiting teams, NHL scouts and various hockey officials. It worked. He rented me a beautiful suite of offices in that noble old building. The offices were fully renovated with a set of French doors opening to a patio that overlooked the river valley. This was the first full-time, year-round office for any junior club in Canada.

Those offices did see many visitors over the years. Visiting scouts came around looking for the skinny on this defenseman or that goalie or just wanting to talk hockey and get a recommendation for a good restaurant. Local sportswriters used to drop in, sometimes to my embarrassment. I'd tell my public relations man, Jim Pelehos, to tell a reporter I wasn't in, then I'd come tearing around the corner and nearly bump into the guy or he'd hear me declaiming over the phone in the next room. I'd have to chew poor Jim out for not telling me the writer wanted to see me, but we both knew it was just a show. And as required I'd go through the same song and dance with the others on my staff: controller Ray Barth, personal secretary Marilyn Noble and receptionist Mattie Middlehurst. Everybody played along.

Ernest Manning, then the premier of Alberta, used to stroll over to the Macdonald for dinner upon occasion. If he saw my light on, he'd stop to say hello. Peter Lougheed used to call. I knew him from his days as a halfback for the Eskimos, and we kept in touch when he entered politics. Peter was a big Oil Kings fan and every time the playoffs came around I knew I'd be getting a phone call: "Bill, have you got any tickets?" I expected the call and always had a couple for Peter. Don Getty, the nicest, most decent man you'd ever want to meet, was another ex-Eskimo turned politician I used to see quite often.

But to make a success of my new team, I had to give it everything I had. That meant I couldn't run another business on the side. I had to sell People's Investors. It was a hard thing to do. I had built that business from the ground up and it had supported my family for years. But I couldn't make a success of both of them, and one had to go. Charles Allard bought People's Investors through Pacific Western Securities.

Dr. Allard was a brilliant surgeon, chief of staff at the Edmon-

*The Edmonton Oil Kings, 1967–68*

ton General Hospital. He also built a real estate and broadcasting empire on the side. He was gentle and soft-spoken but deadly shrewd, and he could size up a deal faster than any man I ever knew. He could sense a good opportunity even before he understood exactly what it was, just like a playmaking center instinctively knows where to position himself on the ice. He once bought a dilapidated old building in downtown Edmonton just because he thought it might come in handy. The building was nearly derelict. Charles took me through it, and when we went upstairs we thought we were going to fall through the floor. But he entered a bid in a silent auction and left on holiday to Florida. He asked me or his assistant, Helen Custer, to let him know what happened. Sure enough, he bid exactly the amount needed to buy the building. And sure enough, while he was on holiday, he met a man on the next beach chair who

*The Oil Kings, Western Canada Hockey League Division Champions, 1968–69.*

was looking for places to expand a his chain of restaurants. It was the perfect match.

For a man who owned a restaurant, Charles was very solitary. He hated crowds and cocktail parties. Sunday nights, he'd call and ask, "Is Bill there?" I'd go over to Charles' home out in the west end and pull up the driveway to where his long, low bungalow was set back from the street. Charles' wife, Gillie, would make us tea and cookies, we'd say good-night to his little daughter, Cathy, and then we'd sit and talk, sometimes until 3:00 A.M. We'd talk business. That was Charles' idea of a good social evening. We were very different, but somehow we hit it off. I did a lot of work with him and used to represent him when a new Allarco building opened up. I'd take his mother and make a little speech on Charles' behalf. He once offered me a vice president's position with Allarco Group, his main compa-

*The Oil Kings, Western Canada Hockey League finalists, 1969–70.*

ny. He plan was to handle Canadian investments for a group of German bankers worth hundreds of millions of dollars, and he needed
someone to go to Germany and represent his interests as the deal
closed. But Charles knew me well enough not to be surprised when
I turned his offer down, even though I knew it would lead to big
money. He knew I needed to be on my own. When I sold People's
Investors to Charles, it was the continuation of a long and mutual-
ly beneficial relationship.

Now I was a hockey man again, owner and general manager of
a championship team in a hockey-mad town, playing in a league I
had helped found. You couldn't ask for a better situation. It was
wonderful to be back in hockey again.

I hired Bob Freeman as my chief scout and brought on a young
man named Wayne Meier to keep an eye on local talent. I made one
thing clear to Wayne right away: "We must bring in Edmonton
boys," I told him. "You have to get their families and their school
friends and their whole community supporting the club." Only a
third of our Memorial Cup team had been local players, and I

*An Oil Kings staff reunion luncheon. L–R: Ray Barth, Mattie Middlehurst, Marilyn Noble and yours truly.*

believed the situation couldn't persist for the long term. I wanted people to really feel the Oil Kings were the home team, and that meant they had to be cheering for their own. Within two years, nearly three-quarters of the Oil Kings were local boys.

I did my share of scouting, too. I saw the inside of every arena in central Alberta and most of the locker rooms. Wayne and his assistants picked out the best prospects from around Edmonton and farther afield, and I looked over every one of them. If I liked what I saw, I'd meet the player personally, and then I'd meet with his mother and father. That meeting was never at a restaurant or café—it was always at the family home. I never picked a player I hadn't seen in his home environment. The reason for that was simple. In many ways I looked for the same things everybody else looks for: skills, size, smarts, speed. But one thing I insisted on was character. I'd look at the commitment a boy had to his family, his school and his hockey. I wanted to see how a boy respected his mother and father.

I wanted to get a sense of what his community thought of him. I wanted to see how he treated his teammates. I wanted to see how hard he worked. You can always teach someone when to go to the net or how to cut off a pass, but you can't teach him the will to succeed. I wanted a team with character.

Many times I sat in a farm kitchen in Camrose or Wainwright with a cup of coffee in my hand and a plate of homemade cookies in front of me, explaining to parents what entering junior hockey meant. The boy, of course, was dying to go and would have signed up that minute even if he had to run the Zamboni himself. His parents and I, however, had to feel each other out a bit. I always said becoming an Oil King was a serious thing and a whole new level of commitment. This wasn't little league anymore. Parents had to understand that their little boy would now answer to me, and that I would have first call on his time. For their part they wanted to hear that I was going to look after their son and make sure he kept up his schooling. Parents who had spent any time at all around junior hockey had usually heard some good things about the Oil Kings, but that didn't stop them from quizzing me closely. I didn't blame them. This sales pitch wasn't over an order of some Maxwell House or a savings plan. It was over the future of their son. I insisted their boy would get the best of two worlds—education both on and off the ice.

Every player was different. Craig Cameron was a wonderful fellow, but he hoarded words like they were thousand dollar bills. He'd say hello at the start of the season and goodbye at the end of it. He sat there throughout my entire Oil Kings sales pitch without saying a word. He gave me no response at all, but I finally signed him. Tommy Bladon was just the opposite, a 17-year-old kid who negotiated me to the wall. Tommy, who was to play on two Stanley Cup teams in Philadelphia, had been talking with a Manitoba team that was going to pay him big money, and he used that leverage expertly.

On a few occasions parents brought lawyers into the room. I'd stand and start collecting my papers. "I'm sorry," I'd say. "There'll be no lawyer representing any player with the Oil Kings." I wasn't about to have a lawyer tell me what to pay or how to play anybody in my organization. Those boys always came back later on their own, bringing their fathers for advice.

Alex Romaniuk, an Edmonton high-school principal, oversaw our education program, and the Oil Kings were always very committed to it. The Oil Kings paid for tuition and books, and I personally guaranteed every one of our players a three-year tuition and books scholarship at the university of his choice. At one point we had five boys at the University of Alberta. When the academic year collided with the hockey schedule one year, I arranged for the university to send a professor on the road with the team. All the players took their exams in the Flin Flon high school, the first time the university had allowed any of its students to take their exams off-campus. We joked their degrees would read "University of Flin Flon."

I sent all my out-of-town boys to Eastglen High School. One year the school principal heard a rumor that I was going to move them to another school. He came to me and said, "Bill, your players are role models for my students and I can't afford to lose them."

When we finally picked our team at the end of training camp, I took everybody to my friend Vic Mah's Blue Willow restaurant. I mean everybody: staff, the new recruits, their parents, the families who boarded our players and last year's returning vets. We'd take over Vic's upstairs dining room and have a great meal. Then I'd get up to speak. I'd tell the players and parents about the Oil Kings and their tradition, and I'd tell them what we expected of their sons. I'd also tell them what we expected of them: absolutely no interference. We were to be their sons' new parents for the year. "I don't come to your town to run your business," I'd tell them. "You're not going to come to our city to run our hockey club." A couple times during the season I had to deliver an ultimatum: "Either your boy goes back with you or you stay away from here." The offending parents always relented, and I very rarely had any trouble.

I had a good idea of what I wanted to see on the ice, too. We played a strong defensive system that allowed us to break fast onto offense. We emphasized strong positional play, as did most other teams. Our attitude was hard-nosed. I wanted a clean but tough team that would go to the corners in both ends of the rink and have no fear of getting hit. I used to set up drills with lots of hitting especially for that purpose. Players would be sprawled all over the ice after, and I'd blow the whistle. "Anyone hurt?" I'd ask. But they'd all be laughing like boys do after they've had a good roughhouse.

If the occasion warranted, the Oil Kings never backed down from a fight. True bench clearers were rare, but it wasn't entirely uncommon to see five or six guys down on the ice, all tangled up in each other's uniforms. We won more of those than we lost, and sometimes they changed the direction of a series.

Our western league was tough. One morning in the sports pages I read that a junior coach felt he had to paint a Red Cross on the side of his team bus to get out of Swift Current. I knew how he felt. That was a team whose fans were known to throw dead ducks on the ice after their Broncos had run up a sufficient lead. One scrappy night against Weyburn, our forward Bob Birdsell punched Ron Pearpoint unconscious for five minutes. That punch-up provoked fighting on the ice and more fighting in the stands. We also had players like the identical twins Bob and Ted McAneeley . In 1969 they had 290 penalty minutes between them after 38 games. Of course, Ted was also a league all-star, and Bob had racked up 26 goals. For a while that season, we led the league in both penalties and points.

We had our biggest and bloodiest battles in Flin Flon, where the Bombers were a great rival. Paddy Ginnell had shaped those boys into a tough, tough bunch. There wasn't a team in the league that took going into that building lightly, and it was war when the Oil Kings came to town. Three years running we met them in the league championship. The first two we lost in close battles, and in 1970 the series was shaping up to be just as physical. In fact, it was hand-to-hand combat: high-sticks, butt-ends, elbows, the whole arsenal of cheap shots hockey players have developed over the generations. I watched, getting angrier and angrier. Finally, I yelled over to the Bomber bench, "Ginnell, enough's enough. Let's you and I go to center ice right now and settle this between us." He was about 30 years younger than I and probably could have laid a licking on me, but I was too furious to care. And when Ginnell just laughed, I became incensed. I yelled back for Ginnell and the whole crowd to hear. "Okay, smart guy. You send out your tough guy and I'll send out mine." A packed, sold-out house and probably a dozen pro scouts watched as I sent out our defenseman Tommy Bladon to face an American kid named McKencery—a nice kid and an intimidating six-foot-three. At first they stood like gladiators, then they started to mix it up as the crowd roared. The players sparred for a bit, then Tommy saw an opening, wound up and leveled McKencery. The poor kid folded up like an accordion and dropped to the ice. The ticking of the time clock was the only sound in the following hush.

After that the Flin Flon crowd started cheering for us. That fight was a turning point for us, and we won the league title four games to one in Flin Flon's building on my fiftieth birthday.

Junior hockey of the sort the Oil Kings played creates excitement because the fans know the kids are playing so hard. Often juniors will make a nice move and not know what to do next. Their mistakes and the effort they make to fix them are sometimes what make the game fun to watch. Darcy Rota, who played for the Oil Kings in the early 1970s, was a perfect example. He could just fly on skates, but he had a tough time controlling his excitement. In one match against Flin Flon, Darcy took a pass at the blue line, wheeled in on net and whipped a wrist shot up in the top corner past the goalie. It was a beautiful goal, with just one problem—he'd scored on our net. Our goalie, a 16 year old named Larry Hendricks, just stood there in amazement.

Back on the bench, all the players were saying, "God, what was Darcy thinking?" But I told them not to say a word when he returned to the bench. I said, "Darcy, come over here and stand by me for a bit." He did and I continued. "Now, Darcy, that was a picture goal. But as you and I know, the trouble is that you scored it on the wrong net. Darcy, I'm expecting that when I send you out on the next shift, you're going to get one back for us just as pretty." Darcy stared back at me, all goggle-eyed, and said, "I will, I will." Sure enough, on his next shift Tommy Bladon fed Darcy a quick pass outside our blue line and Darcy wheeled around the Flin Flon defense as if they were statues. He zapped one into the top corner, just as he had a few minutes ago at the other end of the rink.

You never know what's going to happen, and it all just makes for a better show for the fans. People still come up to me and say, "Wasn't that great hockey?"

The atmosphere at those old home games was electric. For two years we played at the Jasper Place Arena (now the Bill Hunter Arena, I'm proud to say). It was a tiny place, and the fans were so close to the action that playing there was like playing in your living room. Later we moved to the renovated Edmonton Gardens, where we could seat 5,200 fans and almost always did. On a Sunday, loud, loyal and enthusiastic hockey lovers would be hanging from the rafters. The smell of fried onions mingled with the musty smell of old wood. Those that hadn't gotten tickets early enough would be stuck behind the great steel beams that held up the roof. The Gardens had tiny locker rooms, but it did have the league's largest ice surface. As a result Edmonton fans got used to wide-open, fast-skating, fire-wagon hockey.

We wanted the Gardens to be a fun place, and eventually I realized that nothing prevented the show from stopping just because the hockey had. I started doing stunts between periods like Score-O, where we'd get fans to come on the ice and try to shoot a puck into a slot we'd set up in front of the net. Before long everybody in the league was copying it. We had flower night when all the ladies got carnations. At fan appreciation nights we gave away prizes. I dragged out the old used car promotion from my days with the Caps. I even used the same old line: "The only thing we'll guarantee is that it'll get you home." Donkey night was maybe the most unusual thing we did. Between periods, we led donkeys onto the ice and drew names to give them away to fans. They loved it. I'm not so sure how the donkeys felt.

Our top ticket price started at $5 and eventually went to $7. At those prices, the stands were full of families who'd come out for a night of entertainment, and that's what we did our best to bring them. People brought trumpets and all kinds of noisemakers. Fans would be dancing in the stands, and the roar that went up when we scored in a tight game was a force that you could actually feel down on the ice. A sportswriter I know compares old-time junior hockey to the way professional wrestling used to be. It was entertainment, pure and simple.

I'd long ago figured out that the way to build some excitement around town for your hockey club was to get plenty of press. And the way to get plenty of press was to give the reporters plenty of material. Besides, I also figured out early that if I was the one talking, I was the one controlling the interview. Reporters couldn't ask a question if they couldn't get a word in. There were stretches during which I probably saw the local sports reporters more than I saw anyone except my family. We had Al McCann at CFRN, Wayne Overland and Gord Fisher at the *Edmonton Journal,* Wes Montgomery and Bryan Hall at CJCA. Al and Ernie Afganis at CBC were always two of the fairest reporters I ever worked with, and you could always count on them to check a fact and get a quote right. But I had a lot of fun with all the reporters. After all we needed each other, and I did my best to fill their notebooks. We held lots of press conferences. Once I even called a press conference to announce that we'd painted the team bus. One of my media conferences has entered sports journalism myth. I called all the guys down and served them coffee and a few pastries and after we'd chatted a bit I put on my press conference voice. "Gentlemen, I've called you down here today for an important announcement and here it is: Tomorrow, we're going to have a major press conference." They all groaned and some of them made like they were going to throw pastries at my head, but they were laughing, too. And they showed up the next day.

We'd build up the other team coming to play and say how great their stars were, always giving the reporters personalities to write about. Believe it not, I liked to throw in a little hyperbole, too. The Oil Kings never just made a nice comeback in a regular-season game. It was always "The greatest win in Oil Kings history!" Sometimes I'd simply create a story, maybe that I was considering a big trade. Or if we lost two games in a row, I'd suggest this wasn't good enough and that big changes were in the works. After Scotty moved to Calgary and bought the Centennials, he and I took a leaf from those wrestlers I used to promote in Medicine Hat. We'd pick fights with each other in the papers. I'd call him all kinds of names, and he'd call me some more right back. Then we'd telephone each other and have a laugh. Sometimes I'd phone a reporter and offer him an exclusive. Sometimes two or three would get the same offer. Or sometimes I'd pick an argument with one of the writers. If I didn't like what someone had written, I'd storm up to the press box and boom over them as they typed: "I know what you're trying to do! That's blue in my eyes, not scotch mist!" But I always ended up saying, "I need you. And you need us. What would you be writing about if the Oil Kings weren't playing? What beat would you be covering?" Ultimately, you always knew the sportswriters were on your side.

We always paid the reporters' way when they went on the road with us. I'd often host parties for them, too. The Oil Kings had the 400 Club for its top supporters, and we'd occasionally hold social evenings with much food and drink and several cash door prizes. Reporters were welcome to those as guests. At Christmas I'd always host a party exclusively for the media, usually at Charles' Beachcomber restaurant. Those parties were great fun and appropriately well-oiled. I bought them all Christmas presents, usually a shirt and tie from one of my two favorite men's wear stores.

I always had Christmas presents for my players, too: matching shirts, blazers and slacks to wear when we went out on the road or were in public. You couldn't mistake us when we went out, and we went out a lot. The early afternoon before a big game, I'd get all my players dressed up, have them meet me at the Mac, then march them across the street to Hy's for a steak. Things like that made an impression both on the boys and the community.

The Oil Kings traveled mostly by bus. I bought a used Greyhound and had it fixed up inside and our name painted on the sides. We spent days on that bus. We'd start off a road trip going to Saskatoon, more than 500 kilometers away. Then there'd be another 300 to Regina, and from there we'd cruise to Estevan and Weyburn in the eastern part of the province. Swift Current to Calgary to Winnipeg and Flin Flon . . . that bus was like a second home. The players called it the Iron Lung, after the tradition of junior hockey players. Sometimes the atmosphere on the bus was raucous if we were heading out after a big win; sometimes we'd be sullen and frustrated if things weren't going well. Most of the time, to be honest, it was pretty dull. I'd be at the front of the bus, thinking or reviewing papers or talking things over with the coach. Some of the boys studied, some played cards, some read and some slept. We had one player who liked to strip down to his shorts and stretch out in the overhead baggage compartment. We always stayed at good hotels and ate in good restaurants. When you spend that much time on the road, you have to treat yourself well or you get run down. Besides, I liked the way it looked when we got off the bus in our matching suits and marched into the best place in town. It made the players take a little bit of extra pride in being an Oil King.

Being a member of a star junior hockey team has its pitfalls for a young man, but the Oil Kings didn't have too many problems. The players were always in the public eye, and one of my jobs was to keep it from going to their heads. After all, many of them were high school kids and when their names were popping up in the press every day, it was easy for them to get the idea that rules didn't apply to them. There were always girls hanging around the lobby of the Gardens, waiting to meet the players. They'd take off when they saw me coming, but it seems that where there's a will, there's a way. A number of Oil Kings married girls they met when they were with our team.

We made the Oil Kings proud to wear the sweater, and that made team discipline easy. If a player was causing trouble, more often that not the players would look after it themselves. And if that didn't work, one of the captains would come to me. Some infractions, such as being late for practice or talking back to the coach or refusing assignments, merited an immediate walk down the hallway to my office. I'd give a player holy hell, but still try to make him feel good on his way out. "Why have I brought you here?" I'd ask him at the end of my harangue. "It's because you're an exceptional talent. And I don't want to see you damage your opportunities." I all but finished the speech with "go forth and sin no more," and it usually worked. Not always, though. There were players I had to let go. One who was leaving the Oil Kings after repeated locker-room battles with me wanted to come and pick up his skates. "No way," I told him. "I'm selling your skates so I can get back some of the money I wasted on you."

I knew some of the players snickered at my histrionics, and I'd occasionally see eyes roll when I had to explain, probably for the third or fourth time, that what a player lacked was heart, not skill. But no one could accuse me of not making clear exactly what I wanted. Even during games, I'd holler out a constant stream of instruction: "Pick up the wing! Go to the net! Stay on the blue line!" Ultimately, the players knew I could help them win, and they respected me for it. They called me "Mr. Hunter" to my face and "The Great White Father" or "The Fiery Red Leader" in the locker room. Of course, the players didn't exactly hold me in awe. After one afternoon game, I was standing outside the locker room and noticed how it had fallen unusually silent. I slipped in to find Fred Comrie doing an impression of one of my pre-game pep talks. He had it down pretty well: the earnest tone, the references to Athol Murray, the avowals of faith and confidence, the exhortations to "Remember the Oil Kings tradition," and the phrases like "Never before in the history of hockey . . ." I sat behind him and enjoyed the show while Fred went on, oblivious to the horrified looks of his teammates. Finally, he figured it out and turned around.

"That's pretty good, Comrie," I smiled. "Maybe you should deliver it next time."

My relationships with coaches were a little more tangled. Bill Warwick didn't last very long. Ray Kinasewich was a winner, but he eventually left to run a successful business with his brother. Bill Gadsby, after 20 years in the NHL as an all-star defenseman, was a great player—almost too great to make a good coach. He had a lifetime's worth of skills and techniques and understanding. But coming back to junior hockey, he had a tough time realizing that these young men didn't have his instincts or his skills. It would drive Bill crazy when one of his players made a mistake.

And when it came to motivating the players, Bill thought he was still on the Red Wings. You can reasonably expect a professional not to need an emotional windup before a game, but kids do. You have to know how to handle them, which ones need a kick in the pants, which ones need lots of praise, which ones need lots of time and attention. Bill never learned how to handle juniors. He could coach, but even though he ran a hockey school in the summer, he didn't have the patience to teach. Although Bill had a very successful first season for us in 1966, I had to take over during the 1967–68 playoffs. We were floundering, only a loss and a tie away from elimination in the first round. We went on to beat Saskatoon four games in a row.

Jerry Melnyk was a fine coach and a friend, but he just couldn't get results from the team. Coaching is a strange and subtle thing. A coach can understand the game and have all the knowledge and leadership skills he needs, but if his personality doesn't react well with the chemistry on the team, players won't respond to him. I had to let Jerry go. It wasn't his fault. He was working hard, but he couldn't get the team to jell. I felt a couple of the players were being unfair to Jerry, but they were great players. The team needed them and I couldn't get rid of them. I lost a lot of sleep over my decision to release Jerry.

I got off to a terrible start with coach Ken Hodge. I held a press conference to announce his hiring, and I had him behind a curtain while I did the introduction. As I was speaking a reporter arriving late poked his head in the door. It was a reporter I knew well, and I said, "Come on in, you asshole," just ribbing him a bit for being late. But as soon as the word was out of my mouth, Ken popped from behind the curtain, thinking that I was referring to him. Whether that sheds any light on my relationships with coaches over the years is not for me to say.

In 1967 the Oil Kings gave Canadian hockey fans a glimpse at the future of the game when we hosted the Red Army squad from the Soviet Union. I'd heard through hockey circles that the Red Army was interested in touring. By this time our league had made at least a temporary peace with the CAHA, and I called the organization's head, Gordon Juckes, in Toronto.

"Gordon, I understand there's a Russian team that in interested in touring Canada," I said.

"That's right, Bill," said Gordon. "The only problem is we can't find anyone who's willing to pay them."

I asked how much they wanted. Gordon said $10,000 a game.

"B.S.," I said. "I'll give them $5,000." The deal was struck shortly after.

The Russian team was a powerhouse, an elite squad that contained many players from their gold-medal-winning Olympic teams. It boasted Anatol Firsov, their top Olympic goal scorer, and Alexei Yakushev, one of the best wingers in hockey. Alexander Ragulin was an outstanding defenseman and a deadly accurate open-ice hitter. The great Victor Tarasov, a cautious, aloof man, was assistant coach. Very few Canadians had ever seen a great Russian team play. I'd seen their work in the Olympics and knew what we were in for.

Given the strength of the competition, I felt free to beef up my Oil Kings with some of the best talent from around the league. I brought in Bobby Clarke and Reggie Leach from Flin Flon. I brought up Jimmy Harrison from Estevan. Ken Brown came from Moose Jaw. If we were going to ice juniors against a national team, they were going to be the best juniors I could find.

What a game that was. It wasn't just another Oil Kings game. This was Us *versus* Them. From the middle of the second period, everyone in the Gardens was on their feet chanting, "Go, Canada, go."

The Oil Kings became a very successful venture for me although it took a while. In 1966–67, the first year I owned the club, I lost $130,000. Setting up those offices in the Hotel Macdonald hadn't been cheap. I'd also spent too much chartering airplanes and flying my team around. I had go back to a bus, like everybody else. The biggest problem, however, had been that tiny Jasper Place Arena.

Moving into the Gardens gave me a little financial breathing space. So did taking on some partners. The idea actually came from Chris Diamond, who owned Johnson's Restaurant, popular among the sports crowd. "Bill," he said, "why should you carry the burden of the team on your shoulders? I know you must have lost a lot of money. Let some of us come in with you and help out." I was a bit pressed, and Chris's offer sounded good. I sold off 23 percent of the club a board of directors. The money was welcome, but there were other benefits as well. I wanted people to feel the Oil Kings were rooted in Edmonton and were backed by Edmontonians, not just Bill Hunter. It was a good way to build some solid links into the community. I thought the new board was blue chip: Dave Butler, partner in a well-known insurance firm; Jim Chopin from CJCA Radio; Fred Kemp, who had been chairman when the Edmonton

Flyers won the Allan Cup; Chris Diamond; Vic Mah from the Blue Willow; Ron Downey; Jim Pelehos; Bill Tainsh; Ed Trott; Don Scott and Ray Barth. Zane Feldman became vice president.

The board really was a great group. We made the Oil Kings into the flagship junior franchise in Canada. We started off every season by introducing the team to the community with a face-off breakfast. These were social events, and all 750 seats would be snapped up every year. Local businesses fell over themselves to pick up a table. Everybody wanted to be associated with us because in Edmonton, the Oil Kings were kings.

We were winners on the ice, and we did our best to build that image off the ice, too. We sought to operate with a certain style. During one visit to New Westminster, I took the entire club out to The Cave nightclub in downtown Vancouver for dinner and a show after the game. A lot of those kids were right off the farm, and they'd never seen anything like that. People respected the fact that I spent money on the players and on the team. Oil Kings wasn't just a name. We carried ourselves like junior hockey royalty.

After all, there wasn't a lot else in Edmonton in the late 1960s. After the Oil Kings and the Eskimos, there wasn't much. There weren't a lot of other sports on TV, either. In winter the Oil Kings were pretty much the only show in town. There wasn't much to think about other than hockey. Despite its prosperity and growth, Edmonton really was an overgrown small town back then with a small-town homogeneity to it. Most people had similar backgrounds. They'd either grown up in Edmonton or had recently moved from the farm or from a smaller town somewhere else in western Canada. Everybody knew hockey; everybody had hockey in common. It was a language everyone spoke and an atmosphere everyone breathed. That made it easy to focus everyone's attention on the Oil Kings, and it was a perfect atmosphere in which to promote a team.

People in sports circles all knew each other back then. We had a great relationship with the Eskimos. Anytime they were scheduling an event, general manager Norm Kimball would give me a call to make sure it didn't conflict with anything we had planned and I'd do the same for him. We'd buy tables at each other's fund-raisers and show up at each other's press conferences. We both understood we were in the same business and that one team's success only added to the buzz for the other guy. In fact, when the Eskimos went into a slide for a few years under Neil Armstrong, we noticed a decline in our attendance.

There weren't very many parts of the Oil Kings operation I didn't have a hand in. I was running the front office, helping out with scouting, keeping tabs on the players and for a few years I also was chairman of the league. If we weren't playing, I was out looking at other players. We had our own minor teams through the Edmonton Maple Leafs. Night and day I was at the office, at the arena or out on the road. In the winter I spent more time at the Gardens than I did at home. In the summer I'd head out to talk to the players my scouts had identified for me. Eventually, it had to take a toll on my personal life.

Bernie and I split up in 1968. It had been 14 very busy, very fruitful years. But it had become clear to both of us that we wanted different things in life and that neither of us would get them if we stayed together. Our lifestyles had become incompatible, and we decided divorce was the best solution. Our three children stayed with me.

At about the same time Vi and I had a child together. Our wonderful son Greg was born to us the same year Bernie and I split.

Vi and I were now both unattached. I don't really understand why we didn't get together permanently then. Vi said she was no longer interested in marriage to the man she dubbed, with justifiable sarcasm, "Sir William." Despite the birth of Greg, Vi and

I drifted apart. I met Gaye Orris in Winnipeg in August 1969, and we quickly fell in love. We were married although it wasn't to last. This time, however, it was tragedy that broke us up. Gaye was killed in a car accident just a few days after our first anniversary.

I finally married Vi, the woman I'd loved and pursued, in 1972. It had taken us 10 years to figure out that we were destined for each other. We had a quiet ceremony in Edmonton with a few friends. Our home was soon full with seven children: Beverly Anne, Terry Wayne Dodd, Brent Allan, Donna Lynne Dodd, Gwendolyn Jo-Anne Dodd, Bart William, Brent Robert Dodd and Gregory William.

I spent nearly a decade with the Oil Kings. We won two league championships and made it to at least the semi-finals every year but one. The league prospered as well. Between Ben, Scotty and I, we ran the WHL and turned it not only into a junior league second to none, but one that wouldn't take orders from anyone. We proved that in the 1971 Memorial Cup.

The Cup's eastern final was supposed to be played between the St. Catharines Black Hawks, who featured a young Marcel Dionne, and the Quebec City Remparts, who had a fast, flashy forward named Guy Lafleur. It would have been a potent match, but Canada had more on its mind than hockey just then. The October Crisis, when Prime Minister Pierre Trudeau invoked the War Measures Act after Quebec separatists had kidnapped James Cross and Pierre Laporte, was a recent memory. Anything smacking of French–English rivalry carried an extra charge, and that's what happened with that year's Memorial Cup.

Quebec City and St. Catharines were tied after the first two games, which had been divided between the two cities. Things started getting ugly in game three, when the Remparts won at home. The referee handed out 102 minutes in penalties and a linesman was roughed up. The next night the Remparts crushed the Black Hawks

6–1 and things got out of hand. As the game got out of reach for St. Catharines, frustration set in and fight after fight broke out.

The overflow crowd of more than 13,000 fans joined the fray, pelting the Black Hawks with potatoes, tomatoes, eggs, bolts from their seats, golf balls and anything they could find. At least one knife was thrown. The St. Catharines players needed a police escort to return to the dressing room after the game, but not before one player cut a constable for six stitches when he swung his stick at someone who spat on him. A cordon of police tried to protect the Black Hawks as they boarded their bus, but it was barraged by bottles. A mob crushed up to the side of it and began rocking it back and forth. The players lay down on the floor as a police escort got them to their hotel, where some fans circled the building all night long.

The next game was played at Maple Leaf Gardens, and St. Catharines won, bringing them within a game of tying the series. But the Black Hawks refused to return to Quebec City. There had been newspaper reports that the Front de liberation du Quebec, the group responsible for kidnapping Cross and killing Laporte, had threatened members of the Black Hawks.

There things stayed. Eventually, the CAHA awarded the series to the Remparts, but that satisfied nobody. The fans in Quebec felt they had been snubbed by an Ontario team that had resorted to goonery when it was losing. Into the vacuum stepped the Oil Kings. We had won our league championship that year, and I announced that the Oil Kings were willing to take on the Remparts for the Memorial Cup. I called Leo Lebel, head of the Quebec junior league, saying, "Meet me in Toronto. Bring Maurice Filion [coach of the Remparts.] We'll get you a Memorial Cup. We'll play you for it."

Lebel, however, was a timid man and easily led. I walked into a meeting room full of suits from the CAHA. Oh-oh, I thought. The CAHA wasn't crazy about us playing the Remparts. Some of the eastern teams resented the fact that our rules allowed us to use four overage players. And we were again an independent league outside the CAHA. They didn't want us in their sandbox. I turned to Leo and said, "What the hell's this all about? I came to meet you, Leo, not all these guys. What have these fellows ever done for you? You've been ridiculed in the eyes of Canada. An Ontario team has refused to come. They said it's too dangerous. Now that St. Catharines walked out, where's your Memorial Cup? Your team is left stranded. We'll come east and play you for it. Besides, we haven't been on ice in two weeks, so there's no goddamn way you should lose. You'll be a hero."

"Okay," said Filion. Not so fast, said the CAHA guys.

I said, "Look, this is our meeting, not yours. In about five minutes I'll leave here and go straight to Ottawa and I'll see the Prime Minister. And there'll be no way you people will ever stop us from playing for the Memorial Cup." I'd have done it, too. I was fired up. I said, "Come on Leo. Let's get out of here." We marched over to my room and struck a deal. But that remark about the prime minister gave me an idea. I strode out of that room and found the nearest reporter and delivered what might have been my best sound bite of all time: "The burning ambition of every Canadian boy is to play for the Memorial Cup as a junior and the Stanley Cup as a pro," I thundered. "If the prime minister wants to do something right for the west for a change, he'll use the War Measures Act to enforce a Memorial Cup final!"

After that the CAHA backed down. We headed east, and I've never been welcomed in a city like we were in Quebec. Over 5,000 fans met us at the airport and followed us to our hotel, the Chateau Frontenac, with a parade of cars. They carried banners proclaiming, "Vive le Oil Kings!" We were heroes just for showing up. We came and rescued their pride. We had united the west with Quebec after

*The 1971 Oil Kings posed in front of the Chateau Frontenac.*

they had been slandered and brushed off by an Ontario team. Premier Robert Bourassa welcomed us as honored guests at the Quebec National Assembly. Gilles Lamontagne, Quebec City's mayor, held a special dinner for us. We stepped on the ice and the fans (15,000 of them in an arena with an official capacity of 11,000) wouldn't stop clapping. Our kids were in awe.

After all that drama the hockey was an anticlimax. The Oil Kings hadn't seen ice in two weeks. It was too late in the season and we couldn't get on to any ice left in western Canada. We'd spent an hour on the figure skating ice at the Royal Glenora Club, but we hadn't been allowed to use pucks. I tried to keep the guys sharp by having them play soccer, but it wasn't the same. We didn't get back into full kit until the evening before the first game, when we practiced for half an hour at the Colisée. The Remparts won the best-of-three series two games straight. The Coliseé was packed both nights with fans who stood, clapped, sang and danced. When Guy Lafleur scored, the ice was showered in debris. Someone threw down a black brassiere.

I knew the Oil Kings would lose. So did the Edmonton reporters I brought out with me. But we wanted to go east anyway for the hockey, for the notoriety and for the wonderful experience for the players. But for me, the reason to go to Quebec was to show Canada that the CAHA didn't control junior hockey. People like me who had money invested and who spent their time and energy taking care of players, we were the ones who now controlled minor hockey and our own destiny as well.

# 10

# THE WORLD HOCKEY ASSOCIATION

**The referee took his position for the face-off, and the two centers bore down. Gary Davidson, the man who was about to start a whole new professional hockey league, leaned over to me and asked, completely puzzled, "What are they doing?"**

I DON'T STAND PAT. I'VE NEVER BEEN content to play out the clock and be happy with what I've got, no matter what the score. The Oil Kings was a great franchise and became nicely profitable as well, but there was one more rung on the hockey ladder I wanted to climb. I wanted to join the elite club of pro hockey owners, and the time was right.

It was obvious to me that pro sport was growing. There were hundreds of thousands of fans out there with plenty of disposable income, and they were aching for a home team to cheer for. Hockey was in for a period of change when all kinds of opportunities might come up for grabs. Something was going to happen, and I wanted to make sure I was a part of it.

Already in 1968, when I was still chairman of our breakaway junior league and we were fighting with the NHL about travel budgets and other payments, I'd gone out west for private meetings with some people from the Western Hockey League in Portland. I had friends in that league, a professional minor-league circuit that played along the West Coast of Canada and the U.S. in places like San Diego, Los Angeles, Tacoma, Victoria, New Westminster and Vancouver. Al Leiter, a fine man from Seattle, was the president. Hal Laycoe, an old friend of mine, was general manager and coach of the Portland team that dominated the league. He was a former Boston Bruin. Hockey men still talked about his legendary battles with Maurice "The Rocket" Richard during the great Canadiens–Bruins rivalry. I gathered Hall and some of the other owners together. "You guys should come with us," I told them. "The NHL's not treating us right. We'll leave them if your league fully affiliates with us. We've got a thriving junior league right next door to you, and we'll be your farm teams. We've got Canada's finest junior league. We'll have all our players sign contracts to turn pro with you. You have some great buildings, and we'll build new ones where we need them. Here's an opportunity for a second major pro league to start up and challenge the NHL."

Three or four members of the WHL had already been thinking along similar lines for a while, some of them quite vocally. They'd tried to convince the NHL to let them into the league as an entire new division, which had been denied. Some WHL owners thought that merging with our league was a great idea and wanted to sign on then and there. Jim Piggott from Saskatoon owned the Los Angeles team, and he believed it could work. And it would have, too. Bob Brightbart's San Diego Gulls were already drawing 10,000 people a game. Most other teams were also drawing near-capacity crowds. They owned their own player contracts, too. Not depending on players loaned to them by NHL organizations meant the league was already fairly independent.

But the Victoria Cougars were owned by the Toronto Maple Leafs and were managed by Conn Smythe's son Stafford. He was the conduit by which our plans leaked to the NHL's head office. Conn got hold of Al—a real gentleman but not the most daring of men—and laid down the law. Conn had a major interest in the Seattle club, too, and he bitterly opposed my idea. After that we never could get enough owners to go independent, and the plan to start a western major pro league died.

Still, there was plenty of flux in the NHL, and I had a few chances to get my foot in the door. In fact, by this time I'd already let a couple of those chances go by.

The rumblings from the WHL had forced the NHL to create six new franchises for the 1967–68 season. In the spring of 1967, I got a call from Jack Kent Cooke, the Canadian multimillionaire who had been awarded the franchise that was about to become the Los Angeles Kings.

"Bill, are you going to the league meetings in Montreal?" he asked me. He knew I was. Scotty and I always went. He just didn't want to pay my way out there. Nobody ever said Jack Kent Cooke threw around money. Still, he was willing to pay when he had to. When we met in his suite in the Mount Royal Hotel, he had a lucrative salary to offer me along with the post of general manager of his new franchise.

The offer was tempting, and I thought hard about it for a few minutes. But I turned him down. I was still enjoying Edmonton, and I had a feeling that Bill Hunter and Jack Kent Cooke in the same front office would be a volatile combination. Cooke was an outspoken, opinionated, determined man used to getting his way. So am I. I didn't think he could keep his hands off the team, and I knew I couldn't tolerate any meddling. The exchange that ended our meeting probably would have been typical of how our business association would have worked. "Bill, nobody turns down Jack Kent Cooke," he told me. "Mr. Cooke," I told him, "I just did."

Another of the 1967 expansion franchises was the Pittsburgh Penguins. There was no official announcement, but everyone on the inside in the hockey world knew the team was for sale. Edmonton was ready for professional hockey. The city was on the cusp of an important civic vote on building a new, big-league arena to be called the Omniplex. Norm Kimball from the Eskimos and I were co-chairmen of the citizen's committee pushing to get it built. I decided to make a pitch for the Penguins and held a press conference in Edmonton's Chateau Lacombe to say that if the Omniplex vote passed, I would be doing my best to bring in an NHL franchise as a major tenant. I applied for a franchise to the NHL, too, although Clarence Campbell didn't exactly hold out a great deal of hope. Those plans, however, fell apart. Although a city-wide vote on the Omniplex passed by a 78 percent majority, a couple of cranky city councilors found an old bylaw stipulating that a second vote involving only ratepayers had to be held. We lost the second ballot by about 1,000 votes. I couldn't strike a deal on the Penguins, either. I couldn't even find the real owner. The ownership was so shadowy that open rumors circulated that organized crime money was the real backstop for the Penguins. The team was owned by 21 different investors, and I could never seem to find the decision-maker. Even the spokesmen for the club, Art Rooney of the NFL's Pittsburgh Steelers and state senator Jack MacGregor, owned less than 5 percent. It was like negotiating with a committee that never took a vote on anything. Finally I just gave up.

The door to the NHL cracked open again for me in 1969. I got a call from Coley Hall, president and major shareholder of the

WHL's Vancouver Canucks, asking me to come out for a meeting. I got together with him and Cyrus MacLean, who owned a telephone company in Alaska. They wanted me to come aboard as vice president, general manager and coach, which wouldn't have been too exciting a prospect except for the fact that they knew they were joining the NHL the next season. I'd become general manager when they made the jump and be able to hire my own coach and staff. I'd get 10 percent of the club, too. They really wanted me to come, and I would have been happy to accept. But first I had to sell my Oil Kings. I wasn't going to leave them in the hands of some caretaker as I left town. I'd worked too hard to simply abandon the team, and I was determined to find proper ownership before I took up Coley's offer.

Fortunately, I thought I had a buyer. Mitch Pechet was an Edmonton hotelier who loved hockey and had been after me to sell the club for a while. Mitch, however, had sold his Edmonton holdings and was now in Victoria. That delayed our talks. Other delays followed, and we couldn't seem to finalize anything. Meanwhile, Coley was on the phone saying, "Come on, Bill, we've got to have an answer." Finally, after over a month of dancing back and forth, Coley called one day with an ultimatum: "Bill we've got to know today. Are you coming? Yes or no?" I had to tell him no. Turning him down was difficult. The Canucks were a great opportunity and I knew it. At the meetings they had laid their NHL plans out for me. We were going to have the new Pacific Coliseum and it would have been great. Coley had a reputation as a tough, hard-nosed guy, and people speculated that the two of us would never have gotten along. But I had it iron-clad in my contract that there was to be no interference, and I believe he would have honored it. But I couldn't leave my Oil Kings without placing them in good hands.

Eventually, Hall and MacLean hired Annis Stukus, who I think knew he was Plan B. But we were good friends for years, and he never once mentioned the matter.

One other deal tempted me during those years. In 1971 I got a call from Harold Ballard. "Bill, I've got a hell of a deal for you. You just have to get down here right away. It's too good to miss. You can't turn it down."

In London, Ontario, a complex called Treasure Island had just gone into receivership with the collapse of Victoria and Grey Trust Company. The package contained a shopping mall, a hockey arena and the London Knights junior club, which featured a young Darryl Sittler. He was only 17, so I would have had him for at least a few years. I spent a couple of months in London, telling my office staff that I was on holidays. I didn't want anyone to know I was thinking about jumping, and I was thinking about it pretty hard. I could see that the combination of retail and entertainment was a potentially lucrative mix.

I put in a bid for Treasure Island of 50 cents on the dollar, with bonuses that could have returned up to 85 cents. My bid was $900,000 cash, which Harold had helped me arrange, and I thought the deal was all but done. I waited outside in the lobby of the Royal York while my offer was discussed in a long and heated creditor's meeting. My offer was turned down. A year later, when no better offer surfaced, creditors were forced to take 10 cents on the dollar.

By this time Harold and I had become unlikely friends, and I think he shared my disappointment when the Treasure Island deal fell through. We'd had our first dealings years ago when he was refitting Maple Leaf Gardens with new seats. I bought the old ones and made a tidy profit brokering them out all over western Canada. We'd also dealt with each other during the 1966 Memorial Cup. Harold was a very sharp businessman—a genius, I believe. But he was difficult. He was a tremendous philanthropist in private, yet the only word that describes his attitude toward his staff is *cheap*. It was almost as if there were two Harolds. One Harold was always there if a staff member got sick, getting him the best of care and making sure his family was looked after and paying the shot himself. But the other Harold was a miser. Stan Obodiack, Harold's public relations man, was paid $25,000 a year his whole career at a time when everyone else in the league in that position was making at least double that amount. And when Stan died, Harold was instantly on the phone to his widow, wanting the company car back.

I'd now had four opportunities for bigger and better things in the hockey world, and all four of them had fallen through. But I wasn't discouraged. I knew more changes were coming, and I wasn't through yet. I didn't realize it, but the next big change had already begun.

In January 1971 a California sports promoter named Dennis Murphy conceived the idea of a new professional hockey league. He'd been involved with the creation of the American Basketball Association, an independent league that successfully merged with the National Basketball Association to the profit of all concerned. He'd also been with the World Football League, which amalgamated with the National Football League. He had followed the hockey world for the last few years and had concluded the time was right for someone to make the same move on the NHL. He got together with his friend, Gary Davidson, and that April they incorporated the World Hockey Association. Both knew marketing and both knew sports. In fact, Davidson had been a star athlete back in university. But this was hockey, and for their upstart league to have any credibility they knew they'd have to bring a real hockey man on board.

That July I got a call from an acquaintance of mine, a Canadian living in Los Angeles named Walt Marlowe. Walt was a sportswriter. I knew him from the old *Edmonton Bulletin.* Now he was covering the Kings for the *Los Angeles Times.* We exchanged a few pleasantries before Walt got to the point. "Bill, there's a couple guys down here that want to start up a new league, and I'd like to come up and talk to you about it." Walt didn't know I'd had my eye on just such an operation, and I was more than happy to talk.

I was fed up with the NHL, which operated a closed shop run by a few powerbrokers. The owners were making a pile while the players were treated like serfs on skates. But it was the league's attitude toward anyone not in their select club that infuriated me. It was no secret around the hockey world that I was trying to get a franchise. The league knew about my dances with the Penguins and the WHL owners. But as far as they were concerned, the big decisions about hockey would be made by them in the east when they felt so inclined.

When I was trying to buy the Penguins, Clarence Campbell came to Edmonton to speak to the Alberta Medical Association. While he was in town, he took me to dinner. Clarence had been born and raised in Edmonton. He'd played hockey in Edmonton, had refereed there and had graduated from the University of Alberta. But he sat across from me at a restaurant table and said, "Bill, you must be smoking something to think Edmonton could support a National League team. I don't want to see you wasting your time and energy in pursuit of this impossible dream. It'll never happen."

I was angry. I felt as if Clarence thought he could come out here to visit a rube in his hometown, pat me on the head, tell me to go away and I would. He thought he was being kind, but I wouldn't be patronized. "Clarence, you've lost touch," I said. "You've buried your head in the sand. This is great hockey country. Hockey isn't reserved for just the Montreal Canadiens and the Toronto Maple Leafs like you think it is. It isn't the size of the city—it's the size of the heart of the city. Your old big six—hell, we'll outdraw all of them when we get started up." Clarence laughed. "I knew I wasn't going to talk you out of it, Bill," he said, and we parted on friendly terms.

When Walt arrived in Edmonton, I was more than receptive. I told him that if these people were serious they should call me. I didn't really expect anything to come of it, but Dennis Murphy was on the phone the next morning inviting me down to Los Angeles to talk the idea over. I checked into a motel in Anaheim, and Murphy, Davidson, their lawyer, Don Regan, and I met privately for two days. Nobody knew anything about our meeting. We sat by the pool and kicked around their ideas for a new league.

Dennis was a short, heavyset man with plenty of street smarts. He'd been mayor of a small California city and was a campaign advisor for then-governor Jerry Brown. He was a bombastic, garrulous, aggressive, outspoken Irish-American. I liked him immediately. Davidson was a different specimen entirely—tall, blond, movie-star handsome and smooth as they come. He'd been a top athlete in college, and he still had something of the Big Man on Campus air about him. He was always well dressed, but I don't think I ever saw him in suit and tie. Davidson was Mr. California Casual.

The first thing I realized was that these guys knew absolutely nothing about the game of hockey. Nothing. They didn't even know half the teams in the National League or where they played. It was scary how little they knew, something that became abundantly clear when we attended a Kings game that weekend. The anthem had been played, and the players were lined up at the center ice circle. The referee took his position for the face-off, and the two centers bore down. Gary Davidson, the man who was about to start a whole new professional hockey league, leaned over to me and asked, completely puzzled, "What are they doing?"

One thing Davidson and Murphy did understand, however,

*Dennis Murphy, a dynamic Irish promoter and co-founder of the WHA.*
*He was outspoken and aggressive. I liked him immediately.*

was timing. They were promoters, and they knew the timing was right. They knew they needed a hockey man. They had to get me on board, and finally I agreed to join them. I said, "Fine, I'll bring two or three people with me when we have our first organizational meeting." I was thinking about Scotty and Ben. I knew I'd need at least a couple of trustworthy guys who knew hockey. I left Davidson and Murphy with their promise to organize a meeting that fall with a group of prospective owners.

That meeting was held September 23–24 in the Century Plaza Hotel in Los Angeles, and when Scotty, Ben and I showed, the

WHA almost ended before it started. It was immediately obvious that lounging around the boardroom table and leaning against the walls was a crowd of friends, hangers-on and cronies who could no more finance a hockey club than I could score 50 goals in 50 games. Given my experience at the Kings' game, I'd had a feeling it might be like this. Scotty and Ben were appalled. Big Ben turned to me and said, "Let's get the hell out of here. This is a farce."

I had to do some fast talking. "The idea is right, Ben. Let's stick it out and see if we can weed out some of these losers. Let's just play it cool for a day or two. They need us and they know it, and we can end up in control of this situation." So Ben and Scotty agreed to stick it out. Davidson kicked the meeting off with a little sales pitch explaining why the league was necessary and how it was going to work. Regan talked about eliminating the NHL's old reserve clause. I got up and addressed the mob and said, "Look, operating a major-league franchise is a major-league job. It takes a lot of money. You have to be solid financially. You have to be committed. You have to have good buildings. You have to have a community that will welcome the game. You have to have media—radio, TV, newspapers—that will cover and promote the game." They all nodded as if they had some idea of what I was talking about, and we chewed things over for the rest of the day. But the real work got done that night.

Scotty, Ben and I met upstairs in my hotel room to plan our approach. Then we invited Davidson and Murphy to join. I laid out our terms for participating. Ben would become chairman of finance and I would become chairman of hockey operations. We made it very clear that we were running a hockey operation and that hockey people would have to be in charge. The people we'd spent the day with were not going to own teams. Of that roomful of people, we figured maybe one or two might make the cut. "This is nonsense," I said. "This league isn't a plaything. We've got to bring in qualified owners." We agreed that Dennis and I would beat the bushes for some real hockey owners, people respected in their communities, people with stable finances and a serious commitment to putting a team on the ice. We left Davidson and Murphy to thank all the wannabe sports moguls, and the next day we had a much better meeting.

Things started to move quickly. Murphy and I began to plan our search for owners. The ante for a franchise was initially $25,000. We had a few takers immediately. Ben Hatskin was going to come with us in Winnipeg. Scotty and Bob Brownridge led an ownership group in Calgary. I was going to put a team in Edmonton. I had some contacts from my time in the hockey business, and Dennis had some from his experience in the ABA. We set to work.

For a solid month we crisscrossed the United States. I flew to San Diego, where I tried to talk Ron Graham, a wealthy Canadian who had the management contract on the local arena, to join us. From there we went to Atlanta, where we met with Tom and Bob Cousins. From their high-rise office suite, we could see the new stadium being built for their Atlanta Hawks NBA team. I could see it would be perfect for hockey, too. We tried hard to get the Cousins brothers, but while Dennis was a good, thorough, hard-working negotiator, sometimes he came on a little too strong. Tom was extremely wary. He'd just been burned by the NBA, who had promised him he'd be able to sign a promising young local basketball player. The deal hadn't come off, and it had taught Tom an important lesson. "I don't trust a soul in pro sports," he said. We didn't have enough time to spend with them to win their trust, and they eventually went with the NHL.

In Miami we met with Frank Calder. Frank was an elderly gentleman, a multimillionaire who kept a poky little office in the back of an unassuming concrete-block office building. Frank was a huge man constantly wreathed in a nimbus of cigarette smoke. Around him shuffled his secretary, who must have been 70 years old. They both sat behind rickety old desks, files stuffed in battered metal cabinets and typed on manual machines that looked as if they came off the set of *The Front Page*. But Frank owned Calder Racetrack, and he had an old arena in Hollywood, Florida. He promised a massive renovation, but Dennis and I looked at the tin siding and the run-down neighborhood and we had our doubts.

We then went to meet Hal Martin, who was Frank's rival for a Miami franchise and just about his opposite in every way. Frank was like a small-town judge in an old movie—slow moving and worn around the edges but shrewd. Hal was a fast-talker, a go-getter, a developer. His Miami Screaming Eagles were to be developed around a shopping center and hotel. He was going to sell shares for financing. We thought his plan was innovative and solid, so we invited him to join us instead of Frank.

For a while we were angling for Bob Hope to head up a Los Angeles franchise. We met with him, then with his top financial adviser at the Los Angeles arena during a basketball game. But eventually Mr. Hope called and said, "I don't know anything about hockey, and I don't think Los Angeles does, either." I was disappointed. Having Bob Hope on board would have been a major boost to our credibility.

We talked to a group in New York who headed a major advertising agency. They were ready to go but couldn't negotiate an acceptable deal for the use of Madison Square Gardens. Howard Baldwin entered the scene with a group from New England, and they became the New England Whalers.

Many times we just made cold calls. We'd drop into towns that we thought were likely candidates, visit the Chamber of Commerce and ask after the local successful businessmen. Often Dennis or I knew the local sports editor. We'd visit his office and take him into our confidence. We promised that he'd be the first to know if anything happened, then we'd ask, "Who's got money around here?" The sales pitch was pretty simple. In every good-sized city there's somebody who's made a stack of money building apartments or running a widget factory. It's good, worthy work, but the kind of people who tend to make large stacks of money want more than that. They've got big egos. They've made their pile, and they want the world to know it. There isn't an owner in hockey, baseball or basketball that hasn't got a big ego. We dwelt on how being a franchise owner would make them the center of attention, how they'd have people all over them when we made the announcement and how they'd be all over the media. "Look," Dennis and I would say, "everyone around here knows who you are. But get into the world of professional sports and all of a sudden you're on a national, even international, stage. Suddenly, everyone in the country knows who you are." Dennis had one line I heard over and over again: "Would you rather be known as the guy who manufactures brassieres in Muskegon or the guy who owns a hockey team in Detroit?" The WHA offered a bit of rebel appeal, too. We were out to take on the hockey establishment. Our approach worked. Everyone wanted to look closely at our business plan, but it was the appeal to ego that closed many deals.

If we wanted the attention of the world when we announced our new league, I knew we'd have to start sowing the seeds early. Nothing creates interest and buzz like a few unsubstantiated rumors, so we started some. I said to Dennis, "Here's what we'll do. We'll contact certain players I know and ask them if they've heard a rumor about a second professional hockey league starting up. They'll figure out what's going on of course, but it won't stop them from passing the story to other players, and that's what we want."

Before long word spread through locker rooms across North America, and from there it spread to sports reporters. They got the speculation into the papers and that's when the talk really began to pick up speed. Before long even Clarence Campbell deigned to weigh in with his old line: any new league would run out of money before the current hockey powers that be were affected. That was the same tack he'd taken when we started up the new junior league. Clarence hadn't learned a thing.

Some NHL owners took shots at us, too. And their scouts were telling young players not to pay any attention to this upstart league that would never get off the ground. I had lots of it come back to me, too, through the Oil Kings. Scouts staying at the MacDonald Hotel would find their way down to our offices. I was always willing to talk.

"Are you up to something, Bill?" they'd ask. "Starting another league?"

I'd just smile. "Possibly. You never can tell. It's obvious to me the time has never been better."

Eventually, Clarence himself gave me a call. "Bill, what are you doing?" he asked, sounding just a wee bit concerned. I gave him the same line I gave everyone else. He knew where I stood, and I sure knew where that stubborn old man stood.

A quiet little war of nerves was being waged, and it got personal. One of my many trips during that crazy time took me to Toronto. Vi and my sister Bev and her husband, Aird Worsley, were with me and we got some Leafs tickets. Before the game we were socializing with some friends when we ran into Harold Ballard. "You son of a bitch," he thundered. "You're a damn thief, right here in my building." I'd been yelled at by angry owners before. My hide was pretty thick, and I brushed off his comments.

We'd gotten our tickets from Alan Eagleson, and two of them

were prime seats right at center ice. In those days at the Gardens, there was no glass along the boards between the players' boxes. After I got the ladies settled and told them to watch out for flying pucks, my brother-in-law and I went up to our seats. All of a sudden, about the middle of the second period, a slapshot went off the ice and into the crowd. A big commotion followed and sure enough, one of the usherettes came running over, crying, "Mr. Hunter! Mr. Hunter! Come quick! We think Mrs. Hunter's been hit."

And there was Vi, her head cradled in my sister's lap. Bev was screaming. Vi's face was black. She was helped to the Leafs dressing room, where the team doctor examined her and said, "We've got to get Mrs. Hunter over to the Wellesley Hospital right away. I want to get a neurosurgeon on this." She had been hit just above the temple. Right before the puck hit her she had turned to say something to Bev and that had possibly saved her life. Another fraction of an inch and she could have been dead.

It was a dramatic incident, all right, but I could hardly believe the headline in the next morning's *Toronto Star*. There, over Dick Beddoes' byline, it read, "NHL Draws First Blood." Vi wasn't laughing. She was nursing a severe concussion and had barely escaped eye damage.

Such a headline wasn't what I had in mind when we set out to draw some media attention. Otherwise we were happy with the ink our proposed league was getting. We wanted to signal to players that something important was coming down the road. We didn't want them committing themselves to the NHL until they'd had a chance to take a look at our new league. We cautioned everybody, "Don't sign any contracts until you hear from us." While Dennis and I were winging around the continent like a couple of birds not quite sure where they're supposed to be migrating, Davidson and Regan were fine-tuning our plan to lure talent. We had determined to take a direct run at the legal chains the NHL used to bind its players to teams.

The reserve clause had been a standard feature of NHL contracts almost from the start. It tacked on an extra year, the so-called
reserve year, to the end of every contract term. The player was
obliged to stay with the team for that year with only his salary being
negotiable. Because this reserve year could be invoked every season,
it had the effect of locking players into one organization for their
entire careers. The intent was to keep the league evenly balanced by
preventing rich teams from buying up the best players. But the
effect was to rob players of their bargaining power. They couldn't
jump to another club for more money, and both they and the owners knew it. We knew the players resented the reserve clause, and we
didn't even think it would stand up in court. We planned to operate without reserve clauses in our contracts. We would also feel free
to poach NHL players in their reserve year.

On October 20 we held a press conference in the O'Hare
Hilton in Chicago. Davidson did most of the talking. He told the
world that we were going to operate without a reserve clause. He
also announced that we would soon be holding our first draft before
handing the floor to me. I described how we would look at junior,
university and college, professional, semiprofessional, amateur and
European teams. It was pretty audacious talk. I was telling the world
that we were about to hold the largest hockey draft in history while
we hadn't even announced our teams yet. But many of the reporters
were just as fed up with the NHL as we were. They were excited to
hear about our plans, and I sensed a lot of support.

Finally, the time to commit ourselves came. We announced a
press conference in New York for November 1. The ballroom in the
Americana Hotel was packed with news reporters and electric with
excitement. It must have been the largest media gathering in the history of hockey. All the American and Canadian TV networks were
in attendance. On the podium the glare from the TV lights was like

staring into the sun and about the same temperature, too. I didn't care. We had worked so hard, and today we were taking our stand. Maybe it was just the bright TV lights, but I was so excited I felt I was glowing from within. Even jaded old beat reporters felt something historic about to happen. Stan Fischler, a newspaperman, radio commentator and author of a series of hockey books, came up to me. "Bill, this is the greatest idea since sliced bread," he said with more fervor than originality.

I made three simple announcements. I said the World Hockey Association would be launched in the fall of 1972. Our league would have two divisions with 12 teams in total. We would hold a draft in Anaheim, California, on February 2, 1972, and that it would be the largest draft in the history of sport. A flurry of questions followed, but I hardly remember them. We'd made our statement. The game was on.

Immediately after the meeting was the New York sportswriters annual banquet. I went as an invited guest. My table included Sid Solomon, owner of the St. Louis Blues, Bill Jennings, president of the Rangers, and a couple other NHL officials. Bill Wirtz from the Blackhawks was around, too, and Clarence Campbell was the guest speaker. I could sense something was up. These fellows spent the evening wining and dining me, and later in the evening, Clarence found his way over. "Bill," he said, "you've always been a national league man. You can't do this. Going out on your own like this— that's suicide. We'll take care of you. Do you want a franchise? You know the national league is the place to be." He didn't promise me a team, but he came as close as he could. And I have to admit, I felt a little trepidation after that evening. We were taking on one of the most powerful and entrenched Old Guards in the sporting world with a group of owners who made me nervous. Not only that but I'd just stood up and told the whole world about it. We'd built a big stage for a pratfall.

But I soon didn't have any time for doubts. Between a league, a draft and my own team, I had so much to organize and so many places to be that life dissolved into an endless overtime period of hotels, airports, restaurants, meeting rooms. Nervous energy alternated with bone-deep fatigue. We all hit the road, and I stayed on it for II months that year. My travel expenses were so high that Revenue Canada didn't believe my income tax return. I had to show them my day planner.

The draft, which was held in Anaheim, was a big responsibility. We took players from senior hockey, junior hockey, universities, high schools, all levels of pro hockey and the NHL. All the college and NHL players were listed on boards behind the head table. We knew exactly which of the National League players were in their reserve year. All the teams had brought their scouts and their best hockey people. Things moved quickly. Vern Buffey, a former NHL ref whom I'd hired to set up our officiating and serve as draft master, gave us each 30 seconds to make our picks. He set up a big basketball clock at the front of the hall so we could all keep track. The event was a bit like a game show. "Bill, I've never seen anything like this in my life," said Alan Eagleson, head of the National Hockey League Player's Association. I'm sure the intention wasn't to be kind.

Alan Eagleson wasn't the only skeptic I heard from that day. Given our proximity to Disneyland, I heard lots of the inevitable Mickey Mouse jokes.

The big news out of the draft was the Winnipeg Jets making Bobby Hull one of four priority picks. At that time "The Golden Jet" was the most exciting man on ice, the NHL's leading scorer with the wickedest slapshot in the league. Everybody snickered when Bobby's name was called, but the Jets knew what they were doing. Ben had been in touch with Bobby's agent, and he'd held a secret meeting with Bobby in the Hotel Vancouver when the Blackhawks

*The WHA's first draft was the world's largest professional sports draft. We drafted players from all leagues on two continents.*

were in town to play the Canucks. The rumors were going around that Ben and Bobby were talking, but the Blackhawks ignored them, probably hurting Bobby's pride.

Shortly before the draft, Ben called me with excitement in his voice. "Bill, you won't believe this," he said, "but I think we can get Bobby Hull! What do you think?"

I took me about three seconds to say, "Let's get him. What's the tab?"

"One million dollars up front in cash, just for starters," Ben told me.

"I'll tell you what," I said. "We'll get all the teams to chip in. They'll do it because Bobby Hull will fill their buildings and give the whole league a huge boost in credibility with the fans, the reporters and the other players, too."

Ben agreed. I called Murphy and Davidson, and we set up a

league meeting at the O'Hare Hilton in Chicago. I made the pitch for Bobby Hull to the other owners, and Big Ben said he'd kick in a half-million to get things moving. A vote taken about 30 minutes later, however, rejected the plan.

I stood up and one by one stared those owners right in the eyes, millionaires and tycoons from all over the United States. "Gentlemen, you haven't got the message," I said. "There's no way we can afford not to bring Bobby Hull on board." We filibustered, cajoled and pleaded all day. Eventually, we had to use threats. Unless they came through with the money to sign Bobby Hull, Ben and I were gone from the league, and we were going to take our teams with us. "You either do this or we're gone," I said. "There'll be no goddamn league." Our message started to sink in. Twelve hours after the meeting began, the vote passed. "We don't want any cheques from you guys, either," I told them. "It's got to be cash." Some of the owners were still mad as hell about it, but each team agreed to pony up about $100,000 to the Jets to chip in for Bobby's multiyear contract. And on June 27 "The Golden Jet" accepted that billboard-sized million-dollar cheque at the corner of Portage and Main in downtown Winnipeg in front of thousands of cheering soon-to-be Jets fans.

There had been a few notable signings before Bobby Hull. The Screaming Eagles got Bernie Parent, who many thought was the best goaltender around. But the doors on the players box swung wide after word got out that Hull had jumped. In three months our 10 teams signed 89 players from the NHL. I had to tell everyone, "Look, we'd better stop. If this continues we could find ourselves in legal trouble of some kind with the NHL, and we don't need to worry about that right now." So we stopped, more or less. We could have signed another 50 players.

Some exciting talent was joining us. Cleveland got Gerry

Cheevers. J.C. Tremblay went to the Nordiques. So did Marc Tardiff, Serge Bernier and Rejean Houle. I nabbed Jimmy Harrison from the Leafs. Interesting things were happening in Winnipeg, too. The team doctor for the Jets had worked for the Swedish national team. He knew the Swedes were playing some pretty good hockey, and he went over there with chief scout Billy Robinson. As a result Ben Hatskin brought over some of the very first Europeans to play pro hockey in North America. Players like Anders Hedberg and Ulf Nilsson did a lot to fuel Ben's Jets, and they provided the model for fast, puck-control teams like the later Edmonton Oilers. Our coaches included none other than Maurice Richard leading Quebec (although I never saw a man more nervous behind the bench). I talked to him after his first game. "I don't know whether I can do this, Bill," he said. "Maurice, please don't ruin your health," I told him. He quit after two games.

The corporate world was starting to come around, too. Ben, Davidson, Murphy and I were having a finance meeting one afternoon, looking for ways to raise cash. Suddenly, I got an idea. "Why don't we sell our championship trophy? We can get a major company to put its name on it, and we'll throw the proceeds into general revenue." Dennis had a line into Avco, a household finance company. We made a presentation to them, and they came aboard.

Meanwhile, it didn't look like the teams we'd announced back in November were going to be the same ones that would take the ice that fall. The Dayton Arrows fell through and transferred to Houston to become the Aeros. The Screaming Eagles, Bernie Parent and all, folded up and transferred to Philadelphia to become the Blazers. I could almost hear old Frank Calder chuckling all the way from his poky little office over that one. The Calgary Broncos dropped out entirely after failing to post their $100,000 bond.

And Gary Davidson, one of the founders and the first president of the league, decided that he would sell his San Francisco franchise before his players even had their first skate. He never did intend to run a team. He'd given himself a franchise when the league began just so he'd have one to sell after it got going. A group from Quebec was willing to pay $175,000 for it, but it didn't have the cash. We desperately wanted a Quebec team in the league, so I fronted the money myself. I ended up flying to Quebec City and meeting with their group, which included former premier Jean Lesage. The meeting was held around the kitchen table at the home of Paul Racine, who was known as the Banker of Quebec. Lesage had told everyone, "Bring your cheque books." They did, I got my money back, and the Nordiques were in.

That was the end of our game of musical franchises for that year. Although they weren't the ones we'd promised, we did have 12 franchises lined up and ready to play. And by this point I had to stop worrying about the league and look to my own team. The WHA's first season was getting close. The Edmonton Oilers were about to make their debut.

# 11

# THE ALBERTA OILERS

**The powers that be had said over and over again that we wouldn't make it, that we wouldn't manage to drop a puck on an opening face-off. Well, goddamit, here we were.**

Getting the World Hockey Association up on its wobbly skates and into its first season would have been enough of a job on its own, but I also had a team of my own to get on the ice. Murphy, Davidson and I had promised that Edmonton would have a professional hockey team by the fall of 1972, and with less than a year to go, the team had no money, no staff, no players, no name and no place to play. There was much to accomplish, but I wasn't worried, not even for a minute. This was what I'd been building toward my whole life. After 25 years as a hockey man, here was my chance to step up to the big leagues and do it on my terms.

The money question almost took care of itself—or would have if I'd have let it. By the summer of 1971, word about the WHA was getting around. Davidson had formally incorporated the league and the *New York Times* had run a story about our plans. The article named the cities the WHA was targeting, and Edmonton was among them. Now I had to deliver, and this was very much on my mind one day as I gazed out my office window at Edmonton's river valley. I didn't have the kind of money it took to run a pro team. I needed a partner. And I was worried that it might be tough for me to attract the kind of quality partners I needed to join a league that, at least on the surface, looked flaky. Suddenly, the phone rang.

It was Jack Kennedy, a well-known Edmonton lawyer from the firm of Cormie and Kennedy. "Bill, I'd like to get together," he said. "I've got a client who wants to meet with you privately. It's very important." When I asked what it was about, Jack said it would be better to discuss it in person. "But this client of mine wants to discuss coming in with you on this team you're talking about." That got my attention. I found a little time for him on my schedule.

I walked into Jack's office high over downtown Edmonton the next day, and sitting with him was Paul Bowlen, the man many people called the richest in Alberta, who stood at the top of a Calgary-based oil patch and real estate empire. Even more interesting, I knew he was the father of Pat Bowlen, who was then in partnership with Peter Batoni of Batoni Construction. Together they had built much of Edmonton's new skyline, and they could be just the firm to erect the new arena I'd need. Bowlen made me an astonishing offer. He'd back me all the way on both the team and a new 18,000-seat arena in Edmonton. He'd give me a generous contract as president and general manager. He'd take all the risk. I wouldn't even have to take out a bank loan.

"We'll each be 50–50, Bill," he said. "You won't have to assume any financial obligation. If the team loses money, I'll pick up the losses. We can start construction immediately. I've got the land and everything."

I had to pause a minute to let his words sink in. I couldn't believe at first that they were real. Bowlen's offer was fantastic. He was handing me everything I needed to make my dreams come true. My decision should have been simple, but for some reason it wasn't.

I couldn't get past the thought of two of my Oil Kings partners, Charles Allard and Zane Feldman. They'd stepped in to help me after I'd lost money during the team's first year. Without them things would have been a lot leaner than they had been, and maybe I wouldn't have been standing in Jack Kennedy's office listening to the best business deal I'd ever been offered in my life. But the deal that would squeeze them out. Surely, I owed loyalty to those men, I thought. They were my friends. They'd stuck by me when things were tight.

I looked at Bowlen. "I'm sorry," I said. "You've made me a remarkable offer. But my current partners may want to participate in the new team, and they deserve a chance to have a look. My loyalties must lie with them."

Jack Kennedy was puzzled. "I don't see why, Bill," he said. "I don't think they're in a position to do what Mr. Bowlen is prepared to do."

I said I knew that, but my mind was made up. I would stick by the guys that had stuck by me, even though they hadn't asked me to and I wasn't sure if Zane and Charles had the slightest interest in joining me. The meeting ended. We shook hands with slightly baffled expressions on our faces. I don't think any of us could believe what I'd just done.

That still left me with the problem of finding a major backer for the Oilers. I knew I couldn't ask Zane and Charles to assume that role, but I'd been thinking about it long before Jack called. I had a few ideas. I called my old friend Willard "Bud" Estey in Toronto. Bud and I went way back. We had grown up together in

Saskatoon, where our fathers had been friends through sporting circles. Bud was the head of Canadian Cablesystems, at that time the
largest cable company in the country and owner of almost half of
the Famous Players theatre chain. "Bud, I've got an idea I'd like to
discuss with you," I told him. "Can I come down and meet with
you?" Bud was agreeable, as always, and about a week later I hopped
a plane and headed east.

I've been a salesman in one form or another most of my life,
but that morning when I walked into Bud's office high over downtown Toronto I made probably the greatest sale of my career. All day
I outlined for him why it was time for a second major league. I told
him the NHL was ignoring strong markets and the players were fed
up with the deal they were getting. I told him I knew Edmonton
was great hockey country and there were already negotiations under
way for a new building. I told him that down the road the league
would probably merge with the NHL but that it could survive nicely on its own, too. Bud listened intently, and at the end of the day
he had two words for me: "I'm in." I walked into his office with a
crazy-sounding idea about a hockey team with no players, no
coaches, no ticket sales and no building worthy of the name. The
team would play in a league that didn't even exist yet. And I walked
out with a certified cheque for a million dollars. It was more money
than I'd dreamed I would get—in fact, I told Bud I was uncom-
fortable taking that kind of cash for a project that was such a long
way from reality.

Bud just grinned. "Bill, you'll get it going. I know you." He
wasn't investing in a hockey club. He was investing in me. And all
the way home on the plane I carried Bud's cheque in my shirt pocket right next to my heart.

Back in Edmonton I walked into the office of Chuck McDonald, the manager of my Bank of Montreal branch, and put the

cheque on his desk. "I'd like to make a little deposit," I said. Chuck just glanced at it. "Sure, Bill. How are things going with the new team?" Then he took a second look. "A million dollars! My God! I guess this means the team is going just fine." He invited me to lunch the next day, and when I walked in to his private dining room at the bank's main branch on Jasper Avenue, I saw several other business friends of ours. Chuck hauled Bud Estey's cheque from his pocket, slapped it on the table and proclaimed, "This is how Bill Hunter does business!" The news of Bud's money soon got out in the national press, and that was a big deal for the Oilers. Not only did it give us a solid financial start, but it gave us credibility, and that was even more important. People now knew we had the cash to back up our plans.

Canadian Cablesystems had purchased 30 percent of the team. Bud figured his million would be all I needed. "Bill, we don't need any other partners," he told me. "You're off and running, now. This will give you far more money than 99 percent of the other teams in this new league, and there's no need to bring anyone else in on the deal." That was true, too, but I still felt that I owed something to Charles and Zane. I decided to split my remaining share of the team with them and called our lawyer, Danny Pekarsky, to draw up the papers. Danny couldn't believe it. "Why are you doing this, Bill?" he asked. "They wouldn't do it for you. Neither would anyone else. You don't need them. You've got enough cash to get going. It's nothing against Charles and Zane. It's just not common sense to give away your shares like this."

I told him I'd made up my mind and I wanted to share what I was sure was going to be a successful venture with them. Charles, Zane and I got together in Danny's office downtown. "Here's what I'm going to do," I said. "We'll divide the remaining 70 percent of the team three ways."

I'd done what I thought was right, but even at the time I had misgivings. My loyalties had first led me to turn down a very favorable offer and then surrender the bulk of my shares in the team I had dreamed into existence. Both Charles and Zane were very fine men whose advice any businessman would be glad to have. Charles in particular had become very close to me, and I respected him deeply. But Charles didn't understand sports and didn't even like them. He never did understand why you should pay someone tens or hundreds of thousands of dollars to skate around on the ice and bang away at a rubber disk. Charles couldn't fathom paying a hockey player $100,000 when doctors were earning $60,000. In the end it wasn't fair to bring Charles into a business he had no enthusiasm for—and it wasn't a good idea for me, either. I'd just given up control over crucial financial decisions, such as player salary budgets, to two men who didn't know the first thing about running a hockey club and were appalled by what they did know. And as a result we weren't a qualified ownership group and the team suffered. I lost, for example, a five-player package that included Bernie Federko and Brian Sutter because Charles thought they wanted too much money.

By the time 1972 rolled around, this was how the ownership of the new hockey team had worked itself out: I started a new company, called Edmonton World Hockey Enterprises, whose chief assets were a franchise in the WHA and Bud Estey's million, which I then used to buy the Oil Kings for $300,000. That cash got divided between all the Oil Kings partners—enough money to give them all six times the cash they'd backed me with only a few years before. It meant a lot to me to be able to do well by the people who had helped me out when I needed it. That left the new team with four partners: Canadian Cablesystems, Charles, Zane and me. I had $700,000 in cash to get the players on the ice.

And ice was our next concern. We didn't have any. Not big-league ice, anyway. The Edmonton Gardens had done fine for the Oil Kings, but that musty old barn wasn't going to work over the long term for pro hockey.

Our first option was to build our own arena. Charles locked up a perfect piece of property in south Edmonton, near the Labatt's brewery. It had great access from two of the city's major roads and would have worked very well for us. Charles had the financing arranged, and we made our plans public when we announced the team. We even had blueprints drawn up. That's when the exhibition board knocked on our door in a panic. Our plan to construct an arena would scuttle their plans to refurbish the exhibition site. General manager Al Anderson and board member Harry Hole came to me and said, "Bill, it would kill us if you built your own building." Couldn't we come to some sort of arrangement to play in their building? Charles and I agreed to talk, and talk we certainly did. There were three levels of government involved—municipal, provincial and federal—and the meetings dragged on and on. Neither side was willing to stake money until a firm commitment had been made by the other. They wouldn't commit money until we ensured we'd play in their arena, and we wouldn't make assurances until they'd committed their money. There were major fights as we thrashed things out. We had so many meetings and bargaining sessions with the exhibition board and the city that Charles finally said, "To hell with it." He left the negotiating to me and refused to attend another meeting.

At one point Zane and I had to put a little heat on the negotiations by flying down to Indianapolis, Indiana, where a beautiful new facility was waiting for a new tenant. That was only partly a poker move. We were Edmontonians through and through, and we wanted to play hockey in Edmonton. Eventually, however, we reached a deal with the board that would have them build a $15-million arena to house the Oilers. It was to be fully paid for by three levels of government and managed by the exhibition board.

I took the predictable criticism. Laurence Decore, then mayor of Edmonton, said I was getting off easy on the rent and called the whole agreement a sweetheart deal. I fired back in anger. I got on the phone and explained as forcefully as I could that the arena needed a long-term prime tenant to be viable and that I needed a decent rent deal in order to survive. I had signed a 10-year lease that gave the exhibition board all the revenue from concessions and parking—a fair deal for both sides.

We planned to have the Northlands Coliseum ready for the 1973–74 season. Batoni Bowlen Enterprises promised it would be, and although that wasn't the way things worked out, it was good enough for me to start working on the next step.

By this time the team had a name. I'd chosen *Oilers* because of the area. Many Edmontonians earned their living directly or indirectly from the oil patch: on the rigs, in refinery row or out in one of the industrial parks. Edmonton was a blue-collar, hard-working town, and I wanted to give the team a name fans could identify with. A local artist drew the familiar oil-drop logo, and I designed the uniforms and chose the colors. The teams colors were part of a larger idea.

I got Bud Estey to arrange a meeting in Toronto with Charlie Hay, the head of Gulf Western, and his vice president of marketing. I showed him our new logo. I pointed out how it complemented the logo Gulf used at the time. I also told him we would be more than happy to use Gulf's colors: blue and orange. I wasn't going to put Gulf's name on the sweaters, but there wouldn't be much doubt about the reference. Charlie loved the idea, and we shook hands then and there. The deal was worth $10 million, enough to set up the Oilers for years. Approval from Gulf's board would follow shortly, which Charlie insisted was a rubber stamp. But when the deal came before the board chairman, he turned it down. He insisted hockey was already identified with Imperial Oil through its sponsorship of *Hockey Night in Canada* broadcasts. Gulf would look as though it were trying to piggyback on its competition. Down the drain went $10 million. But the name, colors and crest all stuck.

I was juggling important negotiations and maneuverings for everything from an arena to a logo, but one crucial task couldn't be neglected any longer. I had to actually get some players under contract and put a team together.

Recruiting the Oilers (they were the Alberta Oilers at first) really began at the massive draft the WHA held in Anaheim. Bob Freeman was my chief scout with Cec Papke from Calgary and Chuck Catto from Montreal helping him. The final decisions were mine. Whenever we could, we recruited local boys. They were the players we knew best, and they were the players I felt would help Edmonton fans bond quickly with their new team. Players from similar backgrounds would jell quickly as a team, too. And if couldn't find the right local boy, I instructed the scouts to look for draftees from western Canada. This was my choice. I had nothing against players from Eastern Canada or the United States, but I believed prairie boys had a certain strength of character I wanted. We knew they were competitors. I thought any boy who'd come up through those unending bus rides and grueling week-long road trips had developed a special kind of dedication and grit. From the time they were children playing on outdoor rinks, prairie boys were brought up to compete hard.

Our first team was a bit of an Oil Kings reunion. Ray Kinasewich came back from Houston in the Central Hockey League as our coach. He would be helped out by the retired goaltending great

Glenn Hall. Ron Anderson, whom we brought back from the Red Wings farm system, had been on our Memorial Cup team. Doug Barrie, whom I stole from the Los Angeles Kings, had been on that team, too. Ron Walters came back to us. Our goalie, Ken Brown, came home from the Chicago Blackhawks farm system. Former captain Bob Falkenberg returned to Edmonton from the Red Wings farm system. John Fisher signed with us. I stole Bob Wall from Detroit. Eddie Joyal came back to Edmonton from Philadelphia. Dennis Kassian, Jack Norris, Ross Perkins, Rusty Patenaude and Bob McAneeley were all former Oil Kings who joined the original Oilers.

I worked hard to get Al Hamilton back with us. He was doing fine with the Buffalo Sabres, and I had to get his unlisted phone number to get in touch with him and persuade him to jump. Eventually, I flew him out to Ottawa to watch the Memorial Cup and took an unsigned contract with me. I convinced Al to talk and I closed the deal. Sabres owner Seymour Knox got me on the phone. "Bill, I don't want to lose Al, but I understand he's played for you before and he's going back home with you. If you can assure me you're going to take care of him and treat him well, I'm not going to fight you."

Not everyone was so gracious. Jack Kent Cooke laid a lawsuit against me over Doug Barrie, and we had to clear that up before he could play.

We found plenty of western boys to fill the spots not taken by former Oil Kings. Kenny Baird, for whom we had to outbid the NHL's California Seals, came from Flin Flon. We outbid Oakland for Billy "the Kid" Hicke, an ex-Regina Pat. We got Jim Benzelock, who'd been a Winnipeg Jet when that team was in the juniors, and Bernie Blanchette, who'd been a Saskatoon Blade. Brian Carlin was a former Calgary Centennial. Steve Carlyle, a former star with the University of Alberta Golden Bears, came from the college side. I nabbed Wetaskiwin native Val Fonteyne from the Pittsburgh Penguins—a great penalty killer, speedy skater and a solid guy in the locker room.

All through the process I kept a steady stream of press releases flowing over Edmonton sports desks. And if it took a little hype to get the reporters out, so be it. When Jimmy Harrison signed on with us for a four-year contract and a whopping signing bonus of $75,000, I got him to pose with a shopping cart full of money. I pumped up nearly everybody who joined us as a major acquisition that was going to guarantee the Oilers a playoff run if not the championship. Roger Coté from the Cleveland Barons in the American Hockey League was a fan favorite who delivered bone-crushing open-ice hits while playing with a toothpick in his mouth. I knew he was no Bobby Hull, but I built up his signing like he was the second coming of "The Golden Jet." Some players were stars and some weren't. But sports run on excitement, and I knew I had to build some buzz.

Sometimes I just took a flyer. I drafted Rags Ragulin from the Soviet Red Army squad I'd seen play my Oil Kings. I had no idea if I could actually land the guy, but instead I told a sportswriter at the time, "You have to be prepared for the possibility that the entire Russian team might defect."

Some players were eager to jump. The Leafs had offered Jimmy Harrison all of $13,000 a year, and he was glad to come to the Oilers. But some players took considerable reassuring. I had to tell Al Hamilton that his five-year contract was personally backed by Charles Allard. The night before we announced the signing of Roger Coté, Eddie Joyal and Doug Barrie, their agent called to demand that the contracts be guaranteed with some solid assets. Zane had to rush over to his safety deposit box and haul out some share certificates to put in trust.

Putting the Oilers together between 1971 and 1972 was a wild and confusing time. It was like juggling while walking a high wire, and our act was for real money and in front of the entire sporting public of North America. But I was having more fun than I'd had in years. As a hockey man I'd always been able to spot talent, and I was having a ball starting a team from scratch.

In the fall of 1972, I got my first look at what I'd brought together during the Oilers' first training camp at the Edmonton Gardens. The players went through their drills and got to know one another just as they did every fall, but everybody knew this was no ordinary autumn. We knew that our team's finances were sound in Edmonton, but that certainly couldn't be said for every team in the WHA. Many of our players had left solid careers in the NHL, and all of them had all taken a big risk to join our league. I'd told most of them that the goal was to merge our league with the NHL within five years. And to every player who signed with us, I said, "Don't sign this contract if you're not fully confident we're going to be able to meet our obligations to you." But at the same time, the players couldn't be expected not to have had some trepidation going into that first season. I knew there were some fears, and I couldn't blame them. We were attempting something nobody had ever done before. We were going to take on the mighty National Hockey League, the league they'd spent their lives thinking of as the unquestioned bastion of hockey supremacy. Could a league that had folded two teams before its first season even begin to hope to take on hockey's answer to the Catholic Church?

The Alberta Oilers played their first game—one of two on that opening night of the WHA's first season—in Ottawa against the Nationals. It was televised nationally on the CBC, one of only six WHA games the national broadcaster agreed to show that year. On the ice there wasn't any big fuss. No ceremonies, no speeches, just

*The opening ceremony in Quebec City, the second game played by the Alberta Oilers.*

an anthem and a face-off. But that's all I needed. The clack of the sticks on the ice as the puck came down was as beautiful to me as the opening bars of a symphony. All those hours in the Iron Lung traveling from Estevan to Flin Flon had been worth it. It was vindication for every time I'd been turned down for a team or told my town wasn't big-league enough. The powers that be in the hockey world had said over and over again that we wouldn't make it, that we wouldn't manage to drop a puck on an opening face-off. Well, goddamnit, here we were. The puck had just been dropped in front of a packed and enthusiastic house. I knew we could do it. It was game on.

Ron Anderson got the first WHA regular-season goal that night. Billy Hicke got a couple. We won 7–4.

I'd never experienced anything like those first games in the WHA. Everything was a first—first game on the road, first at home, first goal, first shutout, first fight—and nothing was predictable. Different teams had different levels of talent. But at first everybody was starting from the ice up, and any team really could beat any other team on any given night. The players liked that and I did, too. It was exciting. Of course, the flip side of so much novelty means you don't have returning vets or guys who have played together for a couple years. The team doesn't have any history and has to figure out a way to develop some leadership. As well, our teams threw together all sorts of players in a way that didn't tend to happen in the NHL, where a club was staffed by players who'd all come through the same system. We had prominent NHLers, kids from university hockey, players from all kinds of junior leagues, players nearing retirement and players fresh out of junior. Ray and I had to figure out a way to make a team out of them—or rather help them make a team out of themselves. One thing we had going for us was that we had hired a lot of local players. Some had grown up playing together and now were getting a chance to bring the big leagues to their families and friends. I think we all felt good about that.

Some nights were awful. A couple of teams in our league played the role of the old Flin Flon Bombers, and the Los Angeles Sharks were one of them. We played an exhibition game against them. There were about 30 fights, including a bench-clearer, and it took about five hours to finish the game. It was mayhem. In the dressing room after the game, I caught some looks from a few of the players, especially ones that had left the NHL. I knew what they were thinking: What the hell have I gotten myself into? The papers the next day couldn't have been worse. "Huge Brawl," the headline screamed. Dennis Murphy was the general manager of the Sharks, and I told him, "You have set us back 10 years."

Nights like that made for some nervous players at the start, but by the time Christmas rolled around they were happier. Bobby Hull had been cleared to play by a judge who drove the legal stake into the miserly old heart of the reserve clause. People were getting the feeling the WHA was here to stay.

Our travel schedules were brutal, and we tried to make things easier by using our own plane. Our slow twin-engined turboprop didn't speed things up for us, though, especially when we had to stop and refuel on half our flights. Eventually, we returned to commercial flights, but that brought its own problems. It was more cost-effective for our teams to go out on longer road trips less often, so we were away from home a couple of weeks at a time. Even though it felt as if I'd spent half my life in airports, I wasn't used to spending that much time in departure lounges. We'd get terrible connections between Hartford and Quebec City or Winnipeg and Cleveland, zigzagging halfway across the continent to move one state or province over. I've never been a patient man when it comes to waiting. One day I was pacing up and down the aisles, sitting for a couple minutes, popping up again or looking for somebody to talk to. Glenn Hall looked at me and cracked, "Quick, Bill, organize something!"

Not all our destinations were a pleasure to visit, either. When the New England Whalers played at Boston Gardens, the rink used to be surrounded by police guard dogs. And the first few times we played Philadelphia, the players had to change in our hotel room because the dressing rooms weren't finished yet. In New Jersey, another arena without dressing rooms, players said the ice was actually tilted. One night we arrived hours late for a game in New York after our plane got stranded in a blizzard on an airstrip in Ohio, which happened to be the location of our hotel. It was hockey and it was the big leagues, but some days it felt a lot like touring with the Hounds. In a way, though, those times were fun. I was at the head of my team, facing every sort of unpredictable challenge.

Unfortunately, after Christmas the Oilers hit a terrible losing streak. Everything seemed to be falling apart. Our loses mounted to the point that our attendance dropped. I had only 5,200 seats in the Edmonton Gardens. I needed every one full. I couldn't see any way out. I still considered Ray to be a very fine hockey coach, but sometimes a coach is wrong for a team and he can't get through to them. That happens. I had to let Ray go.

With the agreement of Charles and Zane, I took over the team. I knew these players. A lot of them had been with me before, and I knew the background of the other. I knew I could motivate them. We were 11 points out of contention and near the end of the season, but we fashioned an exciting run for the playoffs. Our hopes came down to the final game of the regular season. We were in Philadelphia and had to go through a typical WHA travel schedule to get to Minnesota to play the Fighting Saints. We rose at five o'clock to a catch a 7:00 A.M. flight, made three changes and got into St. Paul at about 1:00 P.M. The players didn't have time to eat anything more than a poached egg or two. And they were dog tired. We'd played three games in three nights. We walked over to the rink just so we could get some air and stretch our legs. I told the players, "Look, for the first period, we've got to just hang on. We'll check, check, check. And every time we get the puck we'll freeze it or dump it down the ice. If we can do that, we can find our stride in the second and go on to win." We won, stunning 18,000 Minnesota fans. And we qualified for the playoffs despite the worst losing skid in, well, Oilers history. Or so we thought.

Shortly after that game, I got a call from somebody at the WHA head office who told me we hadn't quite yet qualified. We were tied in points with the Minnesota Fighting Saints. "But we've won more games than they have," I said, as if that would help. Didn't matter. The owners had voted and the decision had been made. Minnesota

*We won an upset against the Minnesota Fighting Saints on their home ice. What a feeling.*

and the Oilers were locked at 70 points and we would have to play one more game.

It was about money, of course. The league shared in all playoff revenue and knew very well that our building held only 5,200. There was no way the other owners were going to let us into the playoffs if they could possibly avoid it, so out came the tied-in-points ruling. First they tried to get us to play another game in St. Paul, hopefully in front of another record crowd. They offered me half the gate, but I angrily turned them down. We flew back to Edmonton, and I spent hours on the phone haranguing and pleading and arguing. At one point I threatened to sue the league and seize the playoff gate receipts. But I didn't. I'd never sued anyone in my whole life. Eventually, I admitted defeat. We agreed to play a second game on neutral ice in Calgary.

But the players were hurt and angry. Maybe we'd only moved from sixth to fourth in a six-team division, but they felt we'd earned our playoff berth legitimately. I did, too, and I wasn't happy to be treated like that in my own league. We felt we'd been done in by our own and we were a dispirited group on the ice that day. We lost.

It hurt, but the best cure for disappointment is to look forward to something good, and I had just the thing. I was already laying plans for a hockey spectacle the like of which the world had never seen. It would dispel any doubts that the WHA wasn't truly major league.

# 12

# THE SUMMIT SERIES

**The timekeeper was responsible for stopping the game before the end of regulation time. Gerry Cheevers had to be restrained when he threw off his gloves and went after him.**

ANY PEOPLE SCOFFED AT THE WORLD Hockey Association as a second-rate circuit when we were getting it organized in 1971, and nobody felt that keener than Ben and I. We'd made some stellar signings, and we knew our league was going to be first-class. The problem was how to get the sportswriters and the public to agree. Ben and I knocked heads over the issue for hours. What could we do that would grab everybody's attention and prove once and for all that the WHA's best could play with anybody?

One day I was sitting in my office sorting through the day's usual allotment of chaos when I heard that the chairman of the International Ice Hockey Federation, Gunter Sabetzki, was visiting Canada. Inspiration struck. International hockey—that was the answer to our image problem! For years Canadians had been telling themselves that the reason we did so poorly in international competition was that our best players were professionals and everyone else's still qualified as amateurs. We weren't allowed to send our top guns to the tournaments that the Russians were winning with monotonous regularity. We needed to give fans the hockey they wanted—a series between Canadian pros and the best international team the world could bring on. And in 1971 the best meant the Russians. I began to tingle. Canada *versus* Russia, our best against their best with no rules about eligibility and world hockey supremacy hanging in the balance. That would capture everybody's attention. It would be the most-watched hockey series of all time. I got on the phone to Ben, and almost immediately we were on a plane to Toronto to meet with Sabetzki.

John Bassett, owner of the Toronto Toros, helped us set up a meeting at the University of Toronto. He joined Ben and I at the meeting, as did Gordon Juckes from the CAHA and Lou Lefaivre from Hockey Canada. We told Sabetzki that we'd like to open our league's first season by playing a series with the Russian national team. Sabetzki was no fool. His eyes got wide when we outlined our idea for a Canada Cup. He was very excited. He would have signed up right then, but Ben and I couldn't go that far yet. The other teams in the league had no idea what we were about to commit them to and we asked Sabetzki for a little time to get our end of things organized. Sabetzki consented, and Ben and I flew back west with our spirits soaring high as our plane, convinced we'd come up with the ultimate kickoff for the WHA.

Once back in Edmonton, however, I began to have second thoughts. We had so much work to do already: getting the league up and running, dealing with the ongoing game of musical owners, not to mention pulling our own teams together. Was it realistic to stage a major international tournament at the same time? "Besides," I said to Ben, "we'd be icing an league all-star team before we even had our first league game. It seems a little odd. Maybe we're not quite ready for this yet. Maybe we should wait a year or two." After a little thought, Ben agreed. We figured that by 1974 our league would be ready to step out and stickhandle in front of the world, and in early spring 1971 that's what we decided to present to Sabetzki. The World Hockey Association's Team Canada would take on the Russian national team in 1974. It was going to be great and it was going to be a first.

Meanwhile, however, Alan Eagleson got wind of our idea, maybe from Sabetzki himself. Eagleson was well connected in the international hockey world, so he heard most of the scuttlebutt. Eagleson was no fool, either. He knew a good idea when he heard one, and he out-and-out stole it. Immediately, he pitched his own series to Sabetzki, who held him off until he heard from us. Sabetzki had agreed to a series against the WHA in 1974, but he turned around and promised Eagleson the same thing for 1972.

In no time Eagleson went public saying that an NHL Team Canada was going to play the Russians. I felt sick listening to him take credit for what Ben and I had worked up, but there was nothing I could do. That series became the most famous hockey series of all time. It should have been ours.

Still, we had 1974. And there was a lot of work to do on that. You couldn't set up a series with the Russians by simply shaking hands on a university campus. Gordon, Lou and I were the negotiating team that flew to Moscow to set things up. Shortly after we arrived, we were sitting in the lobby of our hotel when we met an old Scottish engineer. He'd been doing business behind the Iron Curtain for years, and he instantly pegged us for the rookies we were.

"You fellows are from Canada, are you?" he asked.

I said we were. "We're here negotiating a hockey series."

"How many meetings have you had?" asked our engineer.

"This will be our first," I said.

"Well, you'll be back two more times."

Sure enough, our old Russia hand was right. It took us three flights to Moscow to get the series finalized.

Our first meeting was held in a rattletrap of a building with tatty old chairs and dim lighting. We couldn't believe they would hold an important international meeting in a building like that, but the Soviets had their reasons. It was the first example of the kind of tactics that would come to characterize our dealings with them. Every time we made progress, the next meeting would be held in a better venue, and when we went back the second time things were much improved. The surroundings weren't luxurious by any means, but at least the lighting let you read the fine print and the chairs didn't wobble. And by the third time we met, I felt as though we were being received at the court of the Czar. The meeting room was magnificent with huge chandeliers hanging from the vaulted ceiling and a red carpet so thick and deep you could lose your keys in it. The furniture was gorgeous and the tables were laid out with candies and caviar. The vodka and champagne was flowing, and if you needed a break mineral water was available by the gallon. Before we started, Russian chief negotiator Alexander Grescoe gave me a hand-tooled, leather-bound copy of the Russian Olympic bid book, a book the International Olympic Committee hadn't even seen yet. I grew to genuinely like Grescoe, who looked a lot like the Hollywood actor Jack Palance: tall and rawboned with a squint in his eye and a seamed face, lined with a scar.

Despite the regal surroundings and gracious behavior, we still weren't signing anything. It was talk, talk, talk and the poker-faced Russians would just nod and whisper among themselves and come back with another *nyet*. Finally, I'd had enough. I got to my feet and proclaimed, "We're getting nowhere with you people. We're packing up and going home and you, my Soviet friends, have just blown $50,000 a game! And one more thing—I know goddamned well you can speak English just as well as I can, so stop hiding behind the interpreter." As the rest of his delegation looked on with their sober negotiating faces, Grescoe burst out laughing. "Bill, we wondered when you were going to snap. At last we get to see the Wild Bill we hear so much about! How's your wife, Vi?" He proceeded to name all our children, and continuing in fluent English talked about the Oil Kings, asked about the Memorial Cup and wanted to know what the Oilers prospects were for the coming season. He knew all about Gordon and Lou, too. My outburst and Grescoe's laughter broke the impasse. That day we signed a deal.

Gordon, Lou and I flew back to Canada and started organizing. Ben was named chairman and I was general manager. The whole show was to be run out of my Edmonton office. Money started coming in when Carling O'Keefe breweries signed a TV sponsorship deal worth $4.3 million. We all agreed that the proceeds would be split in four equal shares, one each for the CAHA, Hockey Canada, the Player's Association and the league.

Bobby Hull and Pat Stapleton would be assistant coaches and players. My choice for head coach was Bill Dineen, who had won the league championship coaching the Houston Aeros. But before I had a chance to name my choice, John Basset forced our hand. He made a public announcement that Billy Harris was going to coach because of his international experience. Billy had coached in Sweden. I got Basset on the phone and gave him hell, but it was too late and Basset knew it. The choice had been announced, and the choice was Harris.

Harris, Hull, Gordie Howe and I got together in Toronto and picked Team Canada for the 1974 Summit Series. There was some discussion at first about whether we'd invite NHL players to join us, but we quickly tossed the idea aside. After all, we wanted to sell our league, and the whole idea was to give our league credibility. In any event the NHL was unlikely to lend us players. So we stuck to our own. We decided we'd limit our picks to 25. That's all the team would need, and it increased the likelihood that every player chosen would actually play.

The whole process took us about two days, and it was remarkably smooth. We all knew hockey, and we knew who we needed. There was some discussion when we got down to the final five or so, but once the decision was made, it stayed made. We promised one another that there wouldn't be any second-guessing and there wasn't. There wasn't a single player who wasn't thrilled when we called him with our invitation. No one turned us down. They all wanted to play for their country against the big, bad Russians.

I believed the team we had assembled was the finest to ever represent Canada. We had Gerry Cheevers in goal, far and away the best international goaltender Canada had. J.C. Tremblay and Pat Stapleton were the best defensive pair I ever saw. Sure picks were Bobby Hull, Gordie Howe with his sons Mark and Marty, Frank Mahovlich, Paul Henderson, Andre Lacroix, Ralph Backstrom and Marc Tardif. Bring on the Russians, I thought. Our guys can take 'em.

That summer we met with all the Team Canada players in Toronto at the Royal York Hotel and laid out our plans. We put the players through a series of physical tests to assess their strength and fitness. Gordie, at the age of 46, registered the stamina and power of a 28 year old. Next we held a training camp in Edmonton. We bunked everybody down at the Westin Hotel, which hadn't even officially opened. I talked the manager, Bob McCauley, into letting us have the whole place to ourselves, just for the publicity it would bring him. A banner hanging outside proclaimed Welcome Team Canada! It was an example of how excitement was just bubbling. We had national TV all over us. I opened our training camp and the Edmonton Gardens to the public, and 5,000 people attended every day to watch the workout. I also set up a four-game exhibition series in Calgary, Medicine Hat, Saskatoon and Edmonton with an all-star junior team beefed up with a few of the younger Team Canada members like Dennis Sobchuk and Pat Price. I knew the series would not only give Team Canada a chance to play together under game conditions, but also generate a huge amount of press and create even more excitement. "We're going to take the game to the people," I told the press. The 1972 team, by comparison, had only played a couple of intersquad games in Toronto. We flew around the prairies in an airplane from one of Charles Allard's companies and played in front of packed houses. And after every game the whole team, led by Bobby and Gordie, would sign autographs until the last child went home.

By the time the series rolled around, our team was ready mentally and physically. We'd trained hard and our exhibition games had brought us together as a team. Winging into Quebec City for the series opener on September 17, we were confident we'd win. Before the game the atmosphere in the dressing room was good—a sort of keyed-up, looking-forward-to-the-battle kind of feel. Prime Minister Pierre Trudeau came in to wish each player well and joined right in with the banter, but there's an edge to a team's mood at such times and Trudeau found that out. The last two players' cubicles before the door were Bobby's and Gordie's. Trudeau stopped to talk to "Mr. Hockey" when all of a sudden he shouted in pain and jumped back. Gordie had taken his stick and given Trudeau a stiff rap right over his elegantly clad ankle. For Gordie it was just a love tap, but Trudeau was hopping around and grimacing. "Well, Mr.

*At a meeting prior to the opening game of the Summit Series. L–R: Yours truly, Paul Racine, "The Golden Jet," Ben Hastkin, "Mr. Hockey."*

Prime Minister," said Gordie, "we just wanted to make sure you were really ready because we may need you tonight." Everyone roared, including Trudeau.

Even Gordie's stickwork couldn't cramp Trudeau's style, and it seemed like he and the opening ceremonies took forever. But words can't describe the feeling of 15,000 people listening in rapt silence to the Russian national anthem and then raising the rafters with "O Canada" sung for real, blending into the cheers as the first puck was dropped. The only cheer louder that night was for the first goal scored by Johnny Mackenzie off Lacroix and Hull. The fans went wild and the game was delayed while officials cleared debris off the ice.

The second period didn't go so well. Bobby got one, but the Russians got three. Their second came from the genius forward Valerie Kharlamov, who got in close, evaded Gerry's poke check, then lifted it over him for a beauty. Finally, in the last five minutes of the third, Bobby came through for us again, finishing tic-tac-toe passes from Mackenzie and Lacroix with a ripping 25-foot wrist shot through the pads of Vladislav Tretiak. With seconds to go the Big M, Frank Mahovlich, broke in on goal home free and beat Tretiak clean with a slick deke. But his shot hit the crossbar and the game ended 3–3.

The doubters had said we were too old (our average age was 30 and the Russians' was 23), but we skated with them all night and outshot them 34–28. I never had any doubts that Team Canada would give the Russians everything they could handle, but I won't deny I was breathing a sigh of relief when I actually saw my prediction come true on the ice. One sportswriter called the game "a moral victory."

The next game, two days later in Toronto, we got the real thing. We whipped the Russians. We played a real Canadian game— tough, physical, close-checking—and we shredded their intricate passing patterns like cabbage into coleslaw. Ralph Backstrom got a goal, Bobby got another, Andre Lacroix scored and J.C. Tremblay finished it off. Alexandr Yakushev was the only redshirt who found the net. There was a disputed call when referee Tom Brown waved off a Russian goal that probably went in, but it wouldn't have changed anything. The fans in Maple Leaf Gardens, all 16,500 of them, went crazy. Their chants of "Go Canada Go" were like the beating of a giant heart. Reporters like Dick Beddoes and Red Fisher, most of whom rated us as scrappy underdogs at best, started to think the WHA was going to pull off one of the great all-time upsets.

"You've got them," said Beddoes. "Play like that and you've got them."

And then the wheels came off the tracks.

As general manager I'd made an agreement with Harris, Hull and Stapleton that no lineup changes were to be made unless the coach had consulted with me. If I had any concerns, all the coaches would discuss the decision. No changes would be made without everybody agreeing, just as when we picked the team. I went ahead of the team to Winnipeg for the next game to make sure all the arrangements were in place. And while I was somewhere in the skies over the Canadian Shield, Billy Harris decided to pull seven players and replace them. He even swapped Cheevers for Don McLeod.

We lost in Winnipeg 8–5. After Toronto we'd had the Russians on the run. Now we'd let them back into the series and were heading to Vancouver on a lousy game. Billy told me he'd promised everybody on the team they'd get a chance to play, but I had a quiet little chat with him and reminded him, forcefully but politely, of our agreement. There were no more lineup surprises after that, and our relationship calmed down.

By now it was clear that the head games the Russians had played during the negotiations would be carried over into the series. They'd come to me in Toronto complaining that they hadn't been given enough ice time in the Gardens to prepare, and I got Harold Ballard to give up some time he'd reserved for the Leafs. But that was only one incident. We met every morning, and every morning there was a fresh list of complaints. Once, they came crying that their bus had "square wheels." I threw up my hands.

Game four in Vancouver, before more than 16,000 fans, was another disappointment. We were leading 5–2 at the end of the first period after a natural hat trick from Bobby Hull. But penalties killed us. Johnny Mackenzie, who was so worked up over the series that he couldn't eat and eventually lost 10 pounds, made a couple of nervous mistakes and spent four minutes in the penalty box in the third. The Russians tied the score and the game ended 5–5.

From coast to coast, we'd played four games in front of loud, sellout crowds. As well, I'd been wining and dining the sports reporters and making sure they had lots to write about, so we'd had more media coverage than any other international series had received. It was positive coverage, too. We didn't have anyone booing our team. Still, after four games we weren't where we should have been. We were deadlocked at one game apiece with a pair of ties, and we should have won them all.

We had plenty of time to think about our play on the plane over to Europe. The 200 of us on the trip found various ways to pass the hours. I played a marathon bridge match with Johnny Mackenzie against Brad Selwood and Mark Howe. We were down 4,500 points by Greenland but were only 10 down by landing. Howie Meeker opined. Serge Bernier stretched out on the floor under a blanket and slept. Bobby Hull took over the intercom to sing "Happy Birthday" to Ron Stewart from Hockey Canada. And all of us chewed through an Air Canada steak.

We spent a few days in Helsinki, Finland, where we'd planned a short two-game exhibition series against the Swedish national team to collect our thoughts and get used to the larger international ice. Before the first game, all the Swedish reporters wrote about the kind of chippy, dirty play they could expect from Canadian professionals. But after the games, we got standing ovations from the fans, and the Swedish press described the series as the cleanest in international hockey they'd ever seen. Then it was on to Russia.

The flight was 85 minutes, but leaving the airport took three hours. Our bags were lost, everything went wrong and no amount of raging could speed things up. My bags disappeared for two days before turning up in a hotel downtown. And I only found them because somebody tipped me off. It was just the next skirmish in the psychological war the Russians waged on us. We were ready for them. Frank Mahovlich and Paul Henderson were among the players who had been with the team in 1972, and they knew what to expect. We had them tell the whole team what the experience would be like, and they were quite accurate. I'd had a good briefing from the RCMP and the diplomats at External Affairs in Ottawa as well.

Our hotel, for instance. We were supposed to be in the Interpol Hotel, the best hotel in town, where most visiting westerners stayed. We wound up in the Rossia, which was no Interpol. The rooms were filthy and full of lice and roaches. After we checked in, Colleen Howe called me and said, "Bill, come on up here. We just want you to have a look at what we're doing." I went to her room, and she and Joanne Hull were down on their hands and knees scrubbing the shower.

Conditions were everything the officials back home had warned us they would be. Every night the phones rang. There'd be voices on the other end, and I'd snarl, "You Russian bastards," and slam the receiver down. The performance would be repeated a few moments later as they tried to keep us from getting a good night's sleep. Finally, I called down to the front desk: "One more call and I'm leaving this thing off the hook!" That worked. The players got the same treatment and used the same solution. Some on the team had harder shells than others. Frank Mahovlich lived in a constant state of tension. "Watch them, Bill, watch them. You can't trust them," he'd say. After a while we called him my shadow because he didn't want to get too far out of sight. But most of the time we just laughed the intimidation off.

Some things, like toilet tissue and Kleenex, we brought with us. We brought our own food, twice as much as the 1972 team had brought, but masses of it went missing. We wanted to bring our own chef (Mike from Hy's Steak Loft), but the Russians wouldn't let us. Their cooks murdered our steaks. They must have boiled them.

The Canadian reporters covering the games ate better than we did. They had a better bus, too, complete with two very attractive young Russian women as tour guides. They'd honk at us as they drove by the old clunker we were ferried around in. And there were difficulties with tickets. A lot of the players brought their wives and girl friends, and we'd been promised excellent seats at the games for them. Excellent seats turned out to mean the very top rows, beside blocks of soldiers who constantly harassed them. We had to lay complaints to get them to stop.

Our first game in Moscow was October 1. Our team was getting ready in its dressing room, and the Russians were down the hall in theirs. I was outside, pacing the halls, on fire with anticipation. I walked past a quiet little room and looked inside. There was Vladislav Tretiak, the great Russian goaltender, methodically strapping on his pads by himself on the opposite side of the building from his teammates. He smiled and I smiled back. We knew we couldn't talk to each other, even though Tretiak spoke a little English. I left him there to collect his thoughts in silence. Goalies are often like that.

I watched the games with Robert Ford, the Canadian ambassador. He walked with leg braces, and found it comfortable to watch the games on a high, padded bench with his feet dangling down. I sat with him in the corner of the arena near the ice. Above us the crowd didn't look like any hockey crowd I'd ever seen before—rows and rows of white shirts and dark suits with big blocks of seats for soldiers in their dark gray and brown uniforms. They applauded things they liked and whistled at things they didn't, but otherwise they sat there quiet and serious, absorbing the game. In contrast, our 3,200 rowdy Canadian fans waved flags and banners, blew into noisemakers and cheered like hell at everything. The Canucks were loud from the face-off through the final buzzer.

Although it was close, we lost the first game 3–2 , with Gordie and his son Mark scoring. We didn't play well. We dumped game six, too, thanks largely to a great game by Tretiak. The score was 5–2 even though the shots were almost dead even. But officiating was beginning to be a real factor. We were getting killed by penalties— 33 minutes in game six to the Russians' nine. Many calls were simply bad officiating. The Russians would spear and spear and spear, and finally our fellows would retaliate and end up with two minutes in the box. If a referee doesn't control the play, the players will lay down the law themselves, and sure enough two fights broke out that night. The second one, between Rick Ley and Kharlamov, started as a stick-swinging duel just before the game ended and continued after the buzzer. The Russian fans chanted their equivalent of "Go home!" to us as Kharlamov got up off the ice with a bloody face. But the Canadian fans, happy to at least see some rough justice, cheered wildly. Ambassador Ford turned to me after the game and said, "Bill, I wouldn't blame you if you took the team home right now. That was disgraceful." The next day the Russian coach, Boris Kulagin, commented that Ley should be jailed.

Tensions were starting to get to us and not just on the rink. We'd taken lots of gum and candies and maple leaf pins to hand out to the kids who clustered around the rinks, hoping to get a look at the hockey superstars. One day, as we were walking into the arena for a practice, two kids approached Gordie Howe for a treat. A soldier came up and cross-checked them with his rifle to shoo them away, and Gordie snapped. He picked that soldier up by the collar of his coat and held him in the air. "You son of a bitch," he snarled. "Don't you ever come near those kids again."

I hustled over. "For Christ's sake, Gordie, put him down before we have a Third World War," I pleaded. He did, but he was fuming.

My day usually began an hour or two before everybody else's.

I'd be up and at the office, calling around, seeing to the day's arrangements. Then I'd check in at breakfast to see if the meal was on time and if all the players had gotten their wake-up calls. Most days we'd hop on our bus and head out to the rink. Our bus driver was an old Russian army man we nicknamed "Colonel Oddjob." Colonel Oddjob was a big Gordie Howe fan, and Gordie played along with him. Gordie would board the bus with a hearty, "Good morning, Colonel Oddjob. And how are the Russian bastards today? What can we do to fix them good?" We'd drive to the rink and spot Russian soldiers, hiding behind trees with drawn bayonets. It got to seem normal after a couple of days.

I had my own personal Russian. Viktor was with me all the time, from when we were negotiating the series to when we were in Moscow playing it. During the Canadian games, he sat on the bench with the Russian players. He stayed in the same hotel as I did, keeping watch in the lobby when I was up in my room. One morning I rose early, unable to sleep because of the time change. There was Viktor, snoozing in the lobby. We spent so much time together that we eventually became friendly. We talked about our families and our educations, and I finally got to like him. I had no doubt he was KGB, though.

Our time in Moscow wasn't entirely spent in rinks and hotels. We saw some wonderful sights. The Moscow Circus was a one-ring marvel of the most beautiful ladies and the handsomest men putting on a truly amazing show. Their Opera House was magnificent, all marble and granite. The Bolshoi Ballet performed Swan Lake for us. I sat in the sixth row with all the Russian aristocrats. All around me were ladies wrapped in sables and hung with jewelry like Christmas trees. A classless society this wasn't.

We spent an afternoon shopping at the GUM store, the department store that was the showpiece of Russian consumer goods, where they were very happy to accept our Canadian dollars. We bought lots of wooden dolls and carvings and toys to take to our kids back home, but there wasn't much else to buy. The shelves were practically empty. I went back later and watched sadly while people squabbled in the lineup for bread.

We had good and bad experiences in Russia, but we didn't let them distract us from our main purpose for being there. We were there to win hockey games, and the spirit on the team remained splendid. We knew we were in a hole, down two games with only two left to play. But we were resolved to come out of this with at least a tie, and we went into game seven determined to return to the form of our first two matches.

Russia led 2–1 after the first period. After 40 minutes the score stood 4–3 Russia in a fast, tight, and for once, clean game. Then Ralph Backstrom scored on a pass from J.C. Tremblay early in the third to tie it up, and the game was really on. Finally, with 27 seconds left on the clock, Bobby Hull grabbed the puck and would not let go until he'd shoved it into the net behind Tretiak. We thought we'd won, and we were delirious with joy—but only for a second. Unbelievably, the Russian officials ruled time had run out. Dick Beddoes and I ran outside to the TV truck. Their tape was synchronized with the game clock, and it showed clearly that Bobby's goal went in with 18 seconds left.

Inside the rink was chaos. Our entire team was on the ice yelling at the ref, Tom Brown, the same zebra who'd missed the Russian goal in game two. But he'd called a good game, and he was helpless to do anything. The timekeeper had been responsible for stopping the game before the end of regulation time. Gerry Cheevers had to be restrained when he threw off his gloves and went after him. Over 3,000 Canadian fans were going crazy with frustration and anger while the Russian soldiers jeered at them. It took most of an hour to get everyone calmed down so we could finish the evening. We complained bitterly to the officials, but it was a waste of breath. They said the time clock had run down. Yeah, sure. A brand-new Swiss time clock installed especially for the series. Game seven went into the books as a 4–4 tie.

After that, game eight was a bit anticlimactic. The Russians started it off with another masterpiece of psychological intimidation. Before the game the announcer informed the fans, "Since the players of Team Canada have repeatedly broken the agreement signed by the WHA and the USSR on adhering to the rules of the International Ice Hockey Federation on dirty play, at the first infringement the USSR Ice Hockey Federation will stop play." It was just enough to take the edge of our aggressiveness for the first part of the game. We lost 3–2.

Our time in Russia ended with a party thrown by the Russians for members of both teams. Many of that generation's greatest players were in that room: Kharlamov, Howe, Yakushev, Hull, Tretiak, Cheevers. We wanted to mix, to share ideas and stories and tell these wonderful athletes how much we respected them and what a thrill it had been to line up against them. But we didn't get the chance. We were seated on one side of the banquet hall, and the Russians were seated on the other. They wouldn't allow their players to cross the floor, and when we came over to them the nameless official-looking types sitting among them waved us off. That's how it had been for me the whole trip. Boris Kulagin, the Russian coach, didn't want to have anything to do with us beyond official courtesies. I ran into Victor Tarasov, the architect of Russian hockey, whom I'd met years ago in Edmonton when his Red Army team came to play the Oil Kings, but there was no friendly spark there, either. They were all on guard, afraid of what the people watching them might think. It was sad.

We had lost the series and that hurt. But I had no regrets. We ran a first-class operation all the way. We should have won, and our team never gave up. And most importantly we had once and for all established the fact that the best in the WHA could play with the best the world had to offer. It was vindication. On that team were the best players and some of the finest people I'd ever worked with. For me personally, it was the most thrilling ride I'd ever been on. We were in a strange land surrounded by strange and sometimes unfriendly circumstances, and we had stuck together. We bonded as a team in a way I'd never seen before, and it was a privilege to be a part of it. For two months we were the center of attention in the hockey world and I thrived on it.

# 13

# THE WORLD HOCKEY
# DISASSOCIATION

**Tales circulated about players on other teams having to take their gear home at night because the club was afraid everything would be repossessed.**

W E HADN'T WON AS MANY GAMES AS we should have, but the Summit Series had been the greatest experience of my hockey career. Even after the plane touched down again in Canada I was still flying. But when I returned to work in the World Hockey Association, I fell back to earth with a bump.

The first news when I got home was that the opening of our new Coliseum in Edmonton was delayed yet again. Things had not gone smoothly from the start. Batoni Bowlen Enterprises had projected that the building would be ready for the end of the 1973–74 season. That sounded great to me. But that early opening wasn't to be. Steel workers went on strike and elevator operators walked off the job. When workers started to sink the pilings, they discovered the site sat on a virtual underground river and the foundation had to be redesigned. It rained so heavily through June that the holes for the pilings had to be pumped out every day. Then there was a country-wide shortage of steel that delayed work for another two months. Peter Batoni and Paul Bowlen had to rustle up steel wherever they could and pay a premium for it, too. Now there was another delay, and the Oilers had to open their season with a two-week road trip while crews finished the Coliseum.

I don't think I've ever been so happy to see the doors open on a building as I was on November 10, when we played our first Coliseum game. Workers were still bolting down seats as the fans came in. Some fans even grabbed a wrench and helped. The Oilers were sitting on wooden boxes since our dressing room had only one bench. It didn't have a shower yet, either. The women in the concession booths worked in their winter coats because of overactive refrigeration. But the Northlands Coliseum was up and running at last. It was ours, and it was beautiful.

There were the usual speeches of welcome, but I was so excited I hardly noticed them. Then came the announcement: "And now, the man that's made it all happen. . . ." I was brought to center ice, and the crowd started chanting "Bill, Bill, Bill." They stood on their feet and roared out an ovation that seemed to last for hours. I stood there, waving and thanking the crowd. I couldn't have been happier.

We gave the Coliseum a proper opening, winning our first game against the Cleveland Crusaders and setting a WHA regular season attendance record of 15,326.

The Oilers were still fun for me. Our first two seasons had been winners, if just barely, with 38–37–3 records. And we were a huge hit with the fans. Despite the small size of the late, unlamented Edmonton Gardens, we led the WHA in attendance for its first two years.

I was working with some true heroes of the game. Jacques Plante, the legendary goalie and the first to use a mask, wasn't happy

*The Edmonton Coliseum, now the Skyreach Centre.*

as coach and general manager of the Nordiques when he came up to me at a league meeting. "Bill, I want to come out of retirement," he said. I was stunned. Jacques was 46. "Are you really serious?" I asked. "Look," he said, "I'm in perfect shape, I've always kept myself in perfect shape, and I'm ready to play." It was true. Jacques trained religiously and watched his diet closely. And so for $150,000 a season, the great Jacques Plante pulled on an Oilers jersey. It was a thrill for me to sign one of the great men of hockey, and it was pretty good publicity, too. I think even Jacques was surprised when he won eight of his first nine games. Fans loved his wild dashes and puck handling, and they would call up to ask if Jacques was playing that night. If he was, we'd sell out. Jacques' comeback, however, didn't last. He only played home games, and when the team was on a road trip, Jacques scrimmaged with the Oil Kings. A puck hit him in the ear, and shortly after he started having equilibrium problems. He called it quits after one year and a 15–14–1 WHA record.

The next year I picked up Normie Ullman. In fact, Norm had been one of our four top draft picks in 1972. But his agent was Alan Eagleson, and it took us a long time to sign him. I knew Alan by this time and trusted him not at all. I wanted to make sure that what I was hearing in negotiations was coming from Norm's mouth, not Alan's. "Before we offer Normie any kind of contract, he's going to be there in room with us," I told Eagleson. So the three of us met in an expensive restaurant in Toronto. Eagleson never chose any other kind, especially since I was paying. I said to Norm, "Here's what we're prepared to pay you. It's a one-year contract and we'll negotiate at the end of that year for a second year or a third—whatever your desire is. You know that if you play well we'll want you back." Normie said, "Yes, I know that, Bill." I gave him a solid offer that was tough to turn down, and he accepted it without countering, right in front of Eagleson. Norm and I cut him right out. It was probably the only time I ever got one over on Alan, and I took great pleasure in it. Normie went on to score his 500th professional goal with the Oilers.

Nick Mileti starting up the Cleveland Crusaders in the league's second year was another bright spot. Getting Nick was a huge coup for us. He was one of the top sports entrepreneurs in the U.S. and owned the Cleveland Indians ball club and the Cleveland Cavaliers basketball team. Nick was another owner angry with the NHL. He felt he'd been promised a franchise, and when it went to someone else he called me up. "I'm with you," he growled. He built a magnificent new coliseum on some Ohio farmland and brought Frank Sinatra in to open it. Those farm roads weren't designed for the kind of traffic Ol' Blue Eyes attracted, though. It caused the biggest traffic jam in the history of the state.

Some good things had happened in the league's front office, too. In our second year we replaced Gary Davidson with Dennis Murphy as league president. It was a decision that had to be made to get the league running on a businesslike basis. Davidson was just not capable of sound administration, and Dennis was a vast improvement.

In many ways, though, the damage had been done. I knew there were going to be problems when we started the WHA, but I had no idea there were going to be so many. At one point we had 48 lawsuits served against us for everything from player contracts to arena management to unpaid bills. We spent almost as much on lawyers as we did on players. In one year alone we paid out a million dollars in lawsuits. That was cash that you could never recover, enough money for half a hockey team. And the American clubs were a constant drain. The Canadians were always there with their money and their fees, but half the time the Americans came up short or were in the middle of some nasty ownership dispute or on the verge of collapse. We could never collect from them, and we always had to make up the difference ourselves. And every time we had to step in to fix problems, it took cash. A television contract bringing in extra revenue could have helped, but we didn't have one. Even though the Oilers had spent two years in the smallest building in the league, the team would have been able to break even at the end of the third year. The league, however, which lost about $20 million in its first two years, kept dragging us down.

Three American owners from Detroit, for example, came to Russia with us to strut around Moscow with their wives. I got a call informing me that they hadn't paid players their meal money during training camp and that they were behind on arena rent. Ben suggestedjokingly we let the Russians take them out back and shoot them, but we quietly shifted them out of the league, grateful that the arena owners didn't hold us to our lease. Other teams come to Edmonton, stayed at the Westin Hotel and left without paying their bills. The Oilers picked up the tab to maintain goodwill in the community. Tales circulated about players on other teams having to take their gear home at night because the club was afraid everything would be repossessed. We heard rumors of teams being refused boarding at the airport because they hadn't paid for their last flight. One day Joe Schwartz, who had owned the San Diego Mariners for a year and a half, called his general manager, Ron Ingram, and said, "Ron, here's a cheque for the payroll and all the bills. We're paid up, and that's the last you'll ever hear from me. I'm out." We never heard from him again. We had another owner, a major chicken farmer from the Midwest who'd sunk $700,000 into the Los Angeles team, pull the same vanishing act.

Where the league had nice professional arenas, we were charged steep rent. Madison Square Gardens charged the New York Raiders a fortune. Harold Ballard charged John Bassett's Toros $50,000 a game for Maple Leaf Gardens. Eventually, after attending a constant string of desperate league meetings, it became clear to me that life was going to stay very, very difficult for a long, long time. Again and again, we'd fix a problem or make some progress and one of the owners would torpedo us.

Merging with the NHL, our original goal, would have ended our problems, and we'd had some talks as early as 1973, only to have them founder on the issue of the reserve clause. Ben and I came very close in 1976 after some secret talks in New York. Sid Solomon from the St. Louis Blues, Bill Jennings, and other NHL representatives met with us to discuss how we could merge. One of the cracks in the ice was over underage players, and Ben and I pledged that the WHA wouldn't sign any. We flew from there to Toronto, where we repeated the promise at a CAHA meeting. The NHL made the same commitment. On the way to the airport for a league meeting in Chicago, Ben and I got some news: John Bassett, now of Birmingham, and Bill Giles of Cincinnati had just signed a whole group of underage players. At the meeting I blew my top. I told them straight out, "The worst goddamned enemies this league has are sitting here at this table." Some of the owners were in shock, some understood why I was so angry, but far too many didn't give a damn. It was after that meeting that I decided I'd had enough. I never got discouraged, but I got more and more frustrated and angry. Finally, I decided this wasn't what I wanted.

My problems weren't just with the league, either. For the last 18 months there had been trouble at home with the partners. Zane and Charles were having serious disagreements and were actually suing each other. There was so much rancor we couldn't even have a meeting. Nobody outside the organization knew the extent of the trouble, and I had to keep covering it up. I was caught in an impossible situation. Meanwhile, Charles' attitude toward hockey salaries hadn't changed a bit. It was impossible for me to sign several outstanding players because the ownership group wasn't willing to cough up enough money.

My first thought was to buy my partners out. I flew to Toronto and made a deal with Wilmot Tennyson, president of Carling O'Keefe breweries. He would back me with all the cash I needed to buy out Charles and Zane. I knew they'd sell. Charles wanted out, anyway. Carling O'Keefe and I would be equal partners with the brewer agreeing to inject $5 million to improve the team's roster, an essential part of the offer because we needed development money. We'd been operating on the cheap for too long. It was starting to show on the ice, and the fans and the reporters were noticing.

The Carling O'Keefe offer was a great deal. With the backing of a major corporation, I'd have control of the club the way I would have if I'd taken Paul Bowlen's offer the first time around. I'd still have the problem of the league, but I figured I could hold out until we eventually amalgamated with the NHL, which had to happen sooner or later. I was overjoyed when Carling O'Keefe said yes.

The next morning Wilmot was to come over to the hotel to sign the papers. I met with Ben Hatskin, who also happened to be in Toronto. Ben, Wilmot and I celebrated with a good meal and a few bottles of wine. But at 7:00 A.M. the next morning Wilmot called me. "We have to see you, Bill," he said. "We're coming over for breakfast." When he arrived he handed me a letter from Carling O'Keefe's controller. The Quebec Nordiques were in financial trouble and had called on Carling O'Keefe to help them out. Wilmot thought that the company had only agreed to finance them through the end of the season, but the controller understood that they had agreed to buy the team if necessary. In the middle of that kind of confusion, they couldn't go ahead with our arrangement. One day I had the greatest deal in the world and the next day I had nothing.

That deal's collapse finally finished me as owner of the Oilers. I'd sold the Oil Kings the previous year, and now it was time to sell the Oilers. I just couldn't go on. Owning the team was no fun anymore. I said to Charles, "We just can't carry on this way." He agreed. I got the same response from Zane.

There was a buyer waiting in the wings—a fast-money, flashy guy from the West Coast named Nelson Skalbania. Charles handled the sale. I had almost nothing to do with it and hardly even met the new owner. Skalbania gave us a horrible offer, but we wanted out, and it was our only choice. It actually cost us money. We didn't sell the club, we gave it away, although we did get Skalbania to promise that the club would stay in Edmonton. Zane and Charles were businessmen getting out of a bad deal, but I was selling off everything I had worked toward since I'd bought the Regina Caps thirty years before. The Oilers were my future and my life. I was heartbroken. On June 10, 1976, I held my last press conference as the general manager of the Edmonton Oilers. About 300 reporters and businessmen came out to hear me say good-bye. If they ever felt that I'd called bogus press conferences in the past, well, this time I had something for them. I guess I was a little bitter.

"My wife and I talked for many hours, and I examined the total picture of my life and what we really wanted and reached a decision that was most difficult to make," I told the assembled scribes.

"I want to make it clear that my decision is not based on some of the malicious criticism we have received, but based on the fact that I have enjoyed over 35 years in the great game of hockey, for which I will forever be indebted.

"I want to take a little time out and perhaps reestablish myself in a field of business which I very much enjoyed and that gives me the environment to contribute and enjoy my wife and family. Besides, I need to make some money."

And that was it. When I walked away from the Oilers, I left them playing in a new building with a solid core of talent. In a league that had become a bad-debt joke, I left a team that paid its bills and treated its players well. But I didn't leave a team that was playing in the NHL, and that had been the whole idea. I'd fallen short. After that press conference, I turned the key in my office door and never went back.

Three years later, the Oilers, the Jets, the Nordiques and the Whalers were accepted into the NHL. Birmingham and Cincinnati were bought out for $3 million each. The merger had finally happened. The Oilers' first home game as an NHL franchise was played at the Coliseum on October 13. Vi and I were invited as honored guests. Bruce Norris from the Red Wings and John Ziegler, president of the NHL, were in town as well, and we all met at a reception before the game. They spent almost the entire time talking with Vi and me. I think Peter Pocklington, who then owned the team, felt a bit left out. Alberta Premier Peter Lougheed and Edmonton mayor Cec Purves spoke before the game. And then the crowd start-

*A trip down memory lane: WHA team logos from start to finish.*

ed to chant, quietly at first, then swelling until it seemed as if all 16,000 Oilers fans were yelling, "We want Bill! We want Bill! We want Bill!"

The hairs prickled on the back of my neck and my eyes welled with tears. I never been so proud. The fans knew who'd done the work and taken the risks to bring the big leagues off their radios and TVs and onto their home ice. They knew who had believed in them when others said that pro hockey couldn't survive in the west. It hadn't taken a genius to figure out that if the NHL wouldn't let us in through the front door, we'd have to kick our way in through the back. The same process had happened in baseball, football and basketball. But someone had had to drop the puck and get the process going in hockey. And he'd had to do it in a town whose love of the game would repay his faith. The fans' outpouring of gratitude that night paid for everything I'd endured in a quarter-century of hockey since C.B. Whitney took off with my money back in 1946. The Coliseum spotlights picked out me and Ben in the stands. We stood and waved.

# 14

# THE SASKATCHEWAN BLUES

**We started selling season tickets for a team that didn't exist to play in a building that was only a pile of drawings, and before long we had 18,694 season ticket pledges . . .**

LEAVING THE OILERS WAS LIKE LEAVING a part of myself behind. But I've always known that the best way to get over a disappointment is to start something new, and it wasn't long before I did.

Edmonton was abuzz with talk of a new newspaper coming to town to take on the established *Edmonton Journal.* The timing was certainly right. Alberta was in the middle of an oil boom. The province was awash in money and $40-a-barrel oil, and the construction cranes over Edmonton's growing skyline were sprouting up like great, ungainly trees. Sun Media had announced it was coming to town with its cheeky blend of saucy headlines, cops and courts, splashy photos, sports, right-wing politics and Sunshine girls. The chain needed someone to take charge of the *Edmonton Sun*'s fledgling ad sales department, and president Doug Creighton called me to ask if I was interested. Doug and I had first met when he'd covered the 1966 Memorial Cup for the *Toronto Telegram*. He knew I could get things done and had plenty of contacts in Edmonton's business community. I agreed to take the job for a year with an option for another. I spent several weeks in Toronto learning how the newspaper advertising business worked, and six months before the tabloid's first issue rolled off the press, I was on the job.

My last journalism experience had been with CFQC Radio in Saskatoon after the Second World War, so it had been a long time since I'd been in the hurly-burly of the news business. It turned out to be just the thing I needed: stimulating, novel and endlessly hectic with its constant deadlines and ringing phones. My job was to set up their ad department, including recruiting and training the sales people. The usual crowd of naysayers gathered round to tell us we'd fail, but we went ahead, got the *Sun* up and running, and it's been a success ever since. I didn't stay long, however. I was gone after the year I'd promised I'd stay.

For a while I went back to First Investors, now the Principal Group. I had a fancy title—general sales manager and senior vice president in charge of sales—and I supervised 450 staff. But something had changed in the company.

When I had started with First Investors, we were small and hungry and knew that the most important element of our success would be the quality, integrity and motivation of our people. Upper management seemed to be losing touch with the fundamentals. They were becoming big, arrogant and forgetful of what had made them successful. Shortly after I rejoined, I was on the company's executive committee. I didn't like what I saw. I didn't like the way the money was being handled. Management was starting to look at government regulations as something to be sidestepped rather than obeyed. Don Cormie had hired me and I had once admired him. But he was starting to make decisions that weren't consistent with the best business practices. I spoke my mind at a couple of meetings, but nothing changed and I decided to leave. First Investors offered to double my salary, but after my concerns were ignored, money wasn't going to keep me around. After about two and half years, I wanted out.

Some years later, when First Investors–Principal Group came crashing down and the government started to investigate what had done with people's life savings, I was glad I'd walked out the door when I did.

Hockey was calling me again. Although I was officially out of the sport, unofficially I had kept my hand in. In the late 1970s my son Bart had played junior hockey in Spruce Grove with an outstanding young center named Mark Messier. Mark was now playing for the Cincinnati Stingers in the WHA. He wasn't having a good rookie year, but I knew where his talent could take him. I got on the phone to Bob Freeman, who had been my chief scout with Oil Kings and was now chief scout for the Oilers. We met for coffee. "Bob, you people just gotta sign Mark," I told him. "Cincinnati probably won't put up too much of a fuss, and he'll do an outstanding job for you." Whether or not it was my suggestion that convinced Bob to sign Mark I never knew, but I knew I had at least tipped him to Messier's potential. Shortly after that I was in Calgary watching my beloved Hounds play in a midget tournament over Christmas. Terry O'Malley, one of the teachers at Notre Dame, was also the playing coach of the Canadian national team, and he took me along to a game the Nats were playing against Sweden. On the ice was a forward the likes of which I'd never seen before—extremely fast and very aggressive going to the net. He was only 16 or 17, but you couldn't take your eyes off him. After the game Terry and I went for a meal and I said, "Terry, this kid looks like something else. He can just fly."

"Yes, he can," said Terry. "He's a bit flaky, but he's got the potential to be a great hockey player."

I met with Bob again. "There's this kid playing with the national team you won't believe, a kid named Glenn Anderson."

Together with some friends including Vic Mah and Wayne Tennant, I even resurrected the Oil Kings into the WHL. Now that the Oilers were in town, though, we couldn't make a go of it. We wound up selling the team to a Portland businessman who moved them to North Dakota.

By the time 1980 rolled around, hockey had gotten its hooks solidly back into me. When I left the Oilers and the flux and chaos of the WHA, I was relieved to get away from the tension. For a while I was simply happy to get up in the morning and not have to wonder what sort of hell was going to break out that day. But after a while I started to miss the tension and uncertainty. I missed the challenge of starting something on my own, of challenging everyone's expectations. And most of all I missed hockey. I wanted back in. And this time I wasn't going to be content in the juniors or with trying to force my way in to the majors through any back door. This time I wanted right into the NHL.

But where? The answer was obvious. There really wasn't any choice.

Saskatchewan was the only province west of the Maritimes without a big-league hockey team. And it had always been hockey heartland. Saskatchewan boys have been among the best in the NHL since the league's inception, all the way from Doug and Max Bentley to Elmer Lach to Gordie Howe. Saskatchewan people love their teams. Given a chance they'd take an NHL franchise to their hearts as deeply and passionately as any fans in the league. And wouldn't it be grand to be the one to bring it home for them, to launch NHL hockey in the province where my dad's Quakers had won championships? The more I thought about the idea, the more it felt like destiny. This would be my greatest challenge. This would be my legacy.

A lot of work needed to be done. For one thing there was no big-league arena in the province. I knew I'd need powerful allies to get one built, so in early 1981 I called Allan Blakeney, then Saskatchewan's NDP premier, and asked for a meeting. I always found Allan very approachable (he used to answer his own phone with the greeting, "Hi. It's Allan."), and we had a productive meeting. Allan put his top bureaucrat in charge of sports and recreation on it. Bill Clarke had been a former Saskatchewan Roughrider, and he was just as enthusiastic as his boss. With Allan and Bill behind the idea, things began to move. But six months after our meeting, Saskatchewan voters tossed out the NDP and elected Grant Devine and his Tories. Vi and I were more than just dismayed watching the news that night. I never thought I'd be pulling for an NDP government, but I was just about sick watching the returns come in. I thought I'd have to start all over again.

Much to my relief, Devine kept Bill Clarke, who set up a meeting with Devine and two of his top men: Eric Berntsen, Devine's right-hand man in cabinet, and cabinet minister Paul Schoenhals, who had once coached the Saskatoon Hilltops, the team that grew out of the ashes of my old Dukes. I was pleased to learn that they were excited at the prospect of pro hockey for Saskatchewan.

"Where do you want to build this arena, Bill?" Devine asked me.

"What about right in Regina here, just north of the city on the highway to Saskatoon?" I suggested.

Regina sounded good to them. But the more I thought about it, the more I realized I really wanted to put the team in my home-town of Saskatoon. I called my old acquaintance Cliff Wright. We'd both attended Nutana Collegiate, and now he was the city's mayor. I told him what I had in mind.

The next Saturday morning the two of us met privately at city hall. He showed me maps of two properties, one south of the city and one north. And after that meeting I knew for certain Saskatoon would be the place. Somehow, it felt right to be returning pro hockey to the town that had once cheered the Saskatoon Sheiks. Saskatoon had been the smallest city in North America to support a pro team back in the 1920s, and I was determined to make history repeat itself.

Of course, first I needed to find a team. And as it happened, an NHL franchise was available. In 1976 the NHL had moved the old Kansas City Scouts to Denver, Colorado, with the hope of stabilizing the franchise, but it hadn't worked out. Owners had changed amid years of financial bleeding, and by 1982 it looked as if the club might be on the move again. The NHL had assigned my old friend Emile Francis, now president and general manager of the St. Louis Blues, to sort things out. Emile said he'd help me get in touch with the owner of the Denver franchise. We figured the club could be had for U.S. $8–10 million. I got in touch with the owner, all right, but he broke every single appointment we made. He'd promise to meet in Denver but wouldn't show up. We'd set something up for another city, and he'd call just before the date to cancel, usually sounding as if he'd had more than a couple drinks. It was frustrating. He obviously wasn't interested in dealing with me, and I gave up.

Things were moving much faster with the arena. I had formed a company called Batoni Hunter Enterprises with Peter Batoni, who had built the Northlands Coliseum. In early 1982 we leased some space in the CN Tower and hired five staff, managed by my daughter Bev. Peter was going to build the arena and become an owner, too, but he had to drop out of that. I had dozens of meetings with the government about that building. Paul Schoenals led the charge for us and eventually we got the government to turn over a parcel of land on the north side of Saskatoon near the airport. We got the land complete with services and a 10-year tax holiday. Access roads would be built and a new bridge put in to speed traffic. Not bad, I thought.

When Peter decided to drop out of the ownership group, I had to find new partners. I quickly got together with Saskatoon businessmen Les Dube, John Sellinger and Bill Mitchell to form the Saskatchewan Coliseum and Hockey Club Ltd. I put together a total financial package of about $78 million to build an arena and ice a team in it. We got a $38 million mortgage on our building with the help of Jim Burns, president and CEO of Power Corp., whom I knew from his days as president of the Winnipeg Jets. We struck a marketing deal with Morgan McAmmond at Molson's Breweries for $28 million, part of it up front. The rest we borrowed from the Royal Bank. I borrowed $8 million myself on the strength of the 18 percent of the shares I would receive. Finally, we cut a deal with the Saskatchewan Securities Commission allowing us to release a public share offering after a year of operation. We estimated that selling 60 percent of our shares could bring in about $75 million.

Our building would cost about $48 million, roughly $38 million of which was covered by a first mortgage. It would be beautiful. Peter Batoni, a dynamic little man who walked about a foot off the ground when he got excited, did the initial design. I described what I wanted to him one day over breakfast, and he whipped off a sketch on a restaurant napkin that became the concept for the whole project.

I had land. I had money. I even had a plan for a building. But I still didn't have a line on a team, and once again Emile Francis came through. In the fall of 1982 Emile and I were in Edmonton

*Prior to announcing our purchase of the St. Louis Blues, the owner-ship group and political leaders met. L–R: Mayor Cliff Wright, Bill Mitchell, Bill Hunter, Premier Grant Devine, Les Dube, Paul Scheonals.*

watching the Oilers take on the Blues. At his hotel suite after the game, Emile asked, "Look, Bill, why don't you buy our team?"

"What do you mean?" I asked. "Is your team for sale?"

"Yes," he said. "It's not publicly advertised, but it's basically always been for sale."

Emile laid the situation out for me. The Blues were owned by Ralston Purina, the giant corporation headquartered in St. Louis. They had bought the team in the late 1970s when the Solomon fam-ily had gone bankrupt. The team nearly folded completely just a cou-ple months before the season was to open. That would have been a disaster for both the local fans and the league, which would have faced a huge public relations problem and would have had to completely revamp its schedule. Out of civic pride Ralston Purina stepped in to

*Peter Batoni, the dynamic builder of much of Edmonton's skyline.*

buy the arena and the team. They even renovated the arena and rebuilt the leaky old roof. But the company told the NHL board of governors that it would be only a caretaker owner and that the NHL was expected to help them find qualified local owners to take over the team. No doubt greatly relieved, the board faithfully promised they would. However, once Ralston Purina was safely aboard, the NHL was in no hurry to replace them. What could be better than a huge corporation with deep pockets owning a key Midwest franchise? Ralston Purina was stable, paid its dues on time and pulled their share of the load in running the league. John Baird, Ralston Purina's member on the board of governors, brought up the subject of new ownership at every annual meeting and he was told, "Oh yes, we're keeping our eyes open." The NHL was quite happy with things as they were.

Ralston Purina wasn't. William Stiritz had recently taken over as the company's CEO and chairman of the board, and he didn't like the $3-million boat anchor the Blues hung on his company's annual bottom line. He was now prepared to sell to anyone and didn't care if the Blues stayed in town.

"Emile," I said, "put me in touch with John Baird."

I called Baird and was delighted when he said he'd be happy to meet with me. In the fall of 1982 we set up the first of a series of secret meetings—at least we tried to keep them secret. Someone had let slip to the sports press that something was up between Saskatoon and St. Louis. For once it wasn't me who planted the rumors. We didn't need to drum up any enthusiasm with leaked reports, and we had every reason to keep things quiet until the deal was closed. We wanted to wring the most publicity we could from a dramatic announcement of the sale. I suspect the information was leaked by someone within Ralston Purina—a Blues fan, maybe—who didn't want to see the team sold and moved.

John Baird and I were in for an interesting time of it. We met all over North America in unlikely and out-of-way places, trying to dodge the media and keep our discussions under wraps. For a while life was like a spy movie. John and I checked into hotels under assumed names. We flew by private jets to meetings in strange cities. A couple times we even met in airplane hangars. I'd get out of the plane to find John sitting at table in the middle of a huge concrete floor. But our maneuvers never shook the reporters for long. Somehow they always found out about our negotiations.

At the same time we were holding all these talks, I was also starting to sell the idea of an NHL team to the people of Saskatchewan. I was on the road across the province, whipping up enthusiasm in those who hadn't caught the fever and keeping it burning in those who had. During the last three months of 1982 and the first three of 1983, I had 196 speaking engagements. Sometimes I'd do three a day—breakfast, lunch and dinner. A friend donated the use of his plane and hired a pilot to fly me around. Once, when we were trying to make a night landing in Kindersley, an airstrip without proper landing lights, local farmers parked their trucks along the side of the runway and turned their lights on so we could see to land. Then we drove to nearby Plenty, a hamlet of 87 souls, where 300 people packed the community hall to hear me speak. Then it was back to the Kindersley International, where the farmers duly lined up their trucks again so we could take off.

Everywhere I went, I pitched the dream of Saskatchewan joining the big leagues. I reminded the people about the long and passionate love they had for the game. I talked about the excitement of professional sports and the pride it would bring. I told them how good it would be for the economy and how it would bring international attention their way for a change. And everywhere I went, I told them, "This team is about you. This isn't Bill Hunter. This is about Saskatchewan standing up on the world stage. We deserve an NHL team." People were hungry for this message. The Rotary luncheons and community halls were packed to hear that someone believed in them. Vi and I stopped for a meals in little roadside restaurants, and people wouldn't take our money. We'd be told, "Mr. Hunter, don't worry about it. Your bill has been covered." Then we'd be signing autographs. People would stop us on the street and say, "We're behind you, Bill."

I decided Don Cherry would make a great head coach when we got a team in place. I knew he'd be the ideal man. He may be from Ontario, but he's Saskatchewan through and through. The province is full of straight-talking, homespun, cocky, confident people like Don. I went down east to meet with him and his wife, Rose. Over dinner I spelled out our plans. Not only could I offer him a great contract, but I had a TV and radio program lined up for him. He accepted. Don accompanied me on 27 speaking engagements, where his no-nonsense style was a big hit. He never let on that he was going to be the coach. We were saving that announcement, so Don spoke simply as a supporter of the idea of professional hockey in Saskatchewan. The people loved him. He praised them as great sports fans and invoked the names of the great Saskatchewan hockey players he'd known and coached. And everywhere we went there'd be a local boy Don could single out as a great future NHL talent.

I made it as easy as I could for people to buy season tickets. I met with the provincial heads of the five major banks, and they agreed to offer interest-free loans to anyone buying a season ticket for the new team. I met with the Saskatchewan Transportation Company, the provincially owned bus line, and persuaded them to set up a park-and-ride system for the entire province. No matter how nasty the weather, hockey fans could bus to the game in safety and comfort. In fact three groups of fans were so excited and confident about the team that they went out and actually bought busses to ride to the games, including one group from a native community in the northeast.

The pace was insane. At one point I tried to work through a bad attack of flu. I came into the office early to read through some documents when I suddenly broke out in a sweat and collapsed. The doctor put me to bed for three days in the Bessborough Hotel, where I was living at the time. "You've run the well dry, Bill," he told me. But I wasn't the only one working hard. Our whole staff routinely worked long in to the night, for we knew that momentum was everything. The mail alone was unbelievable. We were getting 3,500 pieces of mail a day, so much that the post office gave us our own postal code. It took three people every day to enter the ticket sales into our computer. The hard work and frantic pace paid off. I knew Saskatchewan was ready for the NHL, but I had no idea how ready they were. We started selling season tickets for a team that didn't exist to play in a building that was only a pile of drawings, and before long we had 18,694 season ticket pledges backed by letters recorded in a Price-Waterhouse computer. We had ticket-holders into the Dakotas.

Toward the end of 1982, talks with Ralston Purina were nearing an end. With the aid of two young lawyers named Brian Todd and Kevin Scott, who'd helped me all along, I headed to St. Louis for the final, make-or-break session. At that final round at Ralston Purina head office in Checkerdome Square in St. Louis, we sat across the table from a whole player's bench of lawyers and junior executives, centered by John Baird, an amiable giant of a man with whom I got on very well. The final issue to be settled concerned concessions. Ralston Purina had signed a contract with an outside company to handle all the concessions with the Blues. That contract stipulated that any new owner would have to honor the existing arrangement and Ralston Purina tried to hold us to it. Breaking their contract with their concession firm would cost them a lot of money, but I told them that was their problem. We had to run our concessions, both to retain total control of our operation and to make the most of every revenue source we could find.

"Careful, Bill," my lawyers pleaded as we talked during a break. "We're going to lose this."

"Let me handle this," I told them. "You two sit back and I'll consult with you at the breaks. We've got to play hardball here because we absolutely must have our own concessions. That's part of our budget. But we're in the driver's seat here. They're desperate to sell, and we're the first qualified buyers they've seen in years. We can beat them."

Talks stretched out for hours and into the next day. We'd take breaks, huddle up to plan our next move and then get back at it. Stiritz did not take part. But his team sent regular word up to him, and I have no doubt a constant stream of instructions came back down. Stiritz had his own man at the table, too. Right beside John sat someone I came to think of as the Hatchet Man. Solemn, thin-faced and dapper, he sat silently through the whole process. He just took notes and passed them to John, who read them closely. Finally, at four o'clock on the second day of talks, Ralston Purina caved. We had a deal. It included the Blues, the Salt Lake City International Hockey League franchise and all the player contracts for U.S. $14.5 million. John and I reached across the table to shake hands.

After all those years, I finally had an NHL franchise. Things were coming together and nothing could spoil my mood, not even the airport baggage attendant who recognized me from the pictures that had been splashed all over the St. Louis newspapers.

"You're Bill Hunter, aren't you?"

"Yes, I am."

"You're the guy who's trying to steal our team."

"First of all, son, I'm not stealing it," I said. "Secondly, I know how you feel. I'm sorry for you and your friends." After I checked in, I looked over at my two lawyer companions. "I'll bet my luggage doesn't arrive with me."

I was right. The airline lost my bags. They showed up a couple days later.

The actual papers were signed back in Regina at the Royal Bank Saskatchewan regional headquarters. We affixed our names late on a Tuesday night, and I called Bev immediately to tell her to start planning a big splash. She did us proud. Two days later she'd set up a breakfast meeting at the Centre of the Arts in Saskatoon for 800 people. Premier Devine was there. So was Cliff Wright. A sellout crowd was in attendance that morning for our moment of glory. Grant Devine sat beside me at the head table. We looked out at the sea of eager faces and Grant turned to me and said, "Look at how wonderful this is, Bill." Then, as I stood to tell the people the words they'd been waiting to hear, Grant grabbed my hand and raised it in triumph. Everything dissolved into a roar of cheering and a blaze of flashbulbs, loud and bright enough for an entire province. There were tears and hugs and backslaps and handshakes. The picture of Grant and I made front pages across Canada as the rest of the country cheered along with us.

I even went down to Ottawa to meet with Prime Minister Trudeau. He must have forgiven me for being slashed in the locker room before the Summit Series, for he promised all the support the federal government could give us.

That, however, was only half the battle. Ralston Purina had agreed to sell to us. Now we had to convince the NHL to allow us in. Ralston Purina officially notified the league of the sale on January 10, 1983. We had until the board of governors meeting in early May to make our case.

We were confident of our financial plans. Our building was sold out with a waiting list of 5,000. We had plans for 126 skyboxes with no doubt they would be snapped up. Saskatchewan fans stick with their teams, and we knew we'd have full houses for years down the road. We had already booked 196 events such as trade shows, ice shows and concerts. We owned our own concessions. We had major corporate support from Molson's. We also had some behind-the-scenes plans to take advantage of Saskatchewan's provincewide network of fiber optic cables. After the building was sold out and just before the season opened, we planned to announce pay-per-view game broadcasts for those who couldn't get tickets.

We felt our franchise would be good for the league, too. Rivalries crank up fan emotions in any sport, and the Saskatoon Blues would have been natural rivals for the Winnipeg Jets, the Calgary Flames and the Edmonton Oilers. Our entry into the league would have lowered travel costs for everyone by giving them an extra place to play when they came west. And adding a team in western Canada would have plugged the NHL even deeper into the game's heartland.

But it soon became clear that the NHL wasn't going to make our entry easy. We sent Bev down to St. Louis with boxes and boxes of documents the league's officials requested. It would have been impossible to examine all that paper, but the NHL wanted every niggling and nit-picking scrap of it, so we gritted our teeth and jumped through their hoops. Three or four times a day they'd call us with changes and additions to the list of documents.

John Ziegler, then president of the NHL, was smiling and affable in person, but behind our backs he was our worst enemy. In his mind we were stealing an American franchise. That was bad enough to a front office full of Americans, but Ziegler was worried about completely losing the Midwest U.S. market for NHL hockey. He didn't seem to care that the situation there wasn't viable. I'm sure there was a little residual resentment of me from my WHA days, too. Ziegler suggested to each of the owners that agreeing to transfer the Blues to Saskatoon would reduce the value of their franchises. He warned that the sale would lower the price of expansion fees, which are shared by the owners. He hinted that he was close to completing a long-awaited, lucrative deal for national TV rights, which the loss of the Blues to some Canadian hinterland would scuttle.

Many owners had originally been on our side, swayed by the positive press we were getting from people like syndicated sports columnist Jim Murray. But as Ziegler went to work, the owners who had been supportive began to drift away one by one. At one time Jerry Buss from Los Angeles had been such a big supporter of ours that he had invited Vi and I to come down to his estate and talk about making some player trades. Now he called me to say that he might not be able to support our bid after all. I got similar calls from Seymour Knox of the Sabres and Abe Polsen in Washington. It made me angry—not at them but at the people trying to sink us. I argued hard that Ziegler's stories were half-truths and that he had no television contract to jeopardize, that every year he said he was close to closing a television deal. The going was getting tough. A lot would depend on our presentation. We spent $700,000 getting everything just right. Our bid book alone cost $78,000. A German craftsman in Edmonton produced a beautiful scale model of our proposed building at a cost of $18,000.

By this time the story of the Blues coming to Saskatchewan had gone well beyond Saskatchewan and St. Louis. Every news outlet in the continent was following it. Bev was handling my media requests, and every day she'd reserve slots for the two Canadian TV networks and all the papers. NBC, CBS and ABC were covering it. The *Los Angeles Times* sent a reporter to Saskatoon. The *Toronto Star,* the *Globe and Mail* and the *Calgary Herald* all ran front-page surveys asking, "Should Saskatoon get an NHL team?" The results all came back resoundingly yes. I was everywhere, and I have to admit it was exciting. The whole continent was watching to see if this upstart group of prairie boys could pull it off, if we could wrench an NHL franchise home from the U.S. and set it up where everyone knew a pro hockey team rightfully belonged. Canadians love to cheer for an underdog, and we were that, all right.

Finally, May came and it was time to head to New York. Trudeau and Lalonde came through and the House of Commons passed a unanimous motion in our support. The City of Saskatoon gave us a huge send-off. You couldn't move in the airport. Well-wishers packed the place, many carrying posters and signs proclaiming, "Go Bill Go."

Ralston Purina's John Baird believed NHL approval was a done deal. He believed the league would recognize the great favor Ralston Purina had done it by bailing out the Blues when they had almost collapsed, and he was convinced the league would honor that moral obligation by rubber-stamping the sale. I'd been around long enough to have some doubts about the place of words such as *honor* and *moral* in professional sports. But John had asked me to let him do the lobbying. I hadn't spoken to any of the owners other than the

*Saskatoon to New York: Vi and I and our team headed off to New York after a wonderful send-off at the airport. The people of Saskatchewan had given it their all.*

ones who had called me. We were putting all our pucks in one basket: the presentation.

We actually had to make two presentations. The first was in Long Island to a special committee of the board of governors who would make a recommendation to the entire board. We'd expected a few of the governors to know where Saskatoon was, but it was a little disconcerting when we realized that most of them didn't know where Edmonton was, either, despite having had the Oilers in their league for years. In fact, as we were making our proposal for more hockey in western Canada, the team most governors couldn't locate on a map was across town playing the Islanders for the Stanley Cup. It was even more disconcerting when I watched the representative from the Vancouver Canucks fall asleep in the middle of our pitch.

The next day—May 18, 1983—was the big sell in the Helmsley Palace Hotel. Each team was allowed two representatives. We needed a 75 percent majority to approve the transfer.

We gave our presentation in the morning. The governors

seemed apathetic at first. Some were reading the morning papers, and Ziegler had to call the meeting to order to get their attention. Paul Schoenhals said the project had the government's full support and spoke about the history of hockey in Saskatchewan and how much people love the game. Cliff Wright told them about Saskatoon. Boyd Robertson spoke about finances and Peter Batoni about the arena. Les Dube spoke for the owners. I wrapped the presentation up. We all knew our material. We'd practiced our pitches many times. At one point Peter Pocklington from Edmonton leaned over and whispered that we should alter our financial package. He'd be happy to show us how, he said, as if he were on our side. But we weren't about to make any changes. Few questions followed our presentation. Most had been asked the previous day—the predictable stuff about the size of the market, the opening date of the arena and the state of our finances. Bill Wirtz of the Blackhawks, the powerful chairman of the board and a good friend of ours, jumped to his feet and said, "I want you to know that's the finest presentation our league has ever had!" With that the room broke out in applause.

Then came the waiting. We had to return to our hotel room and sit while the governors discussed our bid and took the vote on which my dreams depended. The wait was awful. All the presenters were there, and many of our wives and families had joined us. We ordered food, but nobody could eat. We nibbled away and mumbled conversation. I paced up and down the hallway, trying not to think.

Finally, Ziegler sent a messenger upstairs.

The word, of course, was no. I'd been braced for it, even half expecting it. I knew we'd had some support. Calgary was solidly in our corner. So was Montreal. But I also knew that even some of the Canadian owners had gone against us. Harold Ballard, despite our long relationship, turned me down. Peter Pocklington did, too. Still, I wasn't prepared for the crushing weight that tiny syllable dumped on my shoulders. It was the weight of four decades of traveling with teams from towns the NHL board of governors didn't know existed in leagues they couldn't name. It was the weight of a lifetime of hard work and big risks. It was the weight of forcing my way to the doorstep of the NHL not once, but twice. It was the weight not only of my dreams, but also those of a province. And somewhere in the back of my mind, there was a bit of weight from my father. Jack Hunter was long gone, but somehow I thought that this would have pleased him, wherever he was. Bill Mitchell looked at me and said, "It wasn't right what they did to you, Bill."

After a while we went downstairs for a drink. We couldn't think of what else to do. The hotel was crawling with reporters, and they were all over us, asking questions about our bid. They were incredulous when we told them we'd been denied. Ziegler was in the lounge, too, with some NHL people.

Ziegler walked up to me and said, "I'm sorry, Bill."

I said the only thing I could before turning my back: "Don't tell me you're sorry, John."

# 15

# THE TURNING POINT

**Vi didn't know why it seemed so impor-
tant, but she was driven to get off that
train. She described the compulsion as
an anguish beyond anything.**

W E FLEW BACK TO SASKATOON A QUIET,
exhausted and disheartened bunch while I ran an in-flight movie
inside my head of everything we'd done over the past 18 months. I
wasn't trying to think of anything we'd done wrong—I knew we'd
done our best, and I'm not one to second-guess myself, anyway. But
the effort to bring the Blues to Saskatoon had been so consuming
and had swallowed up so much of my heart that I couldn't let go.
I'd given myself completely over to the Blues. Now that I'd lost them,
I didn't know what else to think about.

There was a civic reception for us when we landed. People were
subdued but proud. They knew they hadn't lost the Blues. The
Blues were taken from them.

The people of Saskatchewan weren't the only ones who felt we'd
been cheated. Cliff Fletcher, president of the Calgary Flames, and

Doc Seaman, one of the team's owners, had been two of our biggest supporters. Doc and I were old friends from Saskatchewan. His family had farmed near Notre Dame when I was at school there, and Doc had been such a good ball player that I'd I tried to talk him into coming with us the summer our team went on the road. Doc now called me to say he thought our plans were worth one last shot at a series of NHL meetings scheduled that summer for Chicago. I hadn't been invited, but Doc said he'd get me a special hearing in front of the board of governors. Les Dube led our original presentation, but Les wasn't a hockey man and nobody around the table knew him. They all knew me, and Doc figured those personal relationships and my ability to put a sales pitch across the table would make the difference. "Bill, if you come on your own and make the entire presentation yourself, you might have a chance to get the decision reversed," Doc told me. A citizen's committee in Saskatoon had been formed to support me, and they figured it was worth a try, too.

I appreciated everyone's support, but I had to turn the idea down. I'd never thrown up my hands in resignation before, but my failure to land the Blues in Saskatoon had taken so much out of me that I had no heart to fight anymore. I figured the NHL's mind was made up. I probably sounded bitter. "To hell with 'em," I told Doc.

Still, I'm always willing to try another tack. Shortly after I chose not to go to Chicago, I got a call from Barry Shenkarow, owner of the Winnipeg Jets. "Maybe you should consider buying our team, Bill," he said. This sounded worth considering. If the NHL wouldn't let us take over an American franchise, maybe they wouldn't kick so hard if we bought one of the Canadian teams. I lined up a couple new partners, a wealthy man from the coast named Ron Dixon and Bill Comrie, who had played for me with the Oil Kings and who now owned The Brick chain of furniture stores. I hopped a plane to Winnipeg and met privately with Shenkarow. Prospects seemed promising, so I met with the mayor and laid out some plans for a new arena in the middle of the city. When that went well, too, my two partners and I met with Shenkarow, and we came to a quick deal to buy the team for $50 million. Shenkarow seemed pleased, and he promised he'd have the legal papers to me within days for my signature.

I flew back to Saskatoon, once again thinking I was in. I guess I still hadn't learned. I waited for those documents for days. Eventually, I called Shenkarow. When I asked where the papers were, he started to waffle. I was a little exasperated. "Barry, are you selling? Yes or no?" I asked him. The answer, of course, was no. Why Shenkarow changed his mind at the last minute after leading us along for weeks only Shenkarow knows.

In 1985–86 Bill Comrie and I considered making another bid for an NHL expansion franchise in Saskatoon. Ottawa and Hamilton were bidding, too. We had Husky Oil willing to come in with us. The Sask Place arena was already built, and we thought we could just expand it and add some skyboxes. We got the expansion book from the NHL, and it looked like the price for getting into the league would be within our means—about U.S. $20–25 million. We felt confident. But at an owner's meeting in Florida, the governors decided to boost the expansion fee to U.S. $50 million, plus another U.S. $10 million for operating expenses. When we heard the news, Bill and I looked at each other. We both knew that the bar had been raised too high for us to clear. In six or seven years, I'd seen the price of an NHL franchise escalate from the U.S. $14.5 million I'd negotiated with Ralston Purina for an existing team to the U.S. $60 million the league now wanted just to join the club.

That round of expansion was the final death knell for my dream of pro hockey in Saskatoon. And to be honest, another disappointment by that time didn't bother me too much. The early 1980s had been tough years for me in the hockey business. It seemed everything I tried was either sabotaged or doomed. I'd been getting sick of the whole thing for a while now, and by the time Bill and I realized that the Saskatoon dream was over, I was up to my ears in an entirely new venture: *Sask Report.*

I'd been in and out of the world of journalism most of my life. I'd filed sports copy for the Regina *Leader-Post* while I was at Notre Dame, covered court, general news and sports for CFQC radio in Saskatoon after the war and helped the *Edmonton Sun* start up its ad sales department. I liked the business and I liked reporting. It kept you in the middle of the action, and there was something about the constant hustle and commotion of it all that I enjoyed. It's a people business, too, and I'm always interested in anything that brings me together with people.

My travels around Saskatchewan preaching the gospel of the Blues had brought me into close contact with the heart of the province. I saw a unique society of proud people where the rest of the country too often saw desolation. I saw a profound sense of community and a feeling for roots that is found nowhere else in the west. Some great stories were going untold, and the market for those was untapped. I felt there was an opportunity for a newsmagazine that spoke to those people about their own place and looked at the world from their point of view. I announced *Sask Report* in April 1985, and we had 40,000 copies of the first issue off the presses by June.

We couldn't have picked a tougher time to start. The Canadian magazine industry is always tenuous, and those days were more difficult than most. Saskatchewan was in the middle of a recession, and money for advertising was tight. But I had a strategy I was certain would make my magazine a success. Every month we'd feature a town—Kelvington or Weyburn or Swift Current. A couple months in advance, I'd visit the town and meet with the mayor, the chamber of commerce, the tourism authority and local business leaders. I'd tell them about our plans to feature their town and ask them for story ideas, written by their own writers if that's what they wanted. Then we'd send in our own scribe to write the feature piece. The town would go on the front cover, too. The concept sold like Round-Up in spraying season. We wrote up a ton of ads for those town features, and they made *Sask Report* financially viable.

The other pot of advertising money we had to dig into was the government's. Government ads are a huge source of revenue for any publication, especially in Saskatchewan with all its Crown corporations. I hunted those dollars hard. I visited all the head offices of SaskPower, SaskTel, the Saskatchewan Transportation Company and more. I went to Premier Devine and my friends in cabinet and told them what I had in mind. I wasn't going to become a propaganda organ for government, but I was going to try to make people feel good about themselves and where they lived. And when they feel good about themselves, that's good for any government, I told them.

I knew I'd need an editor, and I hired Jack Cook, the respected veteran desker from the *StarPhoenix*. I needed a manager and fellow ad salesman, too, and I got a wonderful surprise one day when my son Bart called me. "Dad, I want to go with you," he said. I tried to talk him out of it. He was a rising young sales rep with Xerox Corporation, and I suggested staying there was the more prudent course. "Bart, you can't afford to leave Xerox. We have no pension or medical benefits. We may not even be in business three months from now." He insisted, and to be honest I couldn't have been more pleased. He joined us just before the June issue came out and actually got some ads in our first edition.

We stole ideas from everyone. We learned from *Alberta Report,*
*Macleans, Saturday Night,* whoever we could. But we had our own
style, too. Our forté was success stories—the farmer who had a
unique way of raising cattle or the manufacturer who was competing around the world from some tiny town. Once a year we did an
all-native issue, where we'd feature aboriginal bands from around
the province. We were always adding and trying new ideas from
writers or the public or even advertisers. Many publications put up
a firewall between the editorial and the advertising department, but
not us. Who hears what's going on the business community and in
the public better than those in the ad department? They're out there
every day, talking to new businesses, old businesses, people of all
kinds. And people drive the news business. The ad sales people
never dictated which stories ran, but they gave us lots of ideas.

I wrote a publisher's column. But the rest of the time I was
bringing in money—selling ads, making contacts, meeting with
town and government officials. Like all magazines, we had issues
planned months in advance. And before long we had mayors calling
us up: "When are you going to feature my town?"

Political subjects were touchy for us. If we covered a political
issue, we'd turn over some space to the Tories and the NDP and let
them argue it out between themselves. Sure, we got accused of playing softball with the government. Some even said we had an agreement with the Devine Tories. But the only agreement we ever had
was that the economic development department would supply us
with a series of positive stories on Saskatchewan industry, stories we
would have done anyway. We had to run them, but we could edit
them as we wanted. And in return we got guaranteed ad revenue.
The amount of money the government spent with us even became
an issue in the legislature. I got on the phone to Roy Romanow,
leader of the NDP opposition. "Roy, what the hell are you trying to

do to us?" I pleaded. "Look at the ink we've given your party and your candidates. Your party advertises more in our magazine than the Tories." Roy just laughed. "Bill, that's politics," he said. "Question Period's where you shoot and try to dig up dirt, and Bill, it's all tongue in cheek."

We weren't naive. We knew governments change, and we'd take the chance to give the NDP a bit of a boost sometimes, too. Then I'd get a call from some functionary deep within the Tory bureaucracy: "We'll never take another single ad in your goddamn magazine," he'd rant. I'd just chuckle, wait a couple weeks and then go around and sell him another five spots.

Running *Sask Report* felt good, perhaps because it wasn't the hockey business. Setting out onto the highways and byways of Saskatchewan was a lungful of clean, fresh prairie air and an eyeful of blue sky to boot. Often I was reminded of my early years on the road selling to small-town grocers. With *Sask Report,* I was out with the people and that suited me fine.

*Sask Report* wasn't, however, any less work than the hockey world had been. I was hardly ever in the office. I was on the road constantly. In one issue we did a feature on the Saskatchewan Junior Hockey League, the tier-two league that remained after the Western Hockey League was created. I visited every town in the league and sold the advertising myself. I covered the whole province in 10 days. I'd cut through the back roads and sometimes hit three towns a day. Those sorts of road trips were routine.

I won't say I looked for extra work, but if I saw anything that needed doing, I did it. At the age of 65, I was making a new beginning with *Sask Report.* I wanted to put all my hockey disappointments behind me. I wanted to forget the past. I wanted to make a success of my new life, and to do that I knew I needed to have tunnel vision. I needed to focus on the magazine and give it total commitment. I did. Bart and I routinely worked Saturdays and Sundays. It never stopped being fun, but it was as heavy a workload as any I'd ever shouldered, and the constant travel and the unrelenting deadlines took up almost all my time and energy. I sometimes wonder if I could have predicted what came next if I hadn't been so focussed on escaping my hockey disappointments and building something new.

By the winter of 1989 our son Greg was 21 years old. He was just starting to come into his own, a promising, popular and well-respected young man. He'd been an honors student in high school. One of his professors at the University of Saskatchewan wrote Vi and I a letter telling us what a pleasure he'd been to teach. Greg was just starting to spread his wings. He'd saved his money and gone to travel the world, visiting Singapore and Japan and France. He returned to Canada that Christmas to spend the holidays with his sister Donna and her family. New Year's found him in Banff with some friends, and then he came home through Edmonton, where he stopped to visit his other sister Gwen. He drove home through a snowstorm the way from Edmonton. "I'm so tired, Dad," he said as he walked through the door on January 5.

Vi was visiting Donna in Prince Rupert. I was going out that night with our friends Al Anderson, Lloyd Saunders and Bill Rudichuk. I knew Greg liked them, and I tried to talk him into joining us. Normally, he would have gone. He always had a fun with us, and we enjoyed his laughter and jokes and the way he spiced our conversation. That night he said he just didn't have the energy. I said I'd just stay home with him and we could have a relaxing evening together. "Dad, I don't want you to do that," he said. "You go out and enjoy your friends. I'll be fine. I'm just going to go upstairs to bed." He practically pushed me out the door.

When I returned I went upstairs to check on Greg and found a note on his bedroom door, saying, "I'm resting, Dad. Please don't disturb me." So I let him be. He was still quiet the next morning as I left for work, but after a while something began to bother me. I don't know what it was, but I felt compelled to return home to check on Greg again. I went upstairs to Greg's bedroom and found him. He was dead. Our beautiful youngest son, our baby boy, had taken his life.

I can't describe what I went through that day. I'm not even sure that I remember—or that I even want to remember. Our other children, Bart and Beverley and Brent, came immediately, thank God, and somehow we made it through the next few days.

Vi later told me she had a premonition of that night. On her way out to Prince Rupert to visit Donna, Vi's train had passed through Edmonton, where she knew Greg was still at Gwen's. Vi didn't know why it seemed so important, but she was driven to get off that train. She described the compulsion as an anguish beyond anything. When the train pulled into the station in downtown Edmonton, she got off. She ran to the nearest phone and called Gwen. She got no answer, so she ran back to the train and caught it just as it was pulling out. She never spoke to Greg again.

Greg's death shook me like nothing before. It doesn't do any good to sift the past for blame, but the loss of a son forces you to step back and examine your life. There's no question that all my life I'd worked hard. I'd given total commitment to every challenge I'd faced. I rarely took holidays. And I'd spent so many years on the road. Scouting. Coaching. Selling. Speaking. There were long stretches where I ate more often in restaurants than at my own table. I'd spent so much time in airport departure lounges that sometimes I felt as if I should be paying rent. And I liked it, too. I liked meeting new people and moving around and throwing myself into different situations.

I did my best when I was at home. First thing I'd do when I got back was to call a team meeting of all the kids. One by one they were encouraged to tell me what they'd all been up to, and nobody could interrupt. In reality the phone would be ringing off the hook, and Vi would be trying to get everyone to sit down and eat before somebody had to go off to hockey practice. Those family meetings where we tried to get some serious matters straight usually became free-wheeling gab sessions where we'd tell jokes and take an hour to decide who should take out the garbage. I guess I was just so happy to see everyone that it was hard for me to be a disciplinarian. I know we remained closely knit no matter how much time I spent away from home. And I know I couldn't really have lived any other way. So it's complicated. When I looked back at things, I couldn't say that I would have done anything different.

At the same time there were moments I wish I'd been able to share with my family in person. Our son Bart played goal for a couple seasons with the Portland Winter Hawks in the WHL. One year the Hawks lost in the league semifinals, and the winning Brandon Wheat Kings picked him up for the Memorial Cup finals. The Wheat Kings lost with him in net after a thrilling 1–0 final game, after which Bart won five awards, including Most Valuable Player of the series and of the game. But I was tied up with business and had to watch the game on television. Seeing Bart hoist that hardware in person would have been unforgettable.

You think about other things, too, after the suicide of a loved one. You ask yourself if there were signals you could have caught or if you missed something. Vi and I agreed there had been a huge change in Greg's personality in the last two years of his life. He'd always been so lighthearted and outgoing. He had been so much fun to be around. At the same time he was articulate and mature. He was so responsible that when he was the night manager of restaurant in Saskatoon, the owner used to go home and let Greg run the show. But after he turned 18, he grew more serious and introspective. He was still kind and considerate, but he didn't smile very often anymore. We thought he was growing up. Plus, Vi and I were a little distracted with another of our children who was struggling with a serious bipolar disorder. I guess to some extent our attention was elsewhere when Greg could have used it. Greg probably didn't understand what was happening to him, either. There wasn't a lot of help or understanding for mental illness then.

One thing I did come to realize was how important Vi has been to our family. Family is everything to her. Because of my work and travel, she almost raised our children on her own. Greg's death made me realize the terrific burden she had carried almost by herself. We've had a remarkable marriage. She's had to carry the ball by herself so many times, but she's never complained. So many times I'd call from some hotel room and she'd tell me "Oh yes, everything's fine," when sometimes things weren't. But she didn't want me to worry, so she'd wait until I returned home before telling me the real story. I'd ask her if I was putting too much pressure on her, and she'd always say, "No, Bill. I don't mind." She's always loved being surrounded by kids—our own and everyone else's, too. Our children's friends were always welcome and our house was a social center. I came home for lunch once and there was Vi, setting out plates for 11 kids. We'd both done our best, but our son was dead. His death was a mystery that ate at us.

Losing Greg was like a bomb exploding within our family: it scattered and dispersed us. Before, we had always been together at Thanksgiving and Christmas and even Easter, in addition to the individual visits we shared throughout the year. Now, things fell apart. We no longer sat down together at the same table. We just stopped gathering. We tried once or twice, but it was a hollow thing. Nobody was the same. I was angry and bitter and I knew it, but I couldn't understand why. Everybody suffered terribly. We came to hate Christmas. It became a dreadful time that served only to remind us of Greg. We had to leave our house, too. Greg had helped us chose it, and it was going to be—at long last—a permanent home base for our family. Vi didn't ever want to leave the home that was her link to Greg. But I couldn't even enter Greg's room, and I couldn't stay there. Neither could our other kids.

Confused and sick at heart, I turned again to what I knew best. The NHL was gearing up for another round of expansions, and I made the expected noises about preparing a bid even though I knew the U.S. $50 million I'd need to get a team was more than Saskatoon could afford, especially after the provincial government declined to provide the loan guarantees we'd need. A new outfit, the Continental Hockey League, seemed like a better bet for us. A couple of groups were talking about rival pro leagues (there was the Global League and North American Hockey League), but the CHL was the first to make their plans known. By the summer of 1991 we had teams lined up in Saskatoon, Hamilton, Fort Lauderdale, Cincinnati, Cleveland and Atlanta. We'd even held a draft and had agreements with the Soviet Ice Hockey Federation to join a future European division of the league. It all fell apart, however, in a welter of confusion over delays and arena leases.

A few other opportunities came my way. Ralph Goodale, a powerful federal Liberal cabinet minister, called one day to ask if I had any interest in politics. Ralph and Don McCullough, an old Notre Dame classmate and a longtime Liberal organizer, met with me at the Bessborough and asked if I had any interest in returning to Alberta to lead the provincial Liberal party. "Ralph, it sounds very interesting, but not for me," I told him. I'd had offers from different parties before and I'd turned them down, too. I didn't like politics. It's a game that involves too many compromises and too much nastiness. I've never been good with committees and I'd make a terrible politician.

I was still dissatisfied and still looking to move on. *Sask Report* was still fun, but it was getting harder and harder to keep up with the workload. Bart felt the same way. We were burning out, and in the spring of 1992 we started talking with our employees about a buyout. The buyout happened that June, but our former employees couldn't make the work, and we had to step back in shortly after and close the magazine down for good. That was another pang.

By that time I'd figured out my next move. If the big-league pros couldn't come to Saskatoon, how about a second-tier pro team? I called Bill Comrie and asked him if he was interested in trying to get the International Hockey League to come to town. "It'd be a tremendous winner, Bill," I told him, and he agreed. The IHL board listened to Bill and I make our pitch at an all-star game in Atlanta. We told them how good the market would be and how it would be great for their media profile in Canada, but they turned us down. "We just don't see ourselves going into Canada at this time," they said. The bid, however, wasn't a total loss. They'd been impressed by Bill and me enough to offer us a franchise anywhere in the western United States. "We want the two of you in our league as owners," they told us.

"Bill, this may be the best turn-down we've ever had," I said. "I believe if we went to Denver we'd have a real winner."

Bill agreed. I spent the next three months in and out of Denver with my old Summit Series friend Ralph Backstrom, who had been a university coach in Denver for years. We eventually struck a deal with the city on McNichols Arena. Our deal gave us exclusive professional hockey rights for the city of Denver and area. That was a big deal. Those rights included any professional hockey team, and

I'd got wind that the NHL was trying to get back into Denver. But minutes before the formal signing of the agreement at the mayor's office in Denver, the phone rang. It was for me.

It was Bill Comrie. He'd been on talking to his brother Fred, who owned the IHL's San Diego Gulls. Fred had begged Bill and me not to start a new team in Denver. He wanted us to join him. I couldn't believe my ears.

"Bill, this Denver deal is a gold mine," I said. "The team is going to be a major success, and if the NHL really does want a team in Denver again they'll pay us millions for the rights."

Bill gave me the only answer he could, the same answer that's worked on me before: "Blood is thicker than water," he said. I sighed. Bill and Fred were like sons or kid brothers to me. I looked at the officials assembled in the mayor's office. "A momentary problem has arisen," I said. I had to go.

Fred picked me up at the airport, Mr. Enthusiasm himself. He did have a good operation. The Gulls had a nice arena and averaged more than 6,000 fans a game. And to make a long story short, Bill and I decided to join the Gulls. It wasn't a better deal, but Fred thought he needed us and we were very close. I had to get go back to Denver and explain to a dumfounded city council that something had come up in the Comrie family and that while we certainly thanked them for their offer, we were going to have to turn them down. I joined the Gulls as vice president in charge of operations, and I had a small ownership stake as well.

San Diego was good therapy for Vi and me as we struggled to put our lives back together. We moved into a condominium in La Jolla and Fred filled it with fine furniture for us. It's a beautiful city and the climate wasn't bad, either. The hockey fans were not as educated as Canadian crowds, and we sometimes had to explain the rules over the PA system. But they came to have fun, and they were

*Having our grandson Chase with us in La Jolla for a time helped Vi and I fill our hours with energy and hope.*

loud and boisterous, especially after a couple periods of beer sales. There were loyal, too. We could be losing 7–1, and if we scored a goal it would be as if we'd won the championship. They only time they cheered louder was when there was a fight. All IHL teams had to have a couple real sluggers in their lineup.

We had a great team in the Gulls and once went 26 games without a loss. Our team could have easily played in the bottom third of the NHL, and some from our organization eventually did. Our general manager, Don Waddell, moved on to hold that position in Nashville. Coach Rick Dudley became president and general manager of Tampa Bay. And our captain, Lindy Ruff, went on to coach the Sabres.

I'd been nervous about getting back into hockey after the heartbreak of the Blues, but once I got settled in San Diego I felt right at home again. I wrapped the roar of the crowd, the togetherness of team spirit and the excitement of competition around me like a comforting, familiar old blanket. At first Vi wasn't happy about traveling so far from home, but she was welcomed into our new neighborhood and she soon felt comfortable. Once she got used to driving in southern California—an adjustment that took me a while, too—she was all over the place.

It was a good life. I love to play the horses and we were close to Del Mar racetrack. There were first-class golf courses nearby and plenty of pro baseball and football to watch. But it wasn't to last. We had to leave after about 18 months when Vi's father and mother became very ill. We returned to Edmonton.

San Diego had been a pleasant interlude for us, but when we got back to Canada it seemed as if my bad luck picked up where it had left off. In the fall of 1993 I got involved with the Canadian Football League's attempts to expand into the United States. But being part of the expansion effort was a terrible mistake for me. My job was to drum up new franchises, and I spent time in Boston, Minneapolis and Omaha, but the whole idea was ill-conceived from the start. I thought things couldn't get worse than when we called a league meeting in Orlando to announce the awarding of a new franchise and the prospective owners didn't show up. We'd even booked satellite time so the league could broadcast the press conference live. We knew the owners were financially solid and they'd promised to sign in front of the cameras, but they played us for suckers, and I guess we were. The Orlando fiasco was prelude for what was to come. The night after that abortive press conference, I had a meeting with some CFL officials. I said that after this debacle maybe we should back off the whole U.S. expansion, but Calgary Stampeders owner Larry Ryckman said that we had to go ahead and that he backed me completely. The next day the papers quoted him saying some terrible things about me. In 50 years of involvement in sports, no one had ever said I'd misled him or had called me incompetent. Furious, I resigned from the league.

These were getting to be tough times, even for an old optimist and forward-looker like me. Apart from our idyll in San Diego, it had been awhile since I'd had something go my way. Even harder to bear was the fact that things still weren't right at home. We were still hurting over Greg's death. I couldn't even say what had happened out loud and neither could Vi. The family was still mourning somewhere deep in their hearts and an emotional distance still separated us. We saw each here and there, but we still hadn't gotten together to celebrate anything or reaffirm our love for one another.

What could I do? I moved on to the next thing.

In 1994 the great curler Kevin Martin called. He had just organized the first big cashspiel in West Edmonton Mall and wanted to talk. He and his partner wanted to host another cashspiel, but they had lost a considerable amount of money on the first. They asked me if I was interested in helping them with their second attempt.

I sure was. Car bonspiels had been a great little moneymaker for me back in the Quakers, and I thought it was an idea well worth revisiting. Breaking down the amateur–professional barrier in curling didn't bother me at all. I thought of curling as just entertainment, and the inducement of a new car seemed to add a little sizzle for both the fans and the curlers. It was time, I thought, a little professionalism and promotional pizzazz was brought to the game of curling. I agreed to participate on the condition that we would eventually move the event to Saskatoon. The mall just wasn't set up for it. We had to do things like hang heavy paper over the skylights above the rink so that the sunlight didn't soften the ice too much. Expenses like those were killing us.

So together we started the Husky Curling Classic, the richest cashspiel in the world, which attracted some of the finest rinks. And

*The Husky Curling Classic was the world's richest bonspiel.*

finally I was getting something to click. We did three successful cashspiels in Saskatoon, two in Red Deer and one in Edmonton. Eventually, I bought Kevin out. Husky and other great sponsors such as Nokia and Bruce Saville of Edmonton were solidly on board. Crowds were starting to come around and excitement was building. To be honest, promoting curling wasn't that much different than promoting hockey. What sets them apart is that curling is on the fifth or sixth sports page while hockey is on the front. The game wasn't being that well sold to the public. It needed to generate a little drama, and the best way to do that is to raise the stakes. That's what our prizes did. Skips started rearranging their rinks and dropping the players who weren't measuring up.

It was great to be working with so many of the game's greats. Future Olympic gold medallist Sandra Schmirler, Cathy Borst and World Champion Anne Merkinger were only a few of the women's rinks. We also had Kelly Law, Cheryl Kullman and two-time world champion Connie Laliberte. Among the men, we attracted rinks such as Ed Werenich, the first curler to make more $1 million, as well Kerry Burtnyk, Russ Howard, Rick Folk and Jeff Stoughton. They were all world champions. We had great curlers like Vic Peters and Guy Hemmings, too.

Each year we ranked 32 men's and ladies rinks from around the world. Sixteen of them would be invited to our event, and one year we had both men's and women's Olympic Champions, the two World Champions and the Canadian Champions. They were drawn by the excitement, the high level of competition and the prize pot of $180,000. We billed the Huskey Curling Classic as the richest and greatest bonspiel in the world, and I believe that was the simple truth.

I was having a wonderful time promoting the cashspiels. The crowds were growing, and the media was taking more interest. I was starting to remember how good it felt to be on top of a successful operation. It was so much fun, in fact, that I couldn't stay away from it even when my health started to wobble. For three years I was a sick man, but I refused to stop working.

My health started to fail in 1997. Over the next two years, I had a heart attack that left me with a shunt and an angioplasty. A bout of double pneumonia knocked me on my back for a long time. Then I had to have another operation in Red Deer to clear a blockage in my bladder.

My body may have been failing but my spirits were on the rise for the first time in years. The curling was one reason. The other and more important one was that around the same time the curling started to come together for me, our family finally started to heal itself. Christmas 1997 was the first time our family came together since Greg's death. Being together again was difficult, but it was wonderful, too. And after that, we knew we wouldn't look back.

*Wonderful times with family and friends. Back, L–R: Lee and Stephanie Williamson, Brent and Karen Dodd, Larry Wood, Shona. Front: Dana and Ron Jeppesen.*

*Jordan, Josh, Brady, Brittany, Chase, Samantha, Lexie, Brett and Andrew.*

*With Chase, Brady, Brittany, Josh and Samantha.*

*With Helen and Frank McDonald.*

TOP: With son
Brent and
grandson Travis.
RIGHT: With
the love of my
life, Vi.

Granddaughters
Shelbie and
Carrie.

With Don and Eleanor Funk.    With son Brent.

I'd made a promise to myself after Greg died. I told myself that family would come first. I'd come to understand that life could be harsh and you had to value every moment with the people you love. And now I was getting a beautiful second chance to really put that promise into action. I swear I've done my best to take advantage of it.

Still, my health wasn't getting any better. My family kept telling me I was overworked. I didn't know what it was. Finally, on May 4, 1999—the day before my 69th birthday—I was lying in bed, feeling completely listless. I felt I couldn't move. Vi came in and I could see she was worried. "You're not even drinking any water, Bill," she said. "I'm taking you in." I protested feebly. "I'll just be fine," I said. "Just let me have this weekend."

Vi put her foot down. "No. You're not having any weekend." Vi took me into the Grey Nuns hospital that night. And she made me promise that I wouldn't let the doctors send me back home that night. Vi felt something was deeply wrong, and she wanted me to stay under care until we all knew.

Sure enough, a doctor checked me out and came breezing back into the examination room. "Okay, you can get dressed and go home now," he said. Vi gave me a hard look. I looked at the doctor. "No," I said. "I'm not going home. There's something wrong with me. Besides, you haven't done any blood work on me." So the doctor sent a nurse in to take a blood sample and about an hour later he returned with his new diagnosis. "Well, right this moment you are in kidney failure," he said.

Vi was aghast. Her mother had died of kidney failure and she feared the worst right away. I simply asked, "Well, doctor, how are we going to fix it?" I hadn't grasped what was going on. Fred McDonald, chief of staff at the Grey Nuns, leveled with me. "Bill, you're a very, very sick man. I must tell you, you have maybe a 30 percent chance of making it." I was so worn out and tired that even the odds didn't make much of an impression on me.

I was hustled out of the Grey Nuns in an ambulance to the Royal Alexandra Hospital. For three days doctors and nurses cared for me around the clock, and I finally started to come around. The nurses called me their miracle patient. I have Vi to thank for insisting I spend that first night in hospital.

The ordeal, however, wasn't over. The tests continued, and Dr. Eric Estey came to my room with the results.

"I've got good news and bad news," he said. "The good news is that you're got prostate cancer. We are confident we can clear that problem up. The bad news is that you've also got inoperable bone cancer." His words dropped out of his mouth and fell on the floor with a thud. Vi and I sat there not knowing what to do or say. I asked the only question I could: "Doctor, how long have I got." He knew only that it wasn't much. Vi and I dissolved in tears. We wept for a long, long time.

That was more than a year ago. I have good days and I have bad days, but I'm still here. Four things have helped me fight this disease to a draw. One is that I've stayed active. I really believe that staying busy, meeting new people and trying new things has kept me vital for longer than I would have been otherwise. The other has to do with my attitude. All my life I've been positive and optimistic, and the mental habits of a lifetime keep my spirits up. I smile a lot, and people tell me that smile still goes all the way up to my eyes. The third is a deep and confident faith. Maybe there's a fourth reason, too. I've finally learned to relax. I'm content at last that I've accomplished plenty, even by Jack Hunter's standards.

I love all my children and my grandchildren, but over the last couple years I've probably spent more time with my little eight-year-old grandson, my youngest, than any of the others. Chase and I have great fun together. We go to Oilers games. We go to ball games. Vi takes him to play soccer. I even take Chase to the race track, where we talk about the horses and go through the tout sheets and lay a couple bucks on the ponies.

And sometimes I just watch him play outside, my white-haired face framed by the window while Chase runs and plays in the back-yards, playing fields, alleys and streets of his hometown. The decades roll back for me. The scrape of hockey sticks gives way to baseball chatter which gives way in turn to the counted cadences of football. Eventually, mothers summon the players, maybe two or three times before they actually obey. Then quiet.

# EPILOGUE

Other people call me an eternal optimist.
To them I say, "Thank-you."

**P**EOPLE THINK THAT AFTER A LIFETIME IN sports it's the cheers that you remember, and I'm not saying they're wrong. You never forget those times when joy and excitement surge through an arena like an electric current. I've heard a few roaring crowds in my time. Others say that what sticks with you is your legacy. They say that the most important thing is to leave your mark on the game, and I can lay claim to some of that, too. But cheers fade and legacies, however proud, drift away. The Oil Kings Memorial Cup win seems like a long time ago; Saskatoon never did get its NHL team and the WHA, despite the thrilling hockey it was capable of delivering, is gone. What I've found really matters are the friends you've made.

And I've made so many friends.

Some of them, like my great pals Ben Hatskin and Scotty Munro, are sadly missed. So is Dr. Charles Allard. But I'm fortunate that so many of them are still around. There's Dennis Murphy, the boisterous little Irishman whose friendship has proved more durable than the league we founded. I'm proud that so many of my old Oil Kings have gone from valued team members to trusted friends. There's the Comries, of course, but they're only the start. There's Al Hamilton, Bob McAneeley, Ron Walters, Ross Perkins, Tom Gilmour, Kerry Ketter and more. Our championships may be long in the past, but our friendships are vital and growing. We still see each other almost weekly at luncheons that are filled with laughter and memories and news of one another's lives.

I'm still in regular touch with my old office staff of Mattie Middlehurst, Jim Pelehos, Ray Barth and Marilyn Noble. Vic Mah has stuck by me long after our hockey connection ended. Then there's my good friend and old racing and hockey partner Steve Ruznisky in Prince Albert. I've had some tough breaks from the sports business over my career, but I'd be remiss if I didn't mention some of the wonderful people the financial side of the sport brought me in contact with. I'm proud to call Bruce Saville, a visionary supporter of curling, my friend. Then there are the folks at Husky Oil—Don Ingram, Jim Melvin, Bill Popplewell. My career has taken me all over the west and left me with friends almost everywhere I've been: Gordon Yake, Brian Sutter and Ken Mandrusiak in Red Deer; Cliff Rose, Larry Makelki, Dave Addie, Elmer Franks and Skip Craik in Lloydminster; Bill Rudichuk and Bill "The Kid" Hicke in Regina; Don Funk, Ron and Dave Payne, Bob and Al Anderson, Frank Atcheson and Don McDonald in Saskatoon are just a few. And then there are my close friends who've done so much for me inside and outside of sports: Ed Assaly, Al Korchinski, Hal Spelliscy, Dean Bell, Don Scott, Ed Dauphinais and Lyle Best. I'll never be able to thank them enough for their generosity.

*With Esther Mah,
Vi and Vic Mah.*

*Enjoying a moment
with Al Korchinski
and Ed Assaly.*

*With two lifelong
friends: the late
Lloyd Saunders and
Jim Pelehos.*

I think it's probably fair to say I've seen more hockey players than most over my 70-year involvement in sports. When I began my life in sport, only the original six existed in the NHL, but there were great players and athletes all over this country playing in senior and commercial leagues that most hockey fans these days haven't even heard of. I won't say I've seen them all. But I've seen a few, from the fabulous Bentley brothers to Golden Age greats like Elmer Lach to modern-day heroes like Wayne Gretzky and Mark Messier. When I was so sick, I lay in bed and ran their memory spools in my mind again and again. I can still remember every pass and every move in shifts played 50 years ago—the shooting, stickhandling, skating, body checking.

And because I'm the kind of guy I am, I just couldn't resist conducting the greatest draft of all time in my memory and imagination. Who would you pick, Mark Messier or Ted Kennedy? Terry Sawchuk or Dominik Hasek? I ran three drafts, one for players from my own teams over the years, one for the old senior leagues and one for the NHL.

Of the players I had on my own teams, Emil Francis would have to be in goal. I'd put Vic Myles and Bill Heindl, the toughest fighter hockey's ever seen, on defense. Up front I'd put Tommy Burlington at center, one eye and all. Right wing would feature Cy Thomas and on the left would be Chuck McCullough. As it happens that was my star line when I managed the Quakers.

Many of the finest I've ever seen in senior hockey came from my dad's old Quakers. In goal I'd have Howie Dinsley. Curly Kerr from Saskatoon and Bert LaPrade from Port Arthur would be on defense. Center would have to be played by Max Bentley. Right wing would be Ab Welch and on left wing would be Red Gobel, a little fellow but an artist with a stick. That was my father's first line, and they finished one–two–three in scoring. They were a power play every time they stepped on the ice.

Among the National Hockey League players, I'd pick three teams. The three greatest goaltenders I ever saw, in no particular order, were Glenn Hall, Jacques Plante and Terry Sawchuk. Take your pick. Glenn Hall was so acrobatic you'd have to see him to believe it. He could bend over backward in the net and come bouncing back up. His lateral movement was absolutely outstanding. Sawchuck was a great standup goalie, a tremendous angle player. Every time you looked up, there was Sawchuck. He looked big in the net and he was big out of the net. Jacques Plante was very colorful, always rushing out of the net, always handling the puck. Behind these three I'd have to give honorable mention to Johnny Bower and Gerry Cheevers. Both were great goalies, particularly in the playoffs. Gerry Cheevers was, I think, the greatest playoff goalie ever. But he didn't play long enough in the NHL to measure up to the first four.

My first team's all-star defense would be comprised of Bobby Orr and Eddie Shore. Shore was in a class by himself, rough and tough, always an inspiration to his teammates and the general of his team's power play. Bobby was a beautiful skater, fast and smooth. Before you knew it, he'd be at your end of the ice booming a shot at your goalie. He invented a whole new way to play to defense. I knew he would be one of the all-time greats the moment I first saw him play with the Oshawa Generals. For my next pair I'd match up King Clancy with Doug Harvey. I used to marvel at Clancy. He was small—150 pounds soaking wet—but he would take on anyone. He could steer the biggest men into the corners and hand out tremendous body checks. Exciting to watch, too. When he got the puck he took it right up the ice. Doug Harvey was another rugged guy, a real team leader, an outstanding two-way player and the backbone of all those storied Montreal Canadiens Stanley Cup victories.

My third defense combination would be Larry Robinson and Ray Bourque. They're a lot alike, character players who approach a

*With who else but "The Great One."*

road game in September with the same intensity they chase a play-off spot in March. I used to love to watch Larry use that long reach to poke the puck from frustrated forwards. He could rush, too, and loved to roughhouse in the corners. Ray is every coach's dream, a great team player who's a wizard on the power play.

Up front at center ice my first pick would be "The Great One," Wayne Gretzky. He owns the record book and probably always will. His vision of the ice was uncanny, unlike anything I've ever seen. Enough said. Next, I'd pick Jean Beliveau. Jean, I think, was the epitome of leadership on and off the ice. He too was a brilliant two-way player and as great as he was in the regular season, he always got better in the playoffs. Third, I'd pick Mario Lemieux. In his last years there were times when he even outplayed Wayne. Howie Morenz, Max Bentley, Elmer Lach and Syl Apps get honorable mentions as guys I'd love to draft for a dream team.

On right wing it'd be about an even call between Gordie Howe and Maurice Richard. It's almost unfair to have to choose between them. Both are all-time greats: Gordie for his durability, unsurpassed skill and toughness; "The Rocket" for his unbelievable strength and his sheer will to put the puck in the net. Next I'd take Jarri Kurri. A lot of people underrate Jarri because he's so quiet, but he was a great scorer and also played solid defense. Bernie "Boom Boom" Geoffrion and Guy Lafleur get honorable mentions.

On left wing my first pick would be Bobby Hull, "The Golden Jet." Bobby could excite the fans more than anyone with his skating and terrifying shot. He was as strong as anyone and a tremendous puck carrier. Busher Jackson, an artist with a shifty deke and a big part of the Leafs legendary "Kid Line," would be next. Then I'd take Dickie Moore, a great two-way player and a solid goal-scorer for the Canadiens. Terrible Ted Lindsay, the heart and soul of the old Red Wings, had a snarly style that dominated games. He gets honorable mention.

I saw them all play. Four generations of great athletes. They played in different eras under different conditions, but, at its core, the game they played hasn't changed much. They all laced up skates and taped up sticks. Wayne Gretzky and Howie Morenz could have sat down with each other and traded tips. And they all gave the same thing to their fans, the same thing that keeps people coming out even as salaries and ticket prices climb and commitment to community declines. They all excited us, gave us something to cheer for and brought us together in both victory and defeat. They inspired us. I guess that's why we still go to the rink.

Every now and then I get a call from some reporter who wants my two bits on the latest installment in hockey's ongoing saga, and I'm usually willing to oblige. I tell him that the rich are going to get richer and the poor are going to stay poor. Competing will get tougher and tougher until finally the poor won't be able to compete

*Mayor Bill
Smith unveils
plaque.*

*Bruce Saville
at presenta-
tion.*

*With Bill Smith, Bill Comrie
and Vi.*

*Family gathers in penalty box.*

*Rotary Club Paul
Harris Fellow
Award.*

*Gathering prior to receiving the Companion of the Order of Canada. L–R: Sisters Eileen Haas and Bev Worsley and Vi.*

at all. The NHL's going to devolve into two divisions, one Canadian and one American with Canada playing the United States for the Stanley Cup. That's what's going to happen. The NHL is in dicey shape right now, and most teams are losing money, but I don't see any sign that the owners are willing to think of the interest of the league as a whole or even the game itself. I sometimes think that if Clarence Campbell were around today, he'd sit the owners down and knock some heads until they saw some sense. But most of the owners these days are huge corporations, not individuals who lived and loved the game. The players have to be part of the solution, too. The WHA did them a big favor when it killed the reserve clause and gave them some long-overdue bargaining power, but I can't help but think things are out of hand. I can't even imagine what Charles Allard would have said about today's contracts.

Vi and I live quietly in our home in Edmonton. Not too quietly, though. We both have active social lives and it seems there's always someone new to meet. There's always family passing through

*A hug from grandson Chase at the Bill Hunter dinner.*

or someone's birthday to celebrate. Everyone knows they're welcome at grandma and grandpa's. I've also received a few honors that have made me proud. The City of Edmonton recently gave me their Outstanding Ambassador award and renamed the Jasper Place Arena the Bill Hunter Arena. I sure never anticipated that when I was dying to get my Oil Kings out of it and into the Gardens. The Rotary Club has given me their highest commendation, the Paul Harris Fellowship. And in the spring of 2000, I was made a Companion of the Order of Canada.

*The wheel turns full circle—a salute from the new ownership, management and coaches of the Edmonton Oilers at the alumni golf day, September 5, 2000. Back Row, L-R: Cal Nichols (Edmonton Owners Group Chairman), Patrick LaForge (Edmonton Oilers Hockey Club President), Charlie Huddy (Assistant Coach), Craig MacTavish (Head Coach), Scott Howson (Assistant to the General Manager). Front Row, L-R: Billy Moores (Assistant Coach), Bill Hunter, Kevin Lowe (General Manager), Mark Lamb (Assistant Coach, Player Development).*

Sometimes I wish I'd hung on to a few more dollars. I feel bad that I haven't been able to give Vi some of the comforts she so richly deserves. But back when I was in action, there always seemed to be a new project that needed a little seed money, and that's where it all went. I don't regret a single venture. To be honest, I don't think Vi does, either.

They call me Wild Bill. It's a name I've never really liked, but I've learned to shrug and accept it. If to be passionate and emotional looks wild to some people, so be it. Other people call me an eternal optimist. To them I say, "Thank-you." If that's what Wild Bill means, it's a compliment, and I hope the name always remains appropriate. To this day I keep looking ahead, confident that great things are in store.